Tim Kennedy

Mary Slowinski

SMIL:

Adding Multimedia to the Web

SAMS   201 West 103rd St. • Indianapolis, Indiana, 46290 USA

Trademarks

All terms mentioned in this book that are known to be trademarks or service marks have been appropriately capitalized. Sams Publishing cannot attest to the accuracy of this information. Use of a term in this book should not be regarded as affecting the validity of any trademark or service mark.

Warning and Disclaimer

Every effort has been made to make this book as complete and as accurate as possible, but no warranty or fitness is implied. The information provided is on an "as is" basis. The authors and the publisher shall have neither liability nor responsibility to any person or entity with respect to any loss or damages arising from the information contained in this book or from the use of programs accompanying it.

Executive Editor
Jeff Schultz

Development Editor
Kate Small

Managing Editor
Charlotte Clapp

Project Editor
Elizabeth Finney

Copy Editor
Barbara Hacha

Indexer
Angie Bess

Proofreader
Mary Ann Abramson

Technical Editor
David Warner

Team Coordinator
Amy Patton

Media Developer
Dan Scherf

Interior Designer
Gary Adair

Cover Designer
Dan Armstrong

Page Layout
Rebecca Harmon
Lizbeth Patterson

Overview

Contents

Part III   Using SMIL: The Projects   271

Dedication

Acknowledgments

We'd like to thank the editors of this book, Kate Small and Jeff Schultz, for working diligently and patiently with us to make sure this text came to light.

We'd also like to thank our colleagues and students at Bellevue Community College for being patient with us as well and for acting as sounding boards for some of the ideas and the structure for the book.

Last, but certainly not least, we thank our families who have supported us through late nights, early mornings, and those hair-pulling moments.

Tim Kennedy

Mary Slowinski

About the Authors

Tim Kennedy is the originator of Just SMIL (`http://JustSMIL.com`), the first major informational Web site about the SMIL language. His company, Online Delivery, created the original Streaming Media World (`http://www.streamingmediaworld.com`) site for Internet.com. His speaking appearances include informational sessions at Internet World and RealNetworks conferences. An enthusiast for all types of media production, he is currently Chair of the Media Communication and Technology program at Bellevue Community College.

Mary Slowinski is a full-time faculty member at Bellevue Community College (`http://www.bcc.ctc.edu`) instructing in Web design, digital video editing, and streaming technologies. In the summer, she teaches intensive workshops for teachers and other educators to assist them with mastering and incorporating new technologies into their course curriculum. Her other interests include distance speed skating, world music, and viewing vistas.

Tell Us What You Think!

As the reader of this book, *you* are our most important critic and commentator. We value your opinion and want to know what we're doing right, what we could do better, what areas you'd like to see us publish in, and any other words of wisdom you're willing to pass our way.

As an Executive Editor for Sams Publishing, I welcome your comments. You can e-mail, or write me directly to let me know what you did or didn't like about this book—as well as what we can do to make our books stronger.

Please note that I cannot help you with technical problems related to the topic of this book, and that because of the high volume of mail I receive, I might not be able to reply to every message.

When you write, please be sure to include this book's title and author as well as your name and phone or fax number. I will carefully review your comments and share them with the author and editors who worked on the book.

E-mail: m3feedback@samspublishing.com

Mail: Jeff Schultz
            Executive Editor
            Sams Publishing
            201 West 103rd Street
            Indianapolis, IN 46290 USA

Introduction

Is This Book for Me?

Is this a book I should bother with? You've got to be asking yourself that, especially because time is scarce and your bookshelves are probably already groaning with tech books. So we'll make our case and be brief.

This book is an exploration into the use of the Synchronized Multimedia Integration Language, better known as SMIL. SMIL versions 1.0 and 2.0 allow Web authors to weave together multimedia by writing XML-based markup similar to HTML. You can create powerhouse Web multimedia presentations using a simple text editor. Seems almost too good to be true, but with the backing of the World Wide Web Consortium (W3C, the organization that develops standards for the Web), SMIL is here—and here to stay.

So what can you do with it, you ask? You can place linkable hot spots on a video clip, display a rolling text document with hyperlinks and background music, or create a slideshow of still and moving images with narration and accompanying URLs. As a matter of fact, with the release of SMIL 2.0 in 2001 with its increased flexibility and modularization, the sky's the limit on the ways you can combine and synchronize media using this language.

What this book offers is the tools to write SMIL code. The first part introduces you to SMIL with a brief history of SMIL's development. The second part is a discussion of each module in the new 2.0 spec. Then the book quickly gets to the meat of the issue: how to use SMIL to create projects targeted to the various players. The projects section walks you step-by-step through the creation of a media presentation for each major player/browser. After your tutorials are completed, you can post them on the Web and test them using various platforms and browsers, which will further your real-world understanding of the implementation of this language. And you'll have access to our updates on the companion Web site, where you can get news, updates and so forth.

So should you buy this book? If you are involved in the creation of Web pages or sites and you include (or intend to include) multimedia of any form—sound, images, text, hyperlinks, video, animation—then yes, you should buy this book. If you are a beginner who is working with HTML and is ready to test the multimedia waters, then yes, you should buy this book. If you are a developer who wants to see what all this SMIL hoopla is all about, then yes, you should buy this book.

This is the next multimedia wave. Jump on.

Prerequisite Skills

This book is not a primer on writing Web pages; to get the most from it, you should know HTML and have a basic level of Web mastery. The tutorials will take you from there.

System Requirements

Writing SMIL code itself requires no more than a simple text editor. However, the multimedia portions of the presentations require players. The Web site that accompanies this book contains links to the three major SMIL multimedia players as well as several lesser-known players. We've also included browsers, where appropriate. Be sure you have 30MB–50MB of disk space for the installation of this software.

As for your machine, the faster the CPU and the bigger the hard drive the better. You'll need a minimum of 32MB of RAM. If you plan on working with your own multimedia source files, you'll need software to edit sound, video, and/or images. A graphics editing program would also be helpful.

Using the Book

Some people like to read background development stories, some do not. If you do, start with Chapter 1, "What Is SMIL?," and go from there. If you don't, you can go straight to the projects section. Then follow the instructions regarding the installation of the various players and browsers, and you will be good to go.

Additional Resources

This book, because of the nature of the content, is a work in progress. We've provided a Web site to accompany this book to keep our readers up to date on the developments that inevitably occur with relatively new technology. Feel free to visit us at http://www.smilbook.com to pick up additional authoring tips and to find out the latest SMIL developments.

Part I

Understanding SMIL: The Basics

1. What Is SMIL?
2. SMIL Authoring

1

What Is SMIL?

In the world of Web authoring, HTML is the markup language that pulls everything together. Type a few markup statements into a text editor and you have a Web page that loads graphics and makes hyperlinks.

In the world of multimedia Web authoring, SMIL is the markup language that pulls everything together. Pronounced "smile," it is an acronym for Synchronized Multimedia Integration Language. This friendly sounding, text-based markup language does just what it says: It synchronizes and integrates multimedia.

SMIL is a specification of the World Wide Web Consortium (W3C), a group of researchers and industry representatives that strives to advance the growth of the Web by developing standards. The instructions that make up SMIL are published in specifications maintained by the W3C. Based on XML, SMIL is a text-based language; therefore, you can use the same approach to authoring Web multimedia that you use to author traditional Web pages.

SMIL is still a young markup language. But it is also a powerful tool for creating captivating Web multimedia.

A First Look at SMIL

As a Web designer or developer, you are constantly inundated with complex new technologies. You probably grit your teeth and figure them out the best you can. Still, a bit of technology intimidation may exist that you might not be able to completely shake.

So as you begin this book on SMIL, we'll let you in on a little secret: SMIL is actually pretty easy. You can tell your colleagues that it is mind-blowing stuff—but we all know differently.

Like HTML, you can write SMIL with a basic text editor. As with all languages, SMIL continues to grow in complexity. But even so, you can master some basic SMIL markup with little effort.

The following is a short example of a basic SMIL document:

```
<smil>
<body>
   <par>
      <animation src="myflashfile.swf" />
      <audio src="myaudiofile.rm" />
   </par>
</body>
</smil>
```

In this example, I am playing a streaming Flash animation (`"myflashfile.swf"`) in parallel (`<par>`) with a streaming audio file (`"myaudiofile.rm"`). At first glance, it might look pretty unfamiliar. But if you poke around in the markup, you might notice a few things.

You probably noticed that it is easy to type—just like HTML. You probably also noticed that the tags are similar or even the same as HTML tags you already know. And it is likely that you noticed that the tags reference external sources, the same as an HTML document might reference a graphic.

We will not try to mislead you. Like HTML, SMIL can get complex when you do complex things. But just as with HTML, you can do basic things with very basic markup language.

Why SMIL?

Why use SMIL? It is usually the first question asked. Compared to more established technologies and authoring environments such as Macromedia Flash, SMIL might seem to pale in comparison. What can SMIL do that Flash cannot?

We think that's really the wrong question. SMIL is not a competitive solution. It's not out to replace Flash or any other streaming-media architecture. Because SMIL is "technology agnostic," as shown in Figure 1.1, it allows Web multimedia technologies to collaborate with each other.

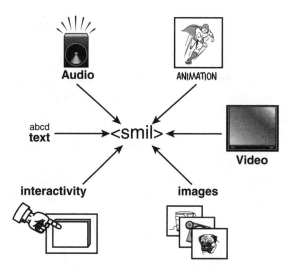

Figure 1.1   *SMIL can pull together a wide range of technologies.*

The growing Web multimedia market is a big business. A lot of dollars are up for grabs. That means that every involved company will continually push the Web multimedia envelope in pursuit of market domination. It would be nice to say that one technology will someday dominate. Then your authoring task would be neat and tidy. But the reality is that the competitive marketplace will always offer a range of technologies to choose from. A solution that helps you meld the strengths of these technologies into a cohesive presentation is just the kind of Web multimedia approach we all need. SMIL is that kind of solution.

Here is an example. Macromedia Flash is a great vector animation tool. It is acceptable for streaming audio but is not so robust with streaming video. RealNetworks' RealMedia is great at streaming audio and video. Why not combine the strengths of each? As illustrated in the code example in the previous section, SMIL allows that kind of collaboration to happen.

As a result, working with Web multimedia is like building a mosaic. SMIL acts as a glue that can hold it all together. But outside of its role as a streaming media referee, there are other good reasons for using SMIL.

The first is that because SMIL is text-based, it's easy for any designer or developer to work with it. Sure, you can buy a powerful SMIL authoring tool. As you'll see later in this book, a growing number are available to choose from. If you want to get started without any investment, however, the text editor that came with your computer will do.

Because SMIL is text based, the door is open for integration with other Web scripting and programming technologies. As long as that Web application can generate a text-based SMIL file, you can create a dynamic streaming presentation. For example, a shopper might fill out an HTML-based form and see a server-assembled Web multimedia presentation of products that match his or her criteria.

Finally, the SMIL effort is led by the W3C. As a group of researchers and industry representatives, the W3C is focused on ironing out standards that everyone can follow. Not all vendors will always agree with the direction that the SMIL specification may go. SMIL has already faced down challenges by major industry players. But as a standards body, the W3C tries to shape a specification that is beneficial to all parties involved. Unlike a proprietary technology owned by just one vendor, SMIL can lean toward general industry and consumer interests.

The Players and Browsers

One of the most amazing revolutions in Internet technology is happening rather quietly. In the early days of streaming, site visitors accessed Web multimedia with helper applications. These applications did little more than take a hand-off cue from the Web browser and play the content. They were accurately called *players*. Browsers browsed Web pages. Players played media content linked from those Web pages. The worlds were very separate.

Today, the differences between a player and a browser are getting pretty fuzzy. The newer player can load a URL directly. Your new player will probably handle traditional hypertext and images along with your streaming media. Your new player will likely let you take a look at the source markup file so that you can see how the Web multimedia presentation was assembled. Your new player might even display standard Web pages. Don't look now, but your new player is starting to sound a lot like a Web browser.

Let's take a look at the main contenders in the multimedia presentation race.

RealPlayer

As SMIL players go, RealNetworks' RealPlayer is one of the best-equipped Web multimedia players around. Officially, RealNetworks still refers to its application as "RealPlayer." "RealBrowser" would probably be a more accurate trade name. Like a Web browser, RealPlayer offers a window for entering URL addresses directly (see Figure 1.2). Like a Web browser, RealPlayer allows users to view the markup source of presentations (see Figure 1.3). The RealPlayer format even allows authors the capability to encode meta information into their clips, making it possible for search engines to connect site visitors with presentations.

Figure 1.2   *RealPlayer in action. Komodo Dragon image ©2000 Online Delivery Inc.*

SMIL support started with the release of the G2 version of the player. At the time, it was the first major streaming player to support SMIL. RealPlayer supports a range of media technologies, including hypertext, still images, audio, animation, and video.

SMIL for RealPlayer is the most dominant use of SMIL today. SMIL has become a central piece of how RealNetworks pulls media technologies together. Through SMIL, RealNetworks content providers glue together animation, video, audio, and interactivity into finished Web multimedia applications.

RealPlayer supports multiple platforms and is available as a free download directly from RealNetworks. A RealPlayer Plus version with a few additional enhancements is available for a fee. For most SMIL situations, the free RealPlayer is sufficient for viewing and authoring.

Figure 1.3 *You can view the source of the document in RealPlayer. Komodo Dragon image ©2000 Online Delivery Inc.*

Currently, most tools that publish or author SMIL do so for RealPlayer. For example, Macromedia Flash exports SMIL to synchronize audio with Flash-based streaming animation. In this way, long animations with audio tracks can stay matched to the visual.

Currently, RealPlayer supports a set of proprietary SMIL-like markup languages for use with SMIL in their player. The two most common RealPlayer proprietary languages are RealPix and RealText. RealPix is a streaming image format that includes a variety of basic transitions and motion effects that can be rendered on-the-fly in RealPlayer. Combined with other media through SMIL, RealPix is a very effective means for delivering a quality multimedia experience on low-bandwidth connections. RealText is a hypertext format that offers scrolling, captioning, and other types of text support. Like SMIL, both RealPix and RealText can be written in a text editor using SMIL-like commands. They're then saved as separate documents that SMIL in turn references as the presentation plays. In the early days of SMIL support in RealPlayer, these RealNetworks proprietary languages were essential to round out RealPlayer's SMIL capabilities. As SMIL develops and there is a greater push toward SMIL that will run in any player, we may see the functions of these proprietary formats replaced by the modules in SMIL itself.

As with many newer Web applications, RealPlayer supports new technologies by automatically linking the site visitor with the appropriate plug-in to play the media content. This approach makes it easier for Web multimedia authors to use the latest features with less fear of losing the audience.

Because RealNetworks was the biggest early supporter of SMIL, it is important to keep an eye on how it is applying the language. Increasingly, RealNetworks seems to hint at its work in developing appliance- and database-driven uses of streaming media. How that will affect RealNetworks' use of SMIL is currently unknown, but it does open the door for exciting possibilities in dynamic Web multimedia authoring.

The latest SMIL 2.0 version of RealPlayer is called RealONE. The name change reflects a RealPlayer that is capable of handling a variety of multimedia playback, Web browsing, and desktop entertainment functions. As we write this, RealOne is currently available as a preview.

QuickTime

The implementation of SMIL in Apple Computer's QuickTime multimedia player, shown in Figure 1.4, started out modestly. Don't let that fool you. QuickTime has a long history in multimedia and supports a wide range of technologies. As a cross-platform player, Windows and Macintosh users alike can take advantage of QuickTime's features. Combined with SMIL, QuickTime makes for a very effective Web multimedia environment.

Figure 1.4 *The QuickTime player has VCR-like controls.*

Just how wide is the range of support for multimedia technologies in QuickTime? It would be an overstatement to say that QuickTime natively supports every digital media technology out there. But that overstatement would not be far from the truth. The QuickTime media architecture supports more than 200 digital media formats, supporting capabilities for audio, text, images, animation, music, interactivity, video, and virtual reality.

Of course, one of those supported formats is SMIL. After your SMIL is loaded, your presentation can call on media in any of those other 200+ formats that QuickTime supports. This alone makes QuickTime a SMIL powerhouse.

SMIL support in QuickTime first appeared in QuickTime 4.1. Initially, it was demonstrated as an easy way to add banner advertisements to a presentation. In this way, the banner ads could be easily changed without having to re-edit the main presentation. It is not a fancy approach to SMIL, but like QuickTime itself, it is solid and practical.

QuickTime system software, including a player, is available as a free download from Apple Computer for both Macintosh and Windows users. A QuickTime Pro version is handy for those authoring QuickTime-flavored SMIL presentations but is not essential for those simply playing presentations.

QuickTime still shows a strong emphasis on the player approach to Web multimedia. Like any Web browser, you can find a Load URL function under a pulldown menu in the QuickTime player. But with large controls and a TV-like appearance, the QuickTime player feels more like a desktop version of a video appliance than a Web browser. This is not a criticism. It is notable that this video-presentation philosophy is reflected in SMIL authoring tools geared toward QuickTime.

Internet Explorer

Although most other companies are approaching SMIL from the player side, Microsoft is approaching SMIL thoroughly from the browser side. Currently, you will not find Microsoft's SMIL support coming from the streaming media unit. Instead, as shown in Figure 1.5, SMIL has been gradually stepping up its appearance in Microsoft Internet Explorer since version 5 of the browser first appeared.

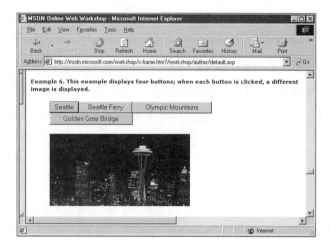

Figure 1.5 *SMIL capability in Internet Explorer.*

To understand Microsoft's approach to SMIL, a little history lesson is in order. Microsoft was initially a contributor to the first W3C-led industry effort to develop SMIL. At the last moment, Microsoft removed itself from the process as the W3C released SMIL 1.0. Depending on your world view, Microsoft made that step for either flattering or unflattering reasons. Nevertheless, it made its own SMIL proposal to the W3C a short time later. Initially called HTML+TIME (Timed Interactive Multimedia Extensions), Microsoft proposed a set of SMIL-based extensions to be used within an HTML Web document. Microsoft even released and later discontinued a companion product for the Office suite that could author Web pages in HTML+TIME.

Now in version 2.0, HTML+TIME is probably best described as special effects for the Web browser. With the release of SMIL version 2.0, Microsoft has rejoined the SMIL effort. It doesn't hurt that the SMIL 2.0 specification includes a subsection called HTML+SMIL that was written by the Microsoft representative to the SMIL effort.

It's hard to predict what the long-term prospects are for HTML+TIME or HTML+SMIL. As of press time, HTML+TIME is supported only in Windows versions of Internet Explorer. In that subset of the browser market, most of the support for HTML+TIME is found in Internet Explorer 5.5 or later. Without cross-platform support and limited to only the newest Internet Explorer Web browsers, HTML+TIME is likely to be considered more of a gimmick for the short term. However, Internet Explorer was one of the first of the major browsers and players to support functions of SMIL 2.0.

Other Players and Browsers

After you get out of the big three (RealNetworks, Apple, and Microsoft), SMIL browsers and players tend to get more experimental and specialized. That should not discount the work that smaller companies are doing. Often, smaller organizations are the ones to push the envelope and show the bigger companies what can be done. However, you cannot expect the widespread adoption that a larger software publisher offers. These players and browsers offer specialized features that are often best limited to use for an intranet or a special purpose. With time, specialized SMIL players and browsers can come and go. The following are the most common that are continually offered.

GRiNS

The GRiNS player is one of the oldest SMIL players around. Short for Graphical Interface for SMIL, GRiNS was originally a research project of the National Research Institute of Mathematics and Computer Science in the Netherlands (known also as CWI). Now spun off as a product of a company called Oratrix, the GRiNS player fits into a larger commercial-product venture that includes a SMIL authoring tool. With its base in research, the GRiNS product typically supports newer versions of SMIL than its larger lumbering competitors do.

The GRiNS player is cross platform and is currently available as a free download from Oratrix (`http://www.oratrix.com/`). Support for various media types is usually accessed through the help of those players. So to view RealMedia in GRiNS, you need to have RealPlayer installed.

SOJA

What if your SMIL player was written in Java? Then you could serve the player and the content at the same time. That is the concept behind Helio SOJA, a Java-based SMIL player shown in Figure 1.6. Short for SMIL Output in Java Applets, SOJA is a convenient solution for content authors who want wider access to their content. Java applets are not always known for their robustness, and that probably limits the use of SOJA by a wider audience more than it should. SOJA is probably best used for SMIL presentations that are based on nonproprietary

Internet media. Helio, the creator of SOJA, is a small, French nonprofit organization. The Java files and tutorials are available for download at the Helio site (`http://www.helio.org/`).

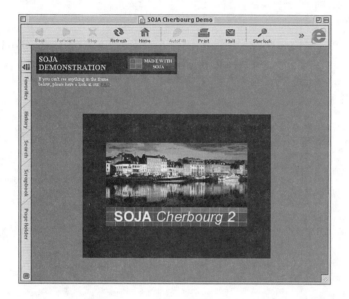

Figure 1.6   *SOJA is a Java SMIL player that plays right in the browser.*

Although Helio has been at it longer, it is not the only Java solution available as a SMIL player. SunTREC Salzburg offers Schmunzel, meaning "little smile" in German. It is no surprise that the home of Java, Sun Microsystems, is a partner in the technology and research center that offers this player.

The Future of SMIL

So what does the future hold for SMIL? If the last couple of years are any indication, SMIL has promise. Each year brings new tools and adopters. SMIL will not solve every problem faced by a Web multimedia author, but it can act as a facilitator to allow multiple media technologies to mix smoothly.

Now that you have a bit of SMIL background, we will dive in and take a closer look at the SMIL language and authoring multimedia for the Web.

2

SMIL Authoring

Authoring with SMIL

It is possible to hand-code your SMIL documents using nothing more than a text editor. In this section, we'll look at the basics of coding SMIL by hand, and in the next, we'll examine authoring tools that do the coding for you.

Basic SMIL Syntax

Writing SMIL is similar to writing HTML; in fact, if you feel comfortable writing HTML, you'll be off and running with SMIL in no time. By using a simple text editor (or any software that can save your work as a plain-text file) and following some basic rules, you can quickly produce a SMIL document that controls where, how, and when your multimedia clips are displayed.

In terms of coding, HTML can be quite forgiving. However, SMIL has some hard-and-fast rules you'll need to observe. Here are the basic rules of the road:

- All code must be written in lowercase. All attributes and tags must be coded in lowercase, without exception.

- Close every tag in the SMIL document, without exception. Some tags with a lot of content can be closed as in HTML; for example, `<smil>…</smil>`. Tags without a corresponding end tag must be closed with a forward slash at the end of the tag; for example, `<region ….. />`.

- Attribute values must be enclosed in double quotes; for example, `<tag attribute="`*`value`*`" />`. Again, no exceptions.

- When stating values for attributes there should be no spaces around the equal sign. Adding spaces will create errors.

- SMIL documents are saved as `.smi` or `.smil` files; use the four-letter extension to decrease playback errors. No spaces are allowed in filenames, although an underscore can be employed. For example, `big bang.smil` is not allowed but `big_bang.smil` is acceptable.

- While not specifically a SMIL rule, it is a good idea to use the standard naming convention of eight characters or fewer followed by a dot and the three-letter file extension (for example, `rollaway.jpg`) when naming files. Again, no spaces are allowed in filenames.

- Recommended for ease when editing your code, but also not specifically a SMIL rule, is the use of HTML-style comments (`<!--` *`comments`* `-->`) that are supported by SMIL, and indenting your code.

So those are the basic rules to keep in mind as you begin composing SMIL files. Other tag-related rules and restrictions exist (for example, the `<head>` section is optional, but the `<body>` section is required), but we'll cover those as we move through the specific tags and attributes in Part II.

SMIL Document Concepts

The structure of a SMIL document essentially revolves around two components: the `<layout>` section, which controls the positioning and display of the media elements, and the `<body>` section, which contains the paths to the media elements and the timing of their display.

A basic SMIL document structure is illustrated next:

```
<smil>
        <head>
            <layout>
                <!-- positioning and display -->
            </layout>
        </head>

        <body>
            <!-- media elements and timing -->
        </body>
</smil>
```

The <head> section of the document, in addition to outlining the layout of the presentation and defining how the elements are displayed, can also contain <meta> tags much like an HTML document does. These <meta> tags can include the presentation's title, author, copyright information, and an abstract describing the content. The <head> section is optional, but recommended, and is necessary for controlling the positioning of media elements on the screen.

The <body> section calls the media elements into the SMIL document by listing the path to the element and by assigning *handles*, or names, to the elements. Media elements can include live-streamed broadcasts, audio or video clips, text files, images, animations, streaming text and other media objects the player supports.

The timing and sequencing for these media elements also occurs within the <body> section. Elements can appear at the same time by grouping them using the parallel tag <par> or sequentially by using the <seq> tag. These tags can also be combined and nested as you like to present the media exactly as you want it displayed.

In addition to naming the elements and timing their appearance, the <body> section also provides several other options. For example, the <switch> tag, which allows the author to provide alternative presentations tailored to a range of options including the viewer's language or connection speed, is part of the <body> section. The capability to use an <a> tag to make elements or regions into links can also be coded into the <body> section.

We'll go into the details of these tags in Section II. Until then, just keep in mind that the <layout> section sets the stage, and the <body> section calls in the media.

Understanding Bandwidth and Data Rates

Bandwidth and Data Rate: the evil twins. Eternally linked and eternally battling.

That is one way to imagine the relationship between bandwidth and data rates. Here's another: Think of your presentation as a bucket of water being poured at a given rate through a hose into a basin. The basin represents the viewer of the presentation. The bucket of water is the file size of the total presentation (determined by adding together the sizes of all the component files in the presentation). The hose represents the available bandwidth. The rate at which it is poured through the hose equates to the average data rate. Data rate is calculated by dividing that total file size (the bucket of water) by the duration of your presentation (the amount of time allowed for water to reach the basin). So, in other words, the data rate is how much water has to move through the hose in a fixed amount of time or, in this analogy, the rate of pour. See Figure 2.1 for a picture of this analogy.

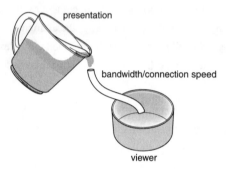

Figure 2.1   *A bandwidth and data rate analogy.*

So if you're trying to pour a big bucket of water very quickly through a drinking straw, all the water is not going to end up in the basin. As a matter of fact, much of the water is going to end up on the floor. That would be the case with a short-duration presentation with a big file size that is attempting to reach the viewer over a dial-up modem. Lots of water, coming in fast, through a very small hose.

This is the dilemma faced by Web multimedia authors because we tend to make large, beautiful presentations and then have to accept the bitter pill that most viewers are still viewing our work using the telephone lines.

Various solutions are available that, of course, all involve reducing data rate, not increasing bandwidth. We'll go into these solutions later. But no matter how you envision these two factors, this much is true: Bandwidth is almost always smaller than we would like, and data rates almost always require reduction. As a Web designer or developer, you're probably already familiar with these terms, but let's do a basic run-through just to make sure that we are all on the same page.

Bandwidth, the hose through which the media is poured, is the amount of data per second that the hardware, software, and connection are capable of delivering to the viewer. It is measured in kilobits per second (Kbps). For example, a

56Kbps modem is technically capable of delivering up to 56 kilobits of data per second.

Keep in mind that it is rare indeed for a viewer to connect at the top speed of a modem. Interference such as line noise, network congestion, and other sundry nuisances can reduce the connection speed, as can the need for error correction, resending lost data, and so on.

A good general rule is to expect only a portion of your viewer's bandwidth to be available for your presentation. For analog connections, such as dial-up modems, reduce the bandwidth figure by 25–30%. For digital connections (such as cable modems or DSL connections) reduce the bandwidth by 10 –15%. In other words, assume that a 56Kbps modem offers 34 – 42Kbps connectivity, and a 256Kbps DSL modem reliably can provide bandwidth of 217–230Kbps (see Table 2.1). Then reduce your data rates accordingly. We'll talk more about that in a moment.

Table 2.1   Connection Speed and Available Bandwidth

Connection Speed/Type	Anticipated Available Bandwidth
28.8Kbps dial-up modem	20Kbps
56Kbps dial-up modem	34 – 42Kbps
128Kbps dual ISDN	90 –100Kbps
256Kbps cable modem/DSL	217–230Kbps
512Kbps cable modem/DSL	435 – 460Kbps
T1 connection (at 1.5Mbps)	1275–1350Kbps

A file's *data rate*, measured in kilobytes per second, is the average amount of data per second that the file delivers. Determining a file's average data rate is simple: take the file size and divide by the file duration. For example, a 100KB file that takes 12 seconds to play has a data rate of 8.3KB per second. File size ÷ duration = average data rate. 100KB ÷ 12 seconds = 8.3K per second.

SMIL presentations typically include several files. To find the data rate for an entire presentation, take the file size of the individual elements and add them. Then divide the total file size by the overall duration of the presentation.

It's important to note that this is the *average* data rate of the file or presentation. In actuality, the data rate of a presentation fluctuates as elements begin or end, most notably when "heavyweight" elements (such as large files or sections of a file that include a lot of motion, transitions, or manipulations) enter or exit. Tools are available that will assist you in visualizing and understanding your data rate so that you can create presentations that flow without clogging the pipe, so to speak. We'll talk about some of the methods for tinkering with this in "Compensating for Bandwidth," later in this chapter.

Now, back to the evil twins.

Calculating Bandwidth and Data Rate

Remember that bandwidth is measured in *kilobits* (Kb) per second and data rates in *kilobytes* (KB) per second. You'll have to convert one to the other to determine whether your data rate is exceeding your targeted bandwidth. We need to also take into account that although a modem Kb is a thousand bits, a file KB is 1,024 bytes. The math will not come out perfectly. So go for the ballpark figure, and leave wiggle room. That's the best you can do.

You can use several methods to convert between bits and bytes, bandwidth and data rates.

Let's use a standard example (see Figure 2.2) and run through a couple of ways to find out whether the presentation is going to stall.

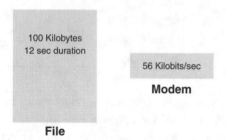

Figure 2.2 *Our sample data used as an example for converting data rate and band-width figures for comparison.*

Method 1

Let's say we've got a 100KB file that takes 12 seconds to play, and we are targeting a viewer with a 56Kbps modem.

1. First determine the presentation's average data rate. To do this, divide the file size by the presentation's duration. Using the

preceding example, our calculation would be 100KB ÷ 12 sec, which gives us an average data rate of 8.3 kilobytes per second.

2. Convert the data rate from bytes to bits. To compare our data rate to our connection speed, we need to multiply by 8 to convert from bytes to bits. The outcome (8.3Kbps×8) is 66.7 kilobits per second (or 66.7Kbps).

Because our example is using the connectivity of a 56Kbps modem, which allows true speeds of approximately 34– 40Kbps (as noted in the previous section on adjusting for overhead), the file's data rate obviously surpasses the available bandwidth. There will either be buffering or lost data.

A quick-and-dirty alternative also is available for estimating whether your presentation's data rate will exceed the bandwidth. First you calculate the average data rate; in our example, it is 8.3Kbps. Then, using a factor of 10, convert the bandwidth kilobytes to kilobits. This makes the math easier to do and covers you for the potential loss of 25% connection speed because of network overhead. Thus, in our example, the viewer is on a 56Kbps modem. Dividing by 10 gives us a connectivity of 5.6 kilobytes for a 56Kbps modem. Because our average data rate for this example is 8.3Kbps and the bandwidth is limited to approximately 5.6Kbps, we come to the same conclusion—just more quickly.

Method 2

The following steps show another way to determine whether the bandwidth and the average data rate of your presentation are suited for one another:

1. First convert your file size from kilobytes (KB) to kilobits (Kb) by multiplying your presentation's total file size by 8. In our example, our 100KB file size would become 800Kb.

2. Divide the converted file size by the bandwidth to find the ideal duration. Again, using our example, for delivery on a 56K modem (and allowing for network overhead), you'd divide the file's size of 800Kb by 34Kbps to get an optimal presentation duration of 23.5 seconds. (File size in kilobits ÷ connection speed = optimal duration. 800 ÷ 34 = 23.5). The outcome is the ideal duration for the file so that it will play back smoothly and without any preloading or buffering.

Because our presentation is 12 seconds in duration, we have again reached the same conclusion. If we attempt to deliver our 100K, 12-second presentation over a 56K modem, there will be buffering, interruptions, and/or lost data because it needs 23.5 seconds to play in its entirety.

Compensating for Bandwidth

No matter which way you calculate it, our presentation example is not going to stream to our user without some delays or potentially lost data. Several things can help.

First, you can reduce the total file size of your presentation (reduce the amount of water in the bucket). Things such as transitions, high-quality images, video that includes a lot of motion, and stereo sound all can add to the file size of your presentation. Try reducing your file size by using the software you used to create the media to crop out unused space, reduce quality, reduce image size and/or frame rate, and eliminate filters and transitions. This is a good first option.

Another option to decrease your file size (which, in turn, reduces your data rate) is to increase the duration of the file (increase the time allowed for pouring). This is automatically done by some players, which won't begin playing a clip until enough data has been cached that will ensure uninterrupted playback (called *buffering* or *preroll*). The other way to extend the duration of your presentation is to add black or another screen matte to your timeline, thus inflating the duration.

You can also choose to begin a presentation with low-bandwidth clips, thus providing the audience with something to view while preloading is occurring. Appropriate choices for this may include simple text titles, a single 8-bit sound file, or a color field that slowly transitions to your first media clip. This is essentially a variant of creating a longer timeline. However, knowing that high-bandwidth clips within a presentation will cause your data rate to spike, you can use these techniques to smooth the way for preloading those high-density clips and smooth out those spikes in your data rate. See Figure 2.3 for a visual depiction of these concepts.

Last, but certainly not least, you can provide alternative versions of your presentation, specifically tailored for particular bandwidths. In some player formats, this has meant creating links to several separate presentations, but with SMIL, it is possible to assess the user's connection and launch the correct version for that connection speed. We'll talk over these options later on in Part III when we discuss the players in detail.

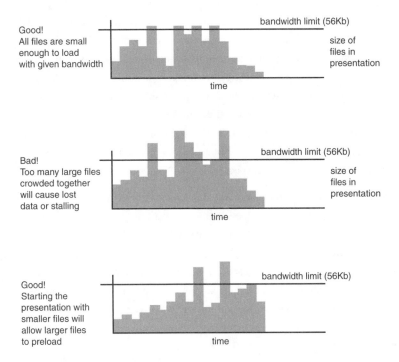

Figure 2.3   *A visual illustration of bandwidth limits and the loading of files.*

Browser Compliance and Compatibility

Although SMIL is a standard, because it is played back using proprietary players, the implementation of that standard becomes the discretion of the software publisher. For example, in the case of RealNetworks, RealPix and RealText are SMIL-based proprietary solutions. QuickTime, in turn, allows some attributes that RealPlayer would not be able to see. And Internet Explorer will do things that RealPlayer or any Web browser will not.

In most cases, Netscape and Internet Explorer will work with the players listed. Gradually, as implementations mature, there will be an increasing number of standard tricks to draw from. Until then, however, it is best if you target most content toward a particular player.

Serving Your Work

Let's say you've mastered SMIL (or perhaps one of the authoring tools) and have produced a completed presentation. How do you go about getting it out to your viewers?

Because RealNetworks, QuickTime, and Internet Explorer all handle the delivery of presentations in their own distinct manner, we'll cover the How-Tos for each when we dissect the players in Section III of this book. For now, suffice it to say that each is considered a *streaming architecture*, meaning that each delivery system contains a client-based player, an encoding scheme, and a server operating system that is distinct unto itself. All can make use of a standard Web server to deliver presentations, but do so in their own distinct manner. So for now, let's look at the general terms and conditions that are common to all, and then in Section III we'll return to the specifics.

First, let's define our terms. *Streaming* has come to be accepted as a rather broad term indicating that a viewer does not have to wait until a file has downloaded to begin viewing the file. Beyond that generality, there are actually two distinct types of streaming protocols. One is typically called "true streaming" with the other usually referred to as "pseudostreaming" or "progressive download." Neither true streaming nor pseudostreaming are superior to the other in every way. Depending on what you are publishing, who your audience is, and how they are accessing your presentation, one may be preferable to the other after you understand the strengths and weaknesses of each.

Here's a quick analogy to help get a picture of the differences between true and pseudostreaming or progressive download. True streaming is like watching a movie on television. It is broadcast, you watch it, and at the end of the show, it's gone. Pseudostreaming is more like watching a movie that is on television but catching it on your VCR. After it has been broadcast and taped, you can watch it again and again if you choose.

Pseudostreaming

Let's start our examination of these two types of streaming with streaming from a Web server. Streaming from a Web server is not considered true streaming because the streaming is not done in real-time. The file will take as long as it needs to completely arrive at the destination, regardless of the duration of the presentation. The two main benefits of this type of streaming are that the presentation received by the viewer can be of very high quality and almost all viewers can access the media. The downside is that the files download (to some extent at least), which takes up space on the viewer's machine, leaves your media at their disposal, and delivery times can be delayed by the protocols used to serve the media. Depending on which architecture you are using, you can limit the extent of this downloading.

First, let's look at the how the file is transmitted. The data is served up using technology that is common for most Web delivery—a standard HTTP server using TCP/IP protocols (Transmission Control Protocol/Internet Protocol). This means that if viewers can access Web pages, they can probably access your presentation. Firewalls rarely present a problem with Web-based serving, which can be a definite plus depending on your target audience.

The TCP/IP protocol is a packet-based system of delivery. The data being sent using this protocol is broken up into small "packets" that are sent independently of one another and then knit back together when they are received by the client machine. The beauty of this system is a little item called CHECKSUM that makes sure all the sent data has arrived. If all packets and data are not accounted for, CHECKSUM signals to the sender to resend the entire file.

This means that all data will definitely arrive at the viewer's machine and makes it preferable when quality is the most important aspect of your presentation. The downside is that this can result in longer buffering or preroll for your presentations until all data is accounted for. Playback begins when enough of the file has been received to ensure constant playback without interruption, and if data is being resent, this can delay the start of playback while data is being cached.

Another downside with this type of serving is that it places the burden on the viewer. The file will, to some extent, download onto the viewer's machine, using hard drive space and leaving the viewer with a portion (or all) of your data. Also, because the amount of data being delivered is fixed, the connection speed of the viewer becomes the determining factor on how long the wait is to see the file (although you can provide alternatives from which the viewer can choose).

Good uses of pseudostreaming or progressive download, which take advantage of these strengths and weaknesses, include advertisements or movie trailers, where quality is key and missed data would be disadvantageous. In these cases, leaving the file on the user's machine for re-review would also be to the media creator's advantage.

True Streaming

In contrast, *true streaming* refers to media being streamed in real-time from a streaming server. The strengths of this type of streaming are the following: The file is not downloaded onto the viewer's machine; The presentation can be automatically matched to the connection speed of the user; The media is received in real-time (meaning that a two-minute presentation will be presented in two minutes); and any point in the presentation can be randomly accessed. The downsides of true streaming are that it requires a streaming server and that data will be discarded if the viewer's bandwidth is insufficient to present all the data of your two-minute presentation in two minutes. Firewalls can also restrict access to files being served from a streaming server.

Files that are served from a streaming server frequently use UDP/IP (User Datagram Protocol), a form of transfer protocol that differs from TCP/IP in several ways. The most critical difference is that UDP does not use CHECKSUM to make sure all the data has been received. In fact, UDP allows for data to be dropped so that files will retain their original duration. In practice, this means that the quality of your presentation may be compromised, but the file will play exactly as long as it is supposed to. Preloading (often called buffering) may still occur, but the file itself, once started, will retain its authored duration. This is very helpful when trying to fit into a block of time or during live broadcasts.

One of the best features of true streaming is the capability to match the viewer's bandwidth and deliver the best quality possible, given this limitation. This is a function of the server's operating system, which first checks the connection speed and then delivers the appropriate file. Although the presentation quality may still be compromised, the viewer will get the best quality possible.

Good uses of true streaming, which take advantage of these strengths and weaknesses, include any live broadcast or situation where adherence to a broadcasting schedule is a reality. The fact that the files will retain their duration allows for a finite start and stop time and often, the files can be crafted so that not much data is dropped out.

Unfortunately, true streaming usually requires a streaming server. The cost of maintaining an additional server may not be an option for some multimedia authors. If not, it's back to Web-based, or pseudostreaming, serving!

Table 2.2 compares true streaming with HTTP streaming:

Table 2.2   True Streaming Versus HTTP Streaming

True Streaming	HTTP Streaming
Streaming server required.	Standard Web server.
UDP delivery protocol-data loss is acceptable and expected.	TCP delivery protocol - no data is lost but may need to be retransmitted, leading to slower delivery times.
Data is sometimes discarded to meet time and/or bandwidth constraints.	High-quality files can be guaranteed because no data is lost or discarded.
Can match user's bandwidth.	File is delivered without regard to user's bandwidth.
Burden on the developer (requires server, multiple versions).	Burden to the user (hard drive space, connection speed).
No file downloads to user's machine.	Files download to user's machine.
May not play behind some firewalls.	Bypasses most firewalls.
Delivers media in real - time - file will play exactly as long as it is supposed to, even if data gets discarded.	Playback will begin when enough of file has downloaded for uninterrupted playback and will for duration of file.

SMIL Authoring Tools

One of the biggest challenges to the adoption of SMIL has been finding good authoring tools. Sure, you can write SMIL in a text editor. But if you're going to author a lot of SMIL, you probably want some kind of authoring environment to make the process easier. Until recently, SMIL authoring tools were few and far between.

Thankfully, SMIL authoring options are starting to rapidly expand. A range of developing applications is now appearing on both the Macintosh and Windows platforms. It is still a little early yet, but the growth in SMIL tools is promising.

Next, let's take a look at some of the authoring tools currently available.

GRiNS

A player and an authoring tool? As you read in Chapter 1, "What is SMIL?", GRiNS is a somewhat experimental but very capable SMIL player. On the authoring side, GRiNS is a capable and powerful SMIL authoring package (see Figure 2.4).

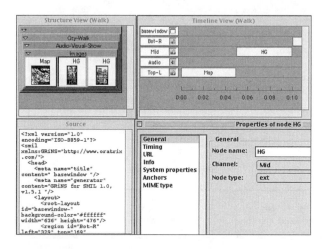

Figure 2.4 *GRiNS in action.*

GRiNS appeals to the multimedia engineer, meaning that it is more menu driven and a bit less visual than other tools. Using an object-oriented approach, the SMIL author can fine-tune a number of details within the presentation. With current versions, some familiarity with SMIL is important to get the most out of the authoring environment.

GRiNS is available from Oratrix (`http://www.oratrix.com`) for both the Macintosh and Windows environments.

Fluition

If GRiNS appeals to the multimedia engineer, Fluition is particularly adapted to the multimedia artist. Like GRiNS, Fluition is object oriented. But where the GRiNS environment leans toward menus and dialog boxes, Fluition is driven more by visual interaction with the author. Fluition, shown in Figure 2.5, is very well suited for SMIL presentations oriented toward video.

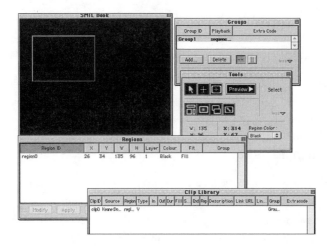

Figure 2.5 *Fluition in action.*

Fluition is available from Confluent Technologies
(http://www.smilsoftware.com) for both the Macintosh and Windows environments.

RealSlideshow

Of all SMIL authoring tools, RealSlideshow is one of our favorites. With other authoring tools, you can expect to have to spend some time getting used to how the application does business. This is not the case with RealSlideshow. As shown in Figure 2.6, the interface to RealSlideshow is simple and intuitive. After a couple minutes with the documentation, you can be up and authoring streaming-image presentations timed to music.

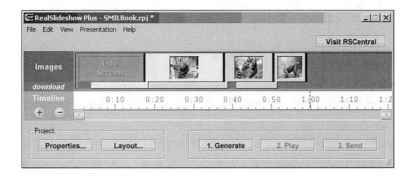

Figure 2.6 *RealSlideshow creates streaming slideshow presentations quickly and easily.*

RealSlideshow leans toward the SMIL-based proprietary RealPix and RealText approaches to authoring SMIL. With market dominance in the streaming-media market, RealNetworks can afford to do that.

RealSlideshow is available for the Windows platform as a free download from RealNetworks (`http://www.realnetworks.com/products/slideshow/`). Users willing to pay can choose to obtain the enhanced RealSlideshow Plus version.

Macromedia Flash

As an animation and Web multimedia tool, Macromedia Flash has wide acceptance and use and offers a range of output options for finished animation. So it was of great interest to the SMIL community when Macromedia, as shown in Figure 2.7, began offering SMIL support with Flash 5.

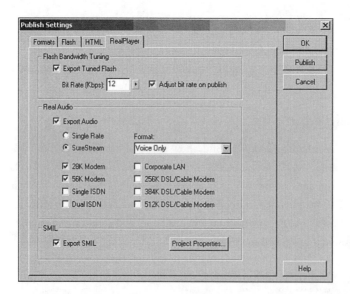

Figure 2.7 *SMIL export capabilities are located in the Flash Publish options.*

One of the available options is to stream the Flash animation from a RealNetworks RealServer. When using this option, the animation is separated from the audio. This enables the RealServer to offer superior streaming audio to accompany the animation. By using SMIL to bring the visual animation back together with the streaming audio, it also allows animators to stream long animations that maintain audio synchronization.

It is a bit of a stretch to call Flash a SMIL authoring tool. Flash currently offers little control over the SMIL output. But the prevalence of Flash makes the SMIL capability worth mentioning.

HomeSite

As the division between players and browsers blurs, so will the division between authoring HTML and authoring streaming-media presentations.

Allaire HomeSite is such a tool that blurs the difference. Long respected as an HTML authoring tool for Windows, HomeSite also supports output to SMIL.

When all is said and done, authoring tools for SMIL are on the rise. But for now, let's go forward and dig into coding this stuff ourselves using what we've learned so far.

Summary

SMIL is a versatile, powerful yet simple language you can use to author multimedia presentations for Web delivery. Authoring tools are rapidly being developed that will assist you with writing your SMIL presentation. This chapter gave you the simple guidelines for SMIL and streaming basics you will need to know before reading the more detailed discussion of how to author multimedia using SMIL 2.0, found in Part II of this book.

Part II

Using SMIL: The Specification Modules

3

Getting Technical: The SMIL Specification

The W3C Builds a Web Multimedia Language

In October 1996, a small group representing the CD-ROM and Web multimedia communities gathered at a workshop hosted by the World Wide Web Consortium (W3C). Their task was to explore the creation of a language that could be used to synchronize multimedia on the Web. Unlike the scripting languages in use for creating multimedia, this new language would be descriptive. It would not require a programmer to make Web multimedia. Encouraged by the discussion, the W3C organized a working group to develop a specification for just such a language. From this working group came the Synchronized Multimedia Integration Language (SMIL).

SMIL 1.0

SMIL 1.0, the first specification of the Synchronized Multimedia Integration Language, was offered as a recommendation by the W3C in 1998 and is a model of simplicity. With only a few SMIL tags under your belt, you can easily create most SMIL presentations.

As stated in the specification, the goals of SMIL 1.0 were basic:

- To describe the temporal (time) behavior of the presentation
- To describe the layout of the presentation on the screen
- To associate hyperlinks with media objects

The resulting language is probably best summed up as HTML for multimedia. With SMIL 1.0, you have a text-based language that is built for multimedia on the Web. What really makes it powerful is that right out of the box, it comes ready to handle time. After years of using CD-ROM multimedia presentation approaches that had been roughly patched up for Web use, SMIL 1.0 showed a new direction.

Timing Media

SMIL 1.0 controls the timing of media with two basic elements: <seq> for the sequential synchronization of media objects and <par> for the parallel synchronization of media objects.

<seq> (for sequential) is used to play one piece of media right after another. With it, you can tell your SMIL player that you want your first media clip to be followed by a second.

<par> (for parallel) ensures that two independent pieces of media play at the same time. For example, using the <par> element, you can instruct a music clip to play in synchronization with a set of images.

Of course, you can combine these two basic building blocks in almost any fashion. For example, by nesting two <par> elements inside a <seq> element, one grouping of media clips running at the same time will be followed by a second block of assorted media objects also running in parallel. See Figure 3.1 for an illustration.

The capability to give the viewer a cohesive presentation from assorted media objects is incredibly important when evaluating SMIL as a potential Web multimedia approach. With other Web multimedia environments, the presentation of media is authored and output as a fixed work. If you want to provide other playback options using those same media objects, you need to recombine and output your content to match your intent. An example of a fixed Web multimedia would be a QuickTime movie that includes an interactive Flash layer. Once the final movie file is created, the interactivity is fixed. Rearranging the media objects and changing the interactivity requires re-authoring the file.

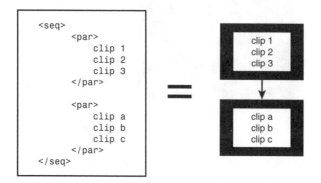

Figure 3.1 *In this example, each block of media clips will play in parallel, but the first block (clips 1-3) will play before the second (clips a-c).*

With SMIL, all the media objects maintain their status as independent media objects that can be pulled together as needed. For example, if you desire a different look for your presentation, a simple rearrangement of the <par> and <seq> elements in the SMIL document can easily achieve this effect. So either by your hand or automatically by a program running on a server, the presentation's organization and use of available media objects can be changed instantly to suit your intent, the viewer's hardware and software parameters, or the viewer's interests.

Media Layout

Timing and synchronization of media objects is very important, but that is only half the problem. HTML authors have long struggled with how to get Web pages to look the way they want them to. Thankfully, SMIL comes with built-in layout control.

The <layout> element determines how objects are displayed in the presentation space. Within the <layout> element, playback areas can be specified using the <region> tag. For example, suppose that you want to display video at the top of the presentation window accompanied by descriptive text at the bottom as in Figure 3.2. The SMIL <layout> element can be employed to create two regions: one for the playback of the video segment and another to display the text.

```
<layout>
  <region id="video" top="50px" left="100px" width="240px" height="180px"/>
  <region id="text" top="360px" left="50px" width="350px" height="20px"/>
</layout>
```

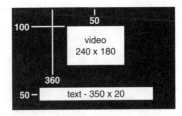

Figure 3.2 *Defining playback areas using <layout> and <region>.*

The <layout> element adds to the object-oriented power of the SMIL timing and synchronization elements. To reach our goal in the preceding example (video accompanied by text) using other multimedia authoring tools, it would be necessary to "burn" the descriptive caption text into the video and output it as such. If you wanted to change that text, you would have to go back to the original source files and create a new version of your video. With SMIL, the descriptive text can be kept as a separate media object and positioned in a <region> below the video with <layout>. Now, changing the captioning requires modifying only your text.

Old-Fashioned Linking

Of course, multimedia on the Web is pretty limited if it stays only within the confines of one start-to-finish presentation. As a delivery mechanism, CD-ROM is currently still more effective at delivering multimedia efficiently. A Web multimedia language needs to offer a functionality that cannot be contained on a single CD-ROM: hyperlinking to other materials and presentations.

SMIL 1.0 did not disappoint. Like HTML, SMIL offers the capability to link through an anchor element to another Web element. Notice the term "Web element" instead of "media element." With a Web-based presentation, a SMIL object can link to another media object, but it can just as easily link to a Web page.

SMIL 1.0 also offers internal anchors. In this fashion, a link can jump within a SMIL document much like an internal reference in a long HTML page might move you down to a specific chapter.

Anyone for a `<switch>`?

Serving Web multimedia to an audience that might come to your presentation from a variety of places with a variety of equipment has the potential for creating authoring headaches. HTML authors have long faced this challenge and have used client-side scripting and server-side detection to offer up content that best matches the individual situations of their site visitors.

To help solve this problem for the multimedia author, SMIL offers the `<switch>` element. Do you have a visitor who speaks French? Give them a French version of your presentation with `<switch>`. Is the visitor using a slow modem or speeding along with a broadband connection? Determine the data rate and `<switch>` to the proper media files to match. Now site visitors can receive content tailored to their personal situations.

The `<switch>` element is indispensable in allowing the author freedom to work directly within the parameters of a specific audience member.

Limitations of SMIL 1.0

The SMIL 1.0 specification was a good starting point for a fledgling Web multimedia language. It is simple enough to learn quickly and generic enough that it can be adapted to almost any Web multimedia player. But, like any first effort, limitations existed.

RealNetworks enthusiastically jumped out front as the first major player to adopt SMIL. To get the most out of its G2 player, however, RealNetworks created two SMIL-based proprietary languages that met the need for low-bandwidth display of streaming text and images. RealText and RealPix provide text effects and transitions not available when using standard SMIL 1.0.

Whereas RealNetworks was a solid advocate for the first SMIL specification, Microsoft responded with criticism. Pulling out of the SMIL effort before the SMIL 1.0 recommendation was made by the W3C, Microsoft later offered a proposal to incorporate SMIL in with standard HTML.

These new interests would require a more powerful and complex language. SMIL 1.0 needed an update.

SMIL 2.0

Named after the city in which it was drafted, SMIL Boston first appeared during the summer of 1999. Later renamed SMIL 2.0, this specification was designed to meet two goals:

- To continue defining an XML-based language that controls the timing and positioning of media objects in a Web multimedia presentation

- To allow use of the SMIL syntax in other XML-based languages, such as eXtensible HTML (XHTML) and Scalable Vector Graphics (SVG)

The latter goal was extremely important to Microsoft because it addresses Microsoft's interest in incorporating SMIL timing elements into HTML and making them available to a Web browser. It also opens the door to much tighter incorporation of SMIL with other technologies, such as the emerging SVG format for graphics and animation.

SMIL 2.0 Modules

Whereas SMIL 1.0 is simple and easy to get into quickly, SMIL 2.0 is more complex—yet much more powerful. Divided into 10 functional areas that contain related modules, the SMIL 2.0 specification includes the following:

- Animation modules—These modules include elements for placing animation into the presentation timeline. They also allow for combining the effects of multiple animations.

- Content Control modules—These modules expand on the `<switch>` element and increase the control of presentation flow and format.

- Layout modules—These modules slightly augment the initial `<layout>` capabilities presented in the SMIL 1.0 specification. Additional support for audio layout is included.

- Linking modules—These modules amplify the hyperlinking capability of SMIL 1.0.

- Media Object modules—These modules further enhance the calling of media objects (such as animation, audio, video, text) as first defined in SMIL 1.0.

- Metainformation module—This module adds more descriptive power to the initial limited `<meta>` element that was offered in SMIL 1.0.

- Structure module—The basic elements of a SMIL 1.0 document gain additional attributes with the introduction of this module, which allows greater presentation control.

- Timing and Synchronization module—Building on the previous <seq> and <par> elements, the SMIL 2.0 Timing and Synchronization module offers more timeline control. The new <excl> element for playing an exclusive set of objects is also included here.

- Time Manipulations module—This module offers control of such time characteristics as the speed or rate of a media object. This is a particularly important module for implementing animation in the timeline.

- Transition Effects module—Absent from SMIL 1.0 was the capability to transition between one media object to another. This module adds the capability to offer standard wipes and fades between media objects.

SMIL Profiles

As you have seen, the SMIL 2.0 modules offer more elements and attributes than the simple capabilities available in SMIL 1.0. But the new specification does not stop there. SMIL 2.0 adds *profiles*, which further enhance the potential for smooth playback of multimedia presentations. Profiles combine modules as an attempt to achieve interoperability across players and browsers. Theoretically, presentations meeting established profile characteristics will be able to hop from player to player with acceptable results. But for the near term, most authors will probably still create presentations for specific players.

Currently, three language profiles make use of SMIL 2.0 modules. Two are host-language conformant, indicating that the profile incorporates a Structure module that contains the root element of the language. (In this case, that would be the <smil> element.) The main profile is called the SMIL 2.0 Language Profile. A subset of this profile is the SMIL 2.0 Basic Language Profile, which is basically a stripped-down profile for use with personal digital assistants (PDAs), mobile phones, and entertainment devices such as MP3 players. Yep. Portable MP3 players with image displays can SMIL.

The third language profile, the XHTML+SMIL 2.0 Language Profile, is based on a proposal by Microsoft and is undergoing development by the W3C. Although it is a subset of the larger SMIL 2.0 Language Profile, it is integration-set conformant, in contrast to host-language conformant. This means that the profile does not include the root (or <smil>) element. With this profile, SMIL is incorporated into the Web page along with HTML. In the past, Microsoft has referred to this approach as HTML+TIME. Extensions to HTML allow for timing and interactivity right within the HTML without using scripting languages.

Deprecation

As can be expected, anytime a language changes, some of its syntax also changes. Deprecation occurs when a portion of the language is no longer included or is marked for phasing out in a future specification.

Thankfully, deprecation between SMIL 1.0 and 2.0 is reasonably digestible. The most notable change between SMIL 1.0 and 2.0 is in the replacement of hyphenated attributes with mixed case (sometimes called *camel case*) attributes. For example, a `clip-begin` attribute would now be `clipBegin`.

Living in Multiple SMIL Worlds

All this talk of specification versions, modules, profiles, and deprecation may have you asking the ultimate SMIL question: Whom do I author for and with what approach?

Any kind of Web multimedia carries with it inherent risk and responsibility. For too long, Web multimedia designers and developers carried a self-righteous attitude about making content available for their visitors. If a viewer did not have the right browser or version of a player to interpret the media, they were doomed to put up with glitches, at best, or no content, at worst. In the lightning growth days of the Internet as a new medium, this attitude was tolerated as the norm.

Today, a designer or developer with that kind of attitude is best referred to as a fool. No company or organization hosting a Web site can afford to turn away potential customers or supporters, and any authors worth their salt will endeavor to meet the parameters set by their visitor's hardware and software. After all, every visitor can bring a sale to the bottom line. Over time, those little sales add up.

So how does Web multimedia fit in given all these potential constraints? Our suggestion is to use it with care and to consider the implications caused by the visitor who cannot see or hear what you create. Every authoring choice should help the site reach its objective or goal. If your Web presentation is mission critical, be sure to ask this question: Is Web multimedia the best way to deliver your content?

Likewise, think carefully about which version of SMIL you use. As we write this book, RealNetworks' RealPlayer and Apple's QuickTime offer solid SMIL 1.0

support, and playback using those players is relatively dependable. However, RealPlayer SMIL does not necessarily work with QuickTime SMIL. As for SMIL 2.0, formal adoption is on the horizon. Microsoft's Internet Explorer on the Windows platform supports some aspects of SMIL 2.0. RealPlayer and QuickTime support is right behind. But even as these new players become available, a large number of people on the Web will still be sticking with their older players for the time being, so SMIL 1.0 still presents a viable option. In any case, you will inevitably excite and motivate some viewers with the multimedia authoring choices you make. And you will leave others behind.

Although we certainly are not discouraging the use of Web multimedia, we do encourage exercising some common sense. For example, when considering viewer accessibility and authoring for a training-department intranet (with control over the access machines), the limitations of using SMIL 2.0 in Microsoft Internet Explorer may not problematic at all. On the wide-open Internet, however, you would not want to limit your viewers to those using Internet Explorer on WinOS machines. RealPlayer with SMIL 1.0 support is currently common across multiple platforms and boasts a large number of users, so this may be the most practical authoring environment for your presentation. At the very least, you should provide multiple paths to your content so that unequipped users do not feel left out. True, they may not get the compelling Web multimedia touch that you have crafted for your luckiest visitors. But those left out are not as likely to leave your site frustrated or annoyed, either.

On to the Specifications

In the following chapters, we walk you through a closer look at the SMIL specification. Working from the outside to the inside of SMIL document construction, we explain the possible elements and their attributes. For your convenience, we highlight differences between SMIL 1.0 and 2.0 elements and attributes. We also inform you of which modules fit within which profiles. Finally, we cover player and browser support based on the current and beta software available at the time that we write this book.

SMIL is a living language that is constantly changing and adapting to the needs of the Web multimedia community. This book is a fixed record of that process. For the very latest news on SMIL, visit World Wide Web Consortium's SMIL information site (http://www.w3.org/AudioVideo/) and the companion site for this book: SMILBook.com (`http://www.SMILBook.com/`). The W3C is the final authority on the SMIL specification, and SMILBook.com is a great way to keep up on how that is impacting the SMIL community.

4

First Things First: The SMIL Structure Module

The Structure module, with its `<smil>`, `<head>`, and `<body>` elements, provides the SMIL package to send your multimedia on its way. Put another way, the Structure module is the wrapper that surrounds all your additional coding. For the most part, you will not find a lot of complexity in this module. The elements it contains were introduced in SMIL 1.0, and because the Structure module of SMIL 2.0 makes use of these same elements, it is essentially backward compatible with SMIL 1.0.

Indeed, despite numerous changes between SMIL 1.0 and 2.0, the code for the structure of your document will stay pretty much the same as it has always been, with some small refinements.

Conformance Profiles and the Structure Module

As explained in the previous chapter, SMIL 2.0 introduces the concept of profiles. *Profiles* combine the various modules to increase interoperability across players and browsers. Presentations meeting profile characteristics should be able to hop from player to player with reasonable results.

Also explained previously are the two host-language conformant profiles (the SMIL 2.0 profile and SMIL 2.0 Basic profile) and one integration-set conformant profile (the XHTML+SMIL 2.0 profile) that currently make use of the SMIL 2.0 modules. Host-language conformant profiles require a Structure module, which contains the `<smil>` element. The integration-set conformant profile does not include the `<smil>` element as a root element; instead, SMIL coding is incorporated into the Web page along with HTML.

As a result, the Structure module is included only in profiles that are SMIL host-language conformant. That means that although you will find the Structure module in SMIL 2.0 and SMIL 2.0 Basic profiles, you will not see it in SMIL Integration Set implementations such as XHTML+SMIL.

That may sound like mind-numbing technobabble, but it actually makes sense if you think about it. With an Integration Set implementation, SMIL is inserted into the markup of a Web page. You would not want the `<body>` and `<head>` elements of the SMIL Structure module to get in the way of the existing `<body>` and `<head>` elements of the Web page in which they sit. For this reason, the Structure module is not included in integration-set conformant profile presentations.

The Structure Module Elements

- Module: Structure
- Conformance: SMIL Host Language
- Profile Compatibility: SMIL 1.0, SMIL 2.0, SMIL 2.0 Basic
- Possible Elements: `<smil>`, `<head>`, `<body>`

As mentioned previously, the use of the Structure module `<smil>`, `<head>`, and `<body>` elements is quite similar to their use in SMIL 1.0. In fact, other than how Structure is written up in the documentation for the two versions, SMIL authors will not see a big difference between SMIL 1.0 and SMIL 2.0.

However, SMIL 2.0 does provide additional attributes for these elements, and these attributes, in turn, offer more choices and control for the author. We'll get to those in a minute.

First, let's take a minute to review what a basic SMIL document looks like:

```
<smil>
<head>
...This is where the markup for information about your content goes...
</head>
```

```
<body>
...This is where the markup for the presentation goes...
</body>
</smil>
```

For conventional Web authors, this simple SMIL Structure should look pretty similar to good old-fashioned HTML. Of course, there is more detail to the Structure module than this code snippet provides. If you understand the concept shown, you are almost ready to jump to the next chapter. But first take a closer look at the elements and attributes of the SMIL 2.0 Structure module.

Element: `<smil>`

- Version Compatibility: SMIL 1.0, SMIL 2.0

- Possible Attributes: `id`, `class`, `xml:lang`, `title`, `xmlns`

- Child Elements: `<head>`, `<body>`

As noted previously, the `<smil>` element is simply the outer container of the markup "sandwich." The `<head>` and `<body>` sit within this outer container. In SMIL 1.0, the `<smil>` element had an optional attribute of `id`. SMIL 2.0 added the attributes `class`, `xml:lang`, `title`, and `xmlns`.

In both QuickTime and RealPlayer, a basic use of the `<smil>` element would take the following form in a text document:

```
<smil>
...presentation <head> and <body> elements and their contents would be
➥inserted here...
</smil>
```

Since Internet Explorer is an Integration Set implementation, the `<smil>` element is not used. Instead, SMIL timing characteristics are identified with the `xmlns` attribute as covered later in this chapter. A sample would look something like this:

```
<html xmlns:t="urn:schemas-microsoft-com:time">
```

Element: `<head>`

- Version Compatibility: SMIL 1.0, SMIL 2.0

- Possible Attributes: `id`, `class`, `xml:lang`, `title`

- Parent Element: `<smil>`
- Child Elements (in SMIL 1.0): `<layout>`, `<meta>`, `<switch>`

The `<head>` element provides information that is not related to the timing of the media elements (called nontemporal information). Some of the choices available include providing metainformation to describe the presentation and media elements involved; layout capabilities, which determine where on the screen the media will appear; and matching your content and delivery to the viewer's situation. In the SMIL 1.0 specification, the `<meta>`, `<layout>`, and `<switch>` elements are established as children of the `<head>` element. Although their location may be the same in SMIL 2.0, the newer specification breaks those elements off to their own modules.

With the exception of the namespace (`xmlns`) attribute, the `<head>` element offers the same attributes as the `<smil>` element. You will be more likely, however, to attach a title to your presentation in the `<head>` element than in `<smil>`. For more information on controlling the `<layout>` of your presentation, visit Chapter 6, "Placing It on the Page: The Layout Modules." The Metainformation module (`<meta>`) is covered in Chapter 5, "Data About Data: The Metainformation Module," and controlling the nature of your presentation with `<switch>` is covered in Chapter 12, "Optimizing Content Delivery: Content Control Modules."

As with the `<smil>` element usage in both QuickTime and RealPlayer, a basic use of `<head>` would take the following form in a text document:

```
<smil>
    <head>
        ...<meta> and <layout> element information is an example of what
        would typically be inserted here...
    </head>
    <body>
    ...This is where the markup for the presentation goes...
    </body>
</smil>
```

In versions of Internet Explorer that support HTML+TIME, the `<head>` element is really the HTML `<head>` element. This would carry the link to the time behaviors supported by HTML+TIME. In an HTML text document, the form would look like this:

```
<html xmlns:t ="urn:schemas-microsoft-com:time">
    <head>
```

```
        <style>
            .time {behavior:url(#default#time2);}
        </style>
        <?IMPORT namespace="t" implementation="#default#time2">
        ...additional <html> head elements as needed by Web page...
    </head>
</html>
```

Element: `<body>`

- Version Compatibility: SMIL 1.0, SMIL 2.0

- Possible Attributes: `id`, `class`, `xml:lang`, `title`

- Parent Element: `<smil>`

- Child Elements (in SMIL 1.0): `<a>`, `<animation>`, `<audio>`, `<img>`, `<par>`, `<ref>`, `<seq>`, `<switch>`, `<text>`, `<textstream>`, `<video>`

The `<body>` element contains content and pathways to your content, as well as all the information related to the timing of the presentation, including start and stop times and sequencing.

With the exception of the namespace (`xmlns`) attribute, the `<body>` element offers the same attributes as the `<smil>` and `<head>` elements. You will be more likely, however, to attach an `id` to your presentation elements in the `<body>` element than in `<smil>` or `<head>`.

In SMIL 1.0, the specification offers the `<a>`, `<animation>`, `<audio>`, `<img>`, `<par>`, `<ref>`, `<seq>`, `<switch>`, `<text>`, `<textstream>`, and `<video>` elements as children of the `<body>` element. Again, although their location may be the same in SMIL 2.0, the newer specification breaks those elements off to their own modules. For more information on controlling the flow of your presentation with `<switch>`, see Chapter 12. Chapter 8, "Bring on the Media: The Media Object Modules," covers the `<animation>`, `<audio>`, `<img>`, `<text>`, `<textstream>`, `<ref>`, and `<video>` elements used to contain and display your media. If you want to link with the `<a>` anchor element, visit Chapter 11, "Making It Interactive: The Linking Modules." Finally, the critical `<par>` parallel and `<seq>` sequential timing elements are covered in Chapter 7, "Grouping Your Content: The Timing and Synchronization Module."

Both QuickTime and RealPlayer make basic use of `<body>` with the following form in a text document:

```
<smil>
    <head>
    ...This is where the markup for information about your content
       goes...
    </head>
    <body>
        ...presentation content instructions would be inserted here...
    </body>

</smil>
```

As with the <head> element in Internet Explorer, <body> in IE is really the
<body> of the HTML document itself. Since an HTML <body> element contains
the content of the presentation, the end goal is the same as a traditional SMIL
<body> element.

The Structure Module Attributes

The <smil>, <head>, and <body> elements all make use of the following attributes. (The only exception is xmlns, or the namespace declaration attribute, which
is used exclusively by the <smil> element.)

Attribute: id

- Version Compatibility: SMIL 1.0, SMIL 2.0
- Possible Values: Valid XML identifier

The id attribute attaches a unique identifier to the element in question. This is
similar to the name attribute in traditional HTML. Assigning a value to id allows
you to reference that element later with another attribute in SMIL.

Attribute: class

- Version Compatibility: SMIL 2.0
- Possible Values: Valid class name or class names separated by spaces

This attribute is used to assign a class name or a set of class names to an element. It is almost identical to id but class allows any number of names to be
assigned to an element or group of elements.

Attribute: `xml:lang`

- Version Compatibility: SMIL 2.0
- Possible Values: Valid language code (with options from Ami to English to Klingon to Xiang)

As covered in the XML specification, this attribute identifies the language used in the presentation content and by the relevant attributes in the markup.

Attribute: `title`

- Version Compatibility: SMIL 2.0
- Possible Values: An alphanumeric text string

This is intended to let the user know something about the element to which it is attached. Implementation depends on its use; the information might be displayed in a title bar or seen as a mouse is rolled over an object, for example.

Attribute: `xmlns`

- Version Compatibility: SMIL 2.0
- Possible Values: A declared namespace

You will find this is the attribute attached to only one element: `<smil>`. `xmlns` declares the appropriate namespace in use in the SMIL document. This attribute allows for a check that compares the SMIL used in your document against standards that are linked to the namespace attribute. As you would expect considering its function, it is found only as an attribute of `<smil>`.

QuickTime makes use of the `xmlns` attribute to reference to Apple's own QuickTime extensions to SMIL:

```
<smil xmlns:qt="http://www.apple.com/quicktime/resources/smilextensions">
```

RealPlayer makes a direct reference to the W3C implementation of SMIL 2.0 with:

```
<smil xmlns="http://www.w3.org/2001/SMIL20/CR/">
```

Like QuickTime, RealPlayer also offers RealNetworks's own extensions to SMIL. The markup form is the same. So, for example, the markup to reference Alpha Channel and Resizing namespaces would look like:

```
<smil xmlns="http://www.w3.org/2001/SMIL20/Language"
➥xmlns:rn="http://features.real.com/2001/SMIL20/Extensions">
```

Probably the most involved use of the namespace attribute is in Internet Explorer browsers that support their HTML+TIME implementation of SMIL. You must declare the namespace, import the tag definitions, and then provide a means to associate elements with their `time2` behavior. To cover the bases, simply use the following code in your HTML document:

```
<html xmlns:t ="urn:schemas-microsoft-com:time">
    <head>
        <style>
            .time {behavior:url(#default#time2);}
        </style>
        <?IMPORT namespace="t" implementation="#default#time2">

    </head>
</html>
```

That use of the `<style>` element is the key that provides a critical link so that your HTML elements can pick up the SMIL behaviors.

Summary

The use of the `<smil>`, `<head>`, and `<body>` elements in SMIL 1.0 and 2.0 is remarkably similar. Additional attributes for these elements in 2.0 offer more flexibility and options. The implementations vary somewhat between the various players and browsers. With Internet Explorer especially, Structure is actually handled by the HTML document itself, so SMIL capabilities are linked to the HTML. But despite all the differences among the implementations, the goal is the same. Structure establishes the framework in which your presentation will sit.

5

Data About Data: The Metainformation Module

The Metainformation module is one of the shortest module sets in the SMIL 2.0 specification. Its purpose is simple: to give Web multimedia authors the power to provide specific data about their presentations, especially for Web-driven indexing and search engines. Much like a book cover provides details about a publication's contents, author, price, ISBN number, Library of Congress catalog data, and publisher, the Metainformation module provides the opportunity to present information about your information.

The Metainformation Module Elements

- Module: Metainformation
- Conformance: Not required for either SMIL host language or SMIL integration set
- Profile Compatibility: SMIL 1.0, SMIL 2.0, SMIL 2.0 Basic, XHTML+SMIL
- Possible Elements: <meta>, <metadata>

SMIL 1.0 introduced basic metainformation capabilities with the <meta> element. SMIL 2.0 continues to support the original <meta> element but further extends the capability to provide information about your presentation with the introduction of the <metadata> element. The older <meta> element is simpler to use, and undoubtedly many SMIL authors will continue to prefer it for this reason. But the new <metadata> element allows SMIL authors to describe almost any imaginable element of their presentation and allows for linking to additional informational resources, thus increasing both the accessibility and range of the information the author can provide.

Element: <meta>

- Version Compatibility: SMIL 1.0, SMIL 2.0
- Possible Attributes: name, content, id, skip-content
- Parent Element: <head>
- Child Elements: None

The <meta> element is the basic building block for machine-to-machine information exchange. Used within the <head> tags, it is very similar in nature to the <meta> element found in HTML.

In RealPlayer, a basic use of the <meta> element would take the following form within the <head> of a SMIL document:

```
<smil xmlns="http://www.w3.org/2001/SMIL20/CR/">
    <head>
        <meta name="title" content="My Presentation"/>
        ...other <meta> element information can be listed here....
    </head>
</smil>
```

A presentation in Internet Explorer will handle metainformation by way of the <meta> tags built into HTML.

Element: <metadata>

- Version Compatibility: SMIL 2.0
- Possible Attributes: Resources, properties, and statements as covered in RDF specification
- Parent Element: <head>
- Child Elements: None

The `<metadata>` element piles on to `<meta>` to allow the content author to specify an almost endless set of metainformation about a document. `<metadata>` follows the W3C's Resource Description Framework (RDF). RDF is made up of resources, properties, and statements. A *resource* is defined as a thing being described by an RDF expression. It can be any material referenced by a URI (uniform resource identifier). *Properties* are defined by the W3C as any specific characteristic, attribute, aspect, or relation used to describe the resource. *Statements* finish up the package. They are what is made up when the resource is tied to a property name, which is then tied to a property value.

If all this sounds repetitively endless, it almost is. Indeed, an author taking full advantage of `<metadata>` may quickly find the metainformation longer than the actual SMIL document.

The Metainformation Module Attributes

Most of the power in the Metainformation attributes lies in the `name` and `content` pairing. The SMIL specification offers possible values but you may find the player supports additional options to get the most out of this attribute combo.

Attribute: `name`

- Version Compatibility: SMIL 1.0, SMIL 2.0
- Possible Values: `base`, `pics-label`, `PICS-Label`, `title`

The `name` attribute is one half of a pair with the `content` attribute. Both are required `<meta>` attributes. The `name` part of the equation assigns a property name. `content` follows up with the actual value to go with that name.

Although a number of options are available, depending on the actual implementation, the SMIL specification suggests the following values for the `name` attribute: `"base"`, `"pics-label"` (or `"PICS-Label"`), and `"title"`.

A `name` value of `"base"` provides a base URI to which all other URIs in the presentation will be relative. `"PICS"` is part of the Platform for Internet Content Selection system. This allows for content to be rated much like movies can be rated for certain audiences. The `"title"` value represents the title of the presentation itself.

RealPlayer supports "abstract", "author", "base", "copyright" and "title" values for the name attribute. So a block of metainformation for RealPlayer might look something like this:

```
<smil xmlns="http://www.w3.org/2001/SMIL20/CR/">
    <head>
        <meta name="title" content="My SMIL Presentation"/>
        <meta name="author" content="Tim Kennedy and Mary Slowinski"/>
        <meta name="abstract" content="A short presentation
        ➥demonstrating the basic capabilities of SMIL 2.0 in
        ➥RealPlayer"/>
        <meta name="copyright" content="(c) 2001 Kennedy and Slowinski"/>
            <meta name="base" content="rtsp://real.onlinedelivery.com/
            ➥mypresentation/"/>

    </head>
</smil>
```

In the RealPlayer itself, the title appears in the playlist—obtained by pulling down the View menu and choosing Playlist. The title, author, copyright, and abstract will appear by pulling down the Help menu and choosing About This Presentation. RealPlayer will also use other name values that you specify. For instance, you might make a corporate Web address available within your About This Presentation information. All name values must be in lowercase:

```
    <head>
                <meta name="web" content="http://www.onlinedelivery.com/"/>

    </head>
```

As described earlier, the name="base" value followed with a URL in content will set the base path to the media items on the server. References to other items on that server may be made by using relative paths. For example, the following reference will link to a clip at
http://real.onlinedelivery.com/video/myfile.rm:

```
<smil>
    <head>
                <meta name="base"
                ➥content="rtsp://real.onlinedelivery.com/"/>
    </head>
        <body>
                <video src="video/myfile.rm"/>
        </body>
</smil>
```

Attribute: `content`

- Version Compatibility: SMIL 1.0, SMIL 2.0
- Possible Values: Dependent on implementation

The content attribute is the other half of the name equation. Whereas name establishes the property name, content attaches a property value to that name. Both name and content are required when using the <meta> tag.

When specifying lengthy content in RealNetworks RealPlayer, you cannot use line breaks or tabs within the content value. You also have to be careful of any characters that would be looked at as markup. Avoid quotes, ampersands, apostrophes, and angle brackets. Use HTML-style equivalents instead. So in the following examples, the first content value is legal and the second is not:

```
<head>
    <meta name="abstract" content="This is my lengthy and
    ➡&qout;legal&quot; abstract that does not include line
    ➡breaks or tabs. I have used codes to represent &qout;,
    ➡&amp;, &apos;, &lt;, and &rt; characters./"/>

    <meta name="abstract" content="This is my lengthy and "illegal"
    ➡abstract that
    includes line breaks.
    I have not used codes to represent ", &, ', <, and >
    ➡characters./"/>

</head>
```

Attribute: `id`

- Version Compatibility: SMIL 1.0, SMIL 2.0
- Possible Values: Valid XML identifier

The id attribute attaches a unique identifier to the element in question. This is similar to the "name" attribute in traditional HTML. Assigning a value to "id" allows for the referencing of that element later with another attribute in SMIL.

Attribute: `skip-content`

- Version Compatibility: SMIL 1.0
- Possible Values: Not implemented

skip-content is a leftover from the SMIL 1.0 specification that was intended to cover changes that would come up in new versions of the language. It allows the newer specification to use older elements but controls what is ignored in the older player. SMIL 2.0 loses skip-content from the specification.

Summary

For an information indexer, all this is the stuff of dreams. For a Web multimedia author, it might seem pretty boring. But it is important to remember that although most Web multimedia is machine readable, it is not machine understandable. The adept author knows that keying a presentation's metainformation so that it will be cataloged by search engines is still relevant and useful. Some day, perhaps frighteningly soon, artificially intelligent search engines will be available that will consume your media, summarize it, index it, and then relate that summary and index to others. Until then, the job is up to you to tell machines how to communicate to visitors what your site contains.

6

Placing It on the Page: The SMIL Layout Modules

- Conformance Profiles and the Layout Module
- The Layout Module Elements
- The Layout Module Attributes
- Subregion Positioning and Attributes
- The Layout Modules Summarized

So far, we've looked at the Structure module, which contains the core structuring of a SMIL document and the Metainformation module, which enables information about your SMIL presentation to be presented to search engines, and indexing services. Now we'll dig into the Layout modules, which control where and how a presentation's visual and audio media are rendered.

Layout module elements and attributes appear in the `<head>` section of a SMIL document and are used to name and define windows and regions for media display. In turn, the media elements refer to these regions by name as the space into which they should be rendered. The Layout module is not required for a SMIL presentation to run; however, if a document does not include the `layout` element, visual positioning becomes implementation dependent, meaning that the player will decide where to display your media. Because this is not a preferred situation, use of the Layout module is strongly recommended.

The SMIL 2.0 BasicLayout module retains much of the visual structuring syntax found in the layout element of SMIL 1.0. However, three additional modules within this section of the 2.0 specification add flexibility and functionality that extend the Layout capabilities far beyond that of SMIL 1.0. The AudioLayout module enables you to control the volume of audible elements in a presentation. The MultiWindowLayout module moves beyond the single window presentations of SMIL 1.0 and enables you to open and close multiple windows, synchronized by the master timeline of the presentation. The HierarchicalLayout module presents a powerful new nesting capability that allows for precise control of media element positioning.

If you combine all this with SMIL 2.0's BasicContentControl module (see Chapter 12, "Optimizing Content Delivery: The Content Control Modules"), which contains the switch element that allows you to program alternative layouts (for example, layouts that use other languages, such as CSS2), absolute control over the positioning and playback of media becomes an authoring reality.

Conformance Profiles and the Layout Module

As one of the basic building blocks in SMIL, you can expect to find the Layout module used in SMIL host-language conformant profiles and most likely in integration-set conformant profiles as well. Programmers wanting to create integration-set conformant language profiles should take special note of the type attribute of the layout element, which acts as a syntax selector.

The Layout Module Elements

As mentioned previously, the basic elements of the Layout modules are very similar to the layout elements found in SMIL 1.0. In the past, these layout elements and attributes from the 1.0 specification have been supported in a similar fashion across most player implementations. As the players begin to implement the 2.0 specification, it would be expected that most of the basic layout capabilities will be supported.

That said, keep in mind that some browser or player implementations will favor absolute positioning, using methods such as Cascading Style Sheets, or even define their own processes for positioning media on the screen. If the methodology is distinctly player specific, the declared language profile will define what elements are allowed and supported. The syntax used with these profiles may vary slightly from what is listed below because it is drawn from both XML convention and that of the SMIL 2.0 Basic Language Profile.

Element: `<layout>`

- Version Compatibility: SMIL 1.0, SMIL 2.0
- Child Elements: `region`, `regPoint`, `root-layout`, `topLayout`
- Possible Attributes: `type`

The `layout` element is the parent element used to establish rendering regions and windows for media playback. If a `layout` element is NOT present in a SMIL document, the player being used to playback the presentation determines where and how the media is displayed. However, using an empty `<layout></layout>` structure forces media to fill and align to the upper-left corner of the presentation window. This is preferable to a document with no `layout` element at all.

The child elements are supported if the `type` attribute of `layout` has the default value of `"text/smil-basic-layout"`, which specifies that the layout language to be used is part of the host-language conformant profile and therefore supports all Layout modules. More information on the `type` attribute is found later in this chapter, as are details about each of the child elements. Non host-language conformant profiles that choose to incorporate the Layout modules need to define which additional elements, if any, are allowed as children. More information on language profiles can be found in Chapter 3, "Getting Technical: The SMIL Specification."

Where the Layout modules are supported, the basic structure of a `layout` element is as follows:

```
<layout>
  <root-layout backgroundColor="black" width="250" height="230"/>
  <region .../>
  <region .../>
</layout>
```

The root-layout element is used to establish the dimensions of the initial presentation window. The region elements are used to define distinct areas for media playback.

Element: <region>

- Version Compatibility: SMIL 1.0, SMIL 2.0

- Parent Elements: layout, topLayout

- Possible Attributes: backgroundColor, background-color, bottom, fit, id, height, left, region, regionName, right, showBackground, soundLevel, top, width, z-index

The region element is the backbone of the Layout module and controls the positioning, size, and scaling of a presentation's media elements. Additionally, the soundLevel attribute can be called on to control the volume of any audible media in a presentation by region.

Regions act as placeholder elements. They don't contain content of their own, but instead create a bounding box, which expresses the width and height of the defined region. After a region is established and named, which occurs within a layout or topLayout element, a media object can identify this region by name as its designated playback space. To accomplish this, the media object lists region as an attribute and uses the name assigned to the region as the value. Thus, the region where the media is to be rendered is designated. Here's a very simple example of this in which a 320×240 pixel region named "images" is defined, and the media file "one.jpg" will be displayed.

```
<smil>
    <head>
      <layout>
          <region id="images" width="320" height="240" />
      </layout>
    </head>
    <body>
      <img region="images" src="one.jpg" />
    </body>
</smil>
```

Although the preceding example uses fixed pixel values for setting the width and height of the region "images", the position and size of a region can also be declared using percentage values. If this is the case, a topLayout or root-layout element with fixed dimensions is a necessary prerequisite. This parent layout then serves as the basis for calculating the relative positioning and size of the nested region. In the simple example that follows, the topLayout element establishes a presentation window that is 400 pixels wide and 400 pixels tall. The region "inset" is given a height and width relative to the dimensions of that topLayout.

```
<layout>
   <topLayout id="base" width="400" height="400" />
     <region id="inset" width="50%" height="50%" />
</layout>
```

The values assigned to the relative-sized region declare its height and width to be 50% of the parent layout. The region would thus be rendered with a height and width of 200 pixels.

Although still adhering to the requirement of an immediate parent layout element, SMIL 2.0 also presents the new concept of nesting regions within one another. Referred to as hierarchical regions, this functionality provides even more fine-tuning for the positioning of media. The syntax for these hierarchical regions is the same for all regions. As an example, the code snippet that follows would be used to create a 200-pixel-square region named "container". Within "container" is the "nested" region, whose dimensions are based on the "container" region dimensions.

```
<layout>
   <topLayout id="base" width="400" height="400" />
     <region id="container" width="200" height="200">
       <region id="nested" width="50%" hieght="50%" />
     </region>
</layout>
```

Since "nested" is 50% of "container" in both height and width, its resulting dimensions would be a 100 pixel square. It is important to note that if a nested region extends beyond the bounding box of its parent, the child region will be clipped to the parent boundaries.

Element: <regPoint>

- Version Compatibility: SMIL 2.0
- Parent Element: layout
- Possible Attributes: bottom, left, right, top, regAlign
- Possible Values: pixels (absolute positioning), percentages (relative positioning)

New to SMIL 2.0, the `regPoint` element provides a means for establishing a point on the presentation display surface that is used to align elements. Because the `regPoint` is relative to the upper-left corner of its `parent` layout, it naturally must have a `layout` element as its immediate parent. The following is an example of the use of the `regPoint` element. In this case, the image "cat.jpg" will be displayed in the region named `"one"`, with its top-left corner placed at a point 10 pixels from the top and 15 pixels in from the left.

```
<layout>
   <regPoint id="topMargin" top="10" left="15"/>
   <region id="one" … />
</layout>
 <img src="cat.jpg" region="one" regPoint="topMargin" … />
```

The `bottom` and `right` attributes for the `regPoint` element work exactly as the `top` and `left` attributes in the preceding example, and also use the geometry of the parent layout to calculate how far from the bottom or right edges the point should be established. Percentage values for the `regPoint` are also relative to the parent layout.

It is very important to note that registration points are an element of their own; they are not tied to a particular region. Therefore, a `regPoint` element can be used with any of the regions included within its parent `layout` element. For example, in the bit of code that follows, a `regPoint` named `"fivein"` is declared that can be used to align media elements 5 pixels in from a left boundary and 5 pixels down from a top boundary. The three regions `"cat"`, `"dog"`, and `"mouse"`, which are part of the parent layout that includes the `"fivein"` regPoint, can all use this `regPoint` to align media within their distinct space, regardless of where they are situated within the larger parent layout.

```
<layout>
   <regPoint id="fivein" top="5" left="5" />
   <region id="cat" . . . />
   <region id="dog" . . . />
   <region id="mouse" . . . />
</layout>
```

Closely tied to the use of the `regPoint` element is the attribute `regAlign`. By default, the `regPoint` element uses the top-left corner of a media object as the point by which to align the media to the defined registration point on the display surface. The `regAlign` attribute allows for the selection of an area of the media object other than the top-left corner to be used for alignment. The `regAlign` attribute is defined in detail in the attributes section of this chapter.

The regPoint element, especially in conjunction with the regAlign attribute, allows for literally pinpointing where media will be displayed. A practical example of this element in use is the display of visual media of varying sizes; a regPoint can be used to center all the media displayed in a given region on this one point.

Element: <root-layout>

- Version Compatibility: SMIL 1.0, 2.0
- Parent Element: layout
- Possible Attributes: backgroundColor, background-color, height, width

This element determines the base or root layout of the presentation, and as such, determines the dimensions of a single browser or media player window in which the presentation is displayed. The regions that are declared within the root-layout element are then arranged within this "top-level" or root presentation window; any regions that use percentages for positioning calculate placement based on the dimensions of this parent window. Only one root-layout is allowed per presentation, unless the switch element is being used to present alternative layouts (see Chapter 12 for more on the switch element). If multiple root-layout elements are present, the presentation will not play, and if either the height or width of the root-layout is not declared, the dimension of the root playback window will be determined by the player.

Element: <topLayout>

- Version Compatibility: SMIL 2.0
- Parent Element: layout
- Possible Attributes: backgroundColor, close, height, open, width

Unlike the single window presentation available using the root-layout element, SMIL 2.0 introduces support for multiple top-level windows that allow greater author control and presentation flexibility. Multiple instances of the topLayout element can appear in a single layout element, with each describing a separate top-level window, or a window that appears on "top" of any other presentation windows that may be open. Regions can then be defined within the topLevel element that provide for specific media playback areas inside each new top-level presentation window.

Like the root-layout element, any regions defined within a topLayout element are arranged inside the window with positions calculated as relative to the coordinate system of that top-level window. Control is also provided for the opening and closing of top-level windows by means of the open and close attributes (which are covered in depth in the attributes section of this chapter); however, the initial display of these windows—and any means of relocating them—are determined by the particular media player that is being used to display the presentation.

The top-level windows act only as containers and do not have a timeline that is distinct from the master presentation timeline, so the closing or opening of these windows does not affect the overall temporal nature of the presentation. Regions can belong to only one top-level window (or a root-layout window). If a region is not defined within a particular topLayout element, it will be assumed to be associated with the root-layout; if no root-layout element exists, playback will occur in a new separate window.

The Layout Module Attributes

The attributes used by the Layout module elements provide control for the positioning and playback of media objects within the defined regions and layouts defined by the elements described previously. The attributes used by SMIL 1.0 to perform these tasks are still present and supported by the SMIL 2.0 Language Profile, although the use of the hyphenated syntax is deprecated in favor of the "camelCase" syntax standardized in XML languages such as SMIL. Language profiles that incorporate the Layout modules would be advised to include support for the hyphenated syntax to increase playback reliability.

Attribute: backgroundColor

- Version Compatibility: SMIL 2.0
- Parent Elements: region, root-layout, topLayout
- Possible Values: keyword colors, hexadecimal equivalents of RGB colors, transparent, inherit

This attribute specifies the background color of a region when the region is actively displaying media. This is especially important if your media element does not fill the region specified; the color behind the media, and whether it is displayed at all, will be determined through the use of this attribute. The background color can be defined by using standard keyword colors such as "blue", "red", or "black" (as found in XHTML), or by the use of the hexadecimal equivalents of RGB colors. If a background color is not defined, the default value of `transparent` makes the background transparent, or colorless. A value of `inherit` will use the parent element's `backgroundColor`, unless it is undefined; in that case, the default value of `transparent` is used instead. When the region is not displaying a media element, the `showBackground` attribute (discussed next) determines whether the background color is displayed.

Attribute: `background-color`

- Version Compatibility: SMIL 1.0
- Possible Values: keyword colors, hexadecimal equivalents of RGB colors

Deprecated and replaced by `backgroundColor`, this attribute can be supported by including it in a language profile.

Attribute: `bottom, left, right, top`

- Version Compatibility: SMIL 2.0
- Parent Elements: `region, regPoint`
- Possible Values: pixel units (absolute positioning), percentages (relative positioning), `auto` (default)

Used in conjunction with the `region` element, these values determine the position or distance the region should be offset relative to the layout that contains the `region`. When used with the `regPoint` element, the assigned value establishes the position of a registration point used to align media elements, which is offset from the boundaries of the containing layout.

When the value assigned is a number, it is calculated as an absolute pixel value; when the value is expressed as a percentage, it is calculated as relative to the parent layout or region. Both absolute and relative values can be used to describe the positioning of a single `region` or `regPoint`. The default value of `auto`, in either case, is computed as a zero or non-calculated value.

Although any combination of these attributes can be used to define the size and position of a `region` or `regPoint`, it is important when authoring to carefully determine the values used and to keep them consistent with the declared height or width of the region or regPoint. The following example establishes several regions and a regPoint alignment point within a single layout element using a combination of relative and absolute positioning.

```
<layout>
   <root-layout height="500" width="500" />
     <region id="middle" top="50% left="50%" />
     <region id="bottombar" top="400" height="100" width="100%" />
     <regPoint id="spot" top="25" left="25" />
</layout>
```

The overall display window is declared as 500 pixels square through the use of the root-layout element. The dimension of this root window will be the basis for any relative positioning of regions and regPoints defined within the same layout; thus the "middle" region is positioned 50% from the top and 50% from the left of the presentation window's top-left corner. The "bottombar" region is absolutely positioned with its top-left corner 400 pixels from the top of the display window. It spans the width of the parent window by declaring a width of 100%. The regPoint "spot" is set using pixel values, and as such, defines a point absolutely positioned 25 pixels in from the left margin and 25 pixels down from the top margin of any of the display spaces defined within the same layout element. Thus, "spot" can be used to position media in the regions "middle", "bottombar" and/or in the root presentation window itself.

Attribute: close

- Version Compatibility: SMIL 2.0
- Parent Elements: topLayout
- Possible Values: onRequest, whenNotActive

The topLayout element allows you to use multiple windows in a single presentation. The attribute close controls the closing of a given topLayout window. The default value of onRequest allows the user to close the window only at the user's discretion; whenNotactive closes the window when the media element is no longer active. A window is considered active when using timed media during playback in any region, and also during any freeze periods that may have been coded into the media element using the Timing and Synchronization module. In the following example, the window called "joe" can be closed when the viewer desires to close it; the window "sam" will close automatically when the media within it has ended its display.

```
<layout>
 <topLayout id="joe" close="onRequest" . . . >
    <region id="1" . . . />
 </topLayout>
 <topLayout id="sam" close="whenNotActive" . . . >
    <region id="2" . . . />
 </toplayout>
</layout>
```

It is important to note that the presentation as a whole follows a master timeline, no matter how many top-level windows have been opened. This allows synchronization between media displayed in separate top-level windows.

Attribute: `fit`

- Version Compatibility: SMIL 1.0, SMIL 2.0

- Parent Element: `region`

- Possible Values: `fill`, `hidden`, `meet`, `scroll`, `slice`

The attribute `fit` defines how the region handles media with dimensions that are either too large or too small for the dimensions of the region. This attribute applies to media that has an intrinsic height and width; media elements with variable dimensions, such as HTML documents, must first be rendered before the `fit` attribute is applied. See Figure 6.1 for an illustration of the effect the various values have on a given media element.

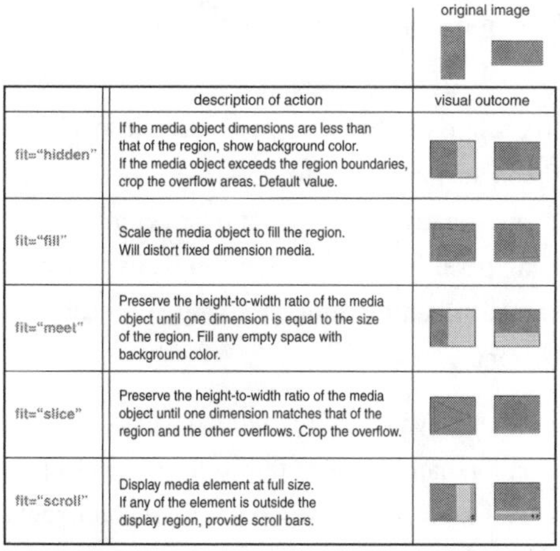

	description of action	visual outcome
fit="hidden"	If the media object dimensions are less than that of the region, show background color. If the media object exceeds the region boundaries, crop the overflow areas. Default value.	
fit="fill"	Scale the media object to fill the region. Will distort fixed dimension media.	
fit="meet"	Preserve the height-to-width ratio of the media object until one dimension is equal to the size of the region. Fill any empty space with background color.	
fit="slice"	Preserve the height-to-width ratio of the media object until one dimension matches that of the region and the other overflows. Crop the overflow.	
fit="scroll"	Display media element at full size. If any of the element is outside the display region, provide scroll bars.	

Figure 6.1 *The values of the `fit` attribute in action.*

Attribute: id

- Version Compatibility: SMIL 1.0, SMIL 2.0
- Parent Element: `region, regPoint, topLayout`
- Possible Values: defined by author

The `id` attribute is used throughout both SMIL 1.0 and 2.0 to assign a unique identifier to an object or element. Within the Layout modules, the `id` attribute can be used to assign a name to a `topLayout`, a registration point (`regPoint`), or a `region`. When used with the region element, the assigned name can then be used by media elements to call for playback in the named region. Although this is similar in function to the `regionName` attribute, `id` must be a unique identifier, whereas multiple regions can share the same `regionName`. An example follows in which the `topLayout` and `regions` are identified by `id`.

```
<layout>
   <topLayout id="top" . . . />
    <region id="main" . . . />
    <regPoint id="spot" . . . />
   </topLayout>
</layout>
```

Attribute: height, width

- Version Compatibility: SMIL 1.0, SMIL 2.0
- Parent Elements: `region, root-layout, topLayout`
- Possible Values: dependent on parent element; see the following

These two attributes are used to declare the size of a presentation window or region. When used with the `region` attribute, `height` or `width` can be given an absolute value using pixel units or a relative value using a percentage of the parent window or region. When using pixel units, the value can be expressed as a simple number; adding a percentage sign after a number value indicates that the measurement is relative to the parent.

In the following example, the first `topLayout` region, named "absolute," uses pixel measurements to create a region named "one" that is 10 pixels from the top of the 200-pixel-wide and 100-pixel-high parent window. The second `topLayout`, named "relative," uses percentages to create a region named "two" that is 125 pixels wide, or 50% the width of the 250-pixel-wide parent window.

```
<head>
  <layout>
    <topLayout id="absolute" width="200" height="100"/>
      <region id="one" top="10"/>
    </topLayout>
    <topLayout id="relative" width="250" height="200"/>
      <region id="two" width="50%"/>
    </topLayout>
  </layout>
</head>
```

When establishing the height or width of the root-layout or topLayout elements, the value must be expressed as an absolute; thus, it must be coded in pixel
units. Because these two elements are parent elements, no basis exists for relative
measurement. Additionally, if either height or width is unspecified for a
root-layout element, the value assigned will be implementation dependent.

Attribute: left (see bottom)

Attribute: open

- Version Compatibility: SMIL 2.0
- Parent Element: topLayout
- Possible Values: onStart, whenActive

The topLayout element allows for multiple windows in a single presentation, and
the attribute open controls when a topLayout window opens. A value of onStart
opens a window when the presentation as a whole begins; whenActive opens a
top-level window (if not already open) when a media element is displayed in one
of the window's regions. The window is considered active during any playback in
any region and also during any freeze periods that may have been coded into the
media element using the Timing and Synchronization module. It is important to
note that the presentation as a whole follows a master timeline, no matter how
many top-level windows have been opened. This allows synchronization between
media displayed in separate top-level windows.

Attribute: regAlign

- Version Compatibility: SMIL 2.0
- Parent Element: regPoint, also used with media objects to fine tune alignment within a region

- Possible Values: `topLeft`, `topMid`, `topRight`, `midLeft`, `center`, `midRight`, `bottomLeft`, `bottomMid`, `bottomRight`

As explained earlier in this chapter, the `regPoint` element defines a point on the presentation's display surface to which a media object's upper-left corner can be aligned. The `regAlign` attribute is used to specify a point other than the upper-left corner of the media element to act as an aligning anchor point.

The values for the `regAlign` attribute are fairly self-explanatory. `topLeft` and `topRight` indicate that the top-left and top-right corners of the media element, respectively, will be aligned to the defined `regPoint`, and `bottomLeft` and `bottomRight` refer to the bottom-left and bottom-right corners of the media object as the alignment point. *Mid* indicates a point that is either half the width or half the height of the media element, so `topMid` and `bottomMid` indicate points that are located halfway across the top and bottom edges of the media object, and `midLeft` and `midRight` indicate points that are located halfway down the left and right sides of the media element. The use of the `center` value aligns the center of the object with the registration point.

In the example that follows, the regPoint named `"cat"` has been assigned a `regAlign` value that will cause the centermost point of a media object to be used as the anchor point for alignment to the `regPoint`. Media objects played back using the `"cow"` regPoint will be anchored to a point located halfway across the bottom of the media object's visual display.

```
<layout>
   <regPoint id="cat" regAlign="center . . .  />
   <regPoint id="cow" regAlign="midBottom" . . . />
   <. . . >
</layout>
```

The `regPoint` and `regAlign` attributes work together with the `fit` attribute for a given region to determine the final rendering of the media object.

Attribute: `regPoint`

- Version Compatibility: SMIL 2.0
- Parent Element: used with media objects to specify positioning within a region
- Possible Values: regPoint id values (from the regPoint element) OR `topLeft`, `topMid`, `topRight`, `midLeft`, `center`, `midRight`, `bottomLeft`, `bottomMid`, `bottomRight`

regPoint refers to a registration point by its previously defined id value (in the regPoint element) and aligns a given media object to the named point. As an alternative, the predefined values for the regPoint attribute indicate points within or bounding a region that can be used without prior definition. For a description of the predefined values, see the information for the regAlign attribute (directly preceding), which features the same set of values. The following example illustrates the use of this attribute. The "tinpan" media object will be displayed in the region "space" and will use the regPoint "spot" to align its upper-left corner 20 pixels down from the top and 10 pixels in from the left of the "space" region. The "cup" media object uses a predefined value of "center" for its regPoint and will have its upper-left corner anchored in the center of the region "space".

```
<layout>
   <region id="space" . . . />
   <regPoint id="spot" top="20" left="10" . . . />
</layout>
. . .
<ref id="tinpan" region="space" regPoint="spot" src="pans.gif" . . . />
<ref id="cup" region="space" regPoint="center" src="cans.gif" . . . />
. . .
```

As mentioned under the previous entry, the regAlign attribute can be used with media objects to further pinpoint their placement. In the following example, the media object "dog" will be displayed in the "stage" region and will use the point "left", which is halfway down the left margin of the region, as an anchor to align itself. However, instead of aligning the upper-left corner of "dog" to this regPoint, as would be the default, the regAlign value attached to "dog" indicates that the bottom-left corner will be aligned to the regPoint "left".

```
<layout>
   <region id="stage" . . . />
   <regPoint id="left" regAlign="midLeft" . . . />
</layout>
. . .
<ref id="dog" region="space" regPoint="left" regAlign="bottomLeft"
➥src="daisy.gif" . . . />
. . .
```

By skillfully combining regPoint elements, regPoint and regAlign attributes, and the fit attribute, authors can determine very precisely where their media will be displayed.

Attribute: `region`

- Version Compatibility: SMIL 1.0, SMIL 2.0
- Parent Element: used with media objects to determine regions for playback
- Possible Values: predefined `region`, `id`, or `regionName` values

After a playback area is named using the `regionName` or `id` attributes of the `region` element, a media clip can declare that it should be displayed in the region by calling it by name. The following is a simple example in which a video file called `dog.mov` will play back in the region named `movies`:

```
<smil>
    <head>
      <layout>
          <region id="movies" width="320" height="240"/>
      </layout>
    </head>
    <body>
      <video region="movies" src="dog.mov"/>
    </body>
</smil>
```

Attribute: `regionName`

- Version Compatibility: SMIL 2.0
- Parent Element: `region`
- Possible Values: defined by author

Used to identify a region and to allow media elements to call for playback in a region by using the assigned name. Although similar in function to the `id` attribute, multiple regions can share the same `regionName`, whereas the `id` attribute is a unique identifier.

Attribute: `right` (**see** `bottom`)

Attribute: `showBackground`

- Version Compatibility: SMIL 2.0
- Parent Element: `region`
- Possible Values: `always`, `whenActive`

showBackground controls whether the background color is displayed when no media is being rendered in a region. The default value of always renders the background color as visible when no media element is occupying the region. If the value is whenActive, the background color will not be shown when the region is not displaying media.

Attribute: soundLevel

- Version Compatibility: SMIL 2.0
- Parent Element: region
- Possible Values: non-negative percentage values

A new feature in SMIL 2.0, this attribute allows for control of audible media elements. Expressed as a percentage, soundLevel values are interpreted as relative to the recorded volume of the media and can be used to increase the volume beyond the source media level. A separate soundLevel can be applied to each instance of a sound source, with a limit of one per region. Unfortunately, the absolute sound level of the media is subject to the hardware limitations of the user and by their system volume settings. The following example illustrates an instance where the volume of media files played back in the region "loud" are increased to 200% of their recorded volume.

```
<layout>
   <region id="loud" soundLevel="200%" . . .  />
</layout>
```

Attribute: top **(see** bottom**)**

Attribute: type

- Version Compatibility: SMIL 2.0
- Parent Element: layout
- Possible Values: text/smil-basic-layout, text/css, other languages and profiles as developed

The type attribute, when used within the layout element, specifies which layout language is to be used by the presentation. The default value of text/smil-basic-layout supports the syntax found in the Layout modules as well as SMIL 1.0 semantics. Setting the value to text/css will allow the use of

CSS2 syntax, but any other languages incorporating the BasicLayout module will need to define what elements are allowed as children of the layout element. If the viewer's player does not understand the designated language, it will skip all the content up until the next </layout> tag.

Use of the switch element (found in SMIL 2.0's BasicContentControl module, which is detailed in Chapter 12) allows multiple type attributes to be present and the player to choose the one that it understands. In the example that follows, two options contained by a switch element are available for playback by the implementing player. If the player supports the SMIL 2.0 Basic Language Profile, it will choose to use the layout with the type of "text/smil-basic-layout"; if it does not support that profile but does support Cascading Style Sheets, it will use the layout with the type of "text/css".

```
<switch>
   <layout type="text/smil-baic-layout">
     <region . . . />
   </layout>
   <layout type="type/css">
     [region="name"] {. . . }
   </layout>
</switch>
```

Attribute: width (see height)

Attribute: z-index

- Version Compatibility: SMIL 1.0, SMIL 2.0
- Parent Element: region
- Possible Values: auto, an assigned number (can be a negative value)

The z-index attribute defines the depth or level of a region by rendering the region with the highest assigned z-index value on top of regions with lower z-index values. In the example that follows, the region "front" with a z-index of 4 will be displayed on top of the region "back" with a z-index of 1.

```
<layout>
   <region id="front" z-index="4" . . . />
   <region id="back" z-index="1" . . . />
</layout>
```

If two sibling regions such as "front" and "back" have the same assigned z-index value, the one that has become active most recently will be rendered on top of the other. If the two also began playback simultaneously, the region that occurs last in the SMIL code will take the top layer.

Hierarchical regions that are nested within another region may also be assigned z-indexes; the nested region's z-index values will be considered as subdivisions of the containing region. For example, if a region is assigned a z-index value of "5" and encloses two nested regions with z-indexes of "1" and "2", each of these children are considered further subdivisions of the parent's z-index of "5".

When regions overlap, parent region z-index values are resolved first, followed by the application of z-index values of any child regions. As with nonoverlapping regions, a higher z-index value places a region on top or in front of a region with a lower z-index value. The default value of auto is equivalent to a zero z-index value and places a region on the same level as their immediate parent.

Subregion Positioning and Attributes

Subregion positioning, which is new to SMIL 2.0, provides for a very detailed level of media element placement through the use of attributes that create temporary child regions within the region selected for their display. The attributes that describe the subregion are assigned directly to the media objects using the region attribute. The media elements, when rendered, override similar attributes of the parent region.

The following example makes use of some of the sub-region attributes. In this case, the image cow.jpg will be displayed in the region one. However, the background color will be black while the jpg is displayed, and it will be offset 5% from the top of region one and 10% in from the left. In addition, the image will not be scaled by the fill attribute found in the parent region; instead, scrollbars will be displayed if any media is outside the subregion boundaries.

```
<layout>
 ...
<region id="one" ... fit="fill"/>
 ...
</layout>
 ...
<img src="cow.jpg" region="one" top="5%" left="10%
➥ backgroundColor="black" fit="scroll">
```

The most practical use of this increased functionality is for displaying one-time-only media objects, or objects that don't fit well into the region selected for their display.

Attribute: `bottom, left, right, top, height, width`

- Possible Values: pixels (absolute positioning) or percentages (relative positioning)

The directional values determine the position or distance the subregion should be offset relative to the region's parent layout measurements, and `width` and `height` define the width and height, respectively, of the subregion. Pixel measurements can be expressed simply as numbers.

Attribute: `backgroundColor`

- Possible Values: keyword colors, hexadecimal equivalents of RGB colors

The color displayed while a media element is playing in the subregion. Overrides any `backgroundColor` attribute that may have been declared for the parent region.

Attribute: `fit`

- Possible Values: `fill, hidden, meet, scroll, slice`

The attribute `fit` defines how the subregion handles media with dimensions that are either too large or too small for the dimensions of the subregion and overrides the parent region's `fit` attribute if any has been declared. See the listing for the region element's `fit` attribute for more information on the predefined values.

Attribute: `z-index`

- Possible Values: an assigned number (can be a negative value)

The `z-index` attribute defines the depth or level of a subregion. The subregion with the highest assigned `z-index` value will be displayed on top of sub-regions with lower `z-index` values. Remember that the `z-index` value of a subregion is considered a subdivision of the parent region's `z-index` value; in other words, the parent region's `z-index` will be observed and applied against other parent regions before the `z-index` of a sub-region is applied.

The Layout Modules Summarized

The SMIL 2.0 Layout modules have expanded the power of the multimedia author or developer to position and present media exactly as desired—a goal that not long ago seemed unreachable. The capability to nest regions within one another, to open and control multiple top-level windows, and to work with subregions that can create temporary children in parent regions is the stuff of dreams for the author who wants to take a media presentation to the next level. But even the BasicLayout module has increased its flexibility and strength. Combining this new control over the appearance of a presentation with the other modules found in SMIL 2.0 makes it possible to ensure user accessibility while also providing ultimate flexibility for the developer.

7

Grouping Your Content: The Timing and Synchronization Module

- Conformance Profiles and the Timing and Synchronization Module
- The Timing and Synchronization Module Elements
- The Timing and Synchronization Module Attributes
- The Timing and Synchronization Module Summarized

At the heart of the Synchronized Multimedia Integration Language lies the Timing and Synchronization module. Orchestrating the timing of various media elements in the presentation is, after all, what makes SMIL different from traditional Web media.

SMIL 1.0 introduced the critical <seq> and <par> elements for the sequential and parallel playback of media. SMIL 2.0 adds to the capabilities by offering an <excl> element for exclusive playback.

Despite how simple it is to implement, Timing and Synchronization is the heftiest and most important module in SMIL. From here, chaos is converted to order and the form of the presentation takes shape.

Conformance Profiles and the Timing and Synchronization Module

As a basic building block in SMIL, you will find the Timing and Synchronization module used both for SMIL Host Language and Integration Set Language Conformance. SMIL Host Language Conformance will lean toward using the <seq>, <par>, and <excl> elements. Because Integration Set Conformance involves incorporating the language into other XML languages, the timeContainer attributes with their seq, par, and excl values become important in that arena.

The Timing and Synchronization Module Elements

- Module: Timing and Synchronization
- Conformance: Required for SMIL Host Language and SMIL Integration Set
- Profile Compatibility: SMIL 1.0, SMIL 2.0, SMIL 2.0 Basic, XHTML+SMIL
- Possible Elements: <seq>, <par>, <excl>

In SMIL 1.0, the <seq> and <par> tags of SMIL Timing and Synchronization were two of the most notable elements of the language. <seq> and <par> act as time containers, allowing you to organize and group your content. <seq> plays contained elements in sequence. <par> plays contained elements in parallel. By listing and nesting these two elements in various ways, you can build almost any presentation.

SMIL 2.0 gains the <excl> element. <excl> plays contained elements exclusively—that is, one grouping at a time. But in doing so, it allows the SMIL presentation to jump and branch for a great deal of interactivity. Supporting <excl> is the <priorityClass> element, which allows the SMIL author to control the playback behavior of the objects that the presentation has not jumped or branched to.

Element: <seq>

- Version Compatibility: SMIL 1.0, SMIL 2.0
- Possible Attributes: begin, dur, end, fill, fillDefault, higher, lower, max, min, pauseDisplay, peers, repeat, repeatCount, repeatDur,

```
restart, restartDefault, syncBehavior, syncBehaviorDefault,
syncMaster, syncTolerance, syncToleranceDefault, timeAction
```

The <seq> element was one of the initial timing building blocks of SMIL. Along with its <par> and <excl> siblings, <seq> can be called a "time container." It contains a child set of elements and specifies how they will relate to each other along a timeline. It plays each child element sequentially, as it is listed. Let's suppose you have two media objects referenced between a pair of <seq> tags. The first media object would play in its entirety, and then the second media object would play. For example, you could use <seq> to play a sequence of images in a slide show presentation.

Using <seq> is not difficult in most implementations. QuickTime uses <seq> in the following traditional manner to play one clip followed by another:

```
. . .
<seq>
    <audio src="myAudio.mp3" />
    <video src="myVideo.mov" />
</seq>
. . .
```

Other than possibly different media types, a sample of <seq> RealPlayer will look almost identical:

```
. . .
<seq>
    <audio src="myAudio.rm" />
    <video src="myVideo.rm" />
</seq>
. . .
```

By contrast, Internet Explorer takes on a decidedly different look when implementing <seq>:

```
. . .
<t:seq>
    <div class="time" dur="2">First line of text</div>
    <div class="time" dur="2">Second line of text</div>
</t:seq>
. . .
```

This difference in code is caused by Internet Explorer's Integration Set approach, in which the SMIL markup is mixed in with the HTML of a Web page.

The <seq> element supports all element timing attributes except for two: endsync and timeContainer. The timeContainer attribute can't be added to a <seq> because this attribute is a type of time container itself.

But you can use timeContainer to attach <seq> (or <par> and <excl>) characteristics to any XML component. This enables you to bring SMIL to languages such as XHTML. So, as seen in Microsoft Internet Explorer, a <seq> using timeContainer would look like this:

```
. . .
<span class="time" timeContainer="seq">
    <img class="time" dur="5" src="bannerad1.gif">
    <img class="time" dur="5" src="bannerad2.gif">
    <img class="time" dur="5" src="bannerad3.gif">
</span>
. . .
```

Element: <par>

- Version Compatibility: SMIL 1.0, SMIL 2.0

- Possible Attributes: begin, dur, end, endsync, fill, fillDefault, higher, lower, max, min, pauseDisplay, peers, repeat, repeatCount, repeatDur, restart, restartDefault, syncBehavior, syncBehaviorDefault, syncMaster, syncTolerance, syncToleranceDefault, timeAction

Another of the initial timing building blocks of SMIL, the <par> element plays child elements in parallel. If you had two media objects referenced between a pair of <par> tags, the two media objects would play at the same time. For example, you could use <par> to play an animation presentation and its audio soundtrack simultaneously.

Like <seq>, putting <par> to work is not difficult. QuickTime uses <par> in the following way:

```
. . .
<par>
    <audio src="myAudio.mp3" />
    <video src="myVideo.mov" />
</par>
. . .
```

QuickTime will play both media objects in parallel. As with <seq>, RealPlayer is almost identical in its use of <par>:

```
. . .
<par>
    <audio src="myAudio.rm" />
    <video src="myVideo.rm" />
</par>
. . .
```

As expected, the SMIL Integration Set approach of Microsoft Internet Explorer provides a different look:

```
. . .
<t:par>
    <div class="time" dur="10">First line of text</div>
    <div class="time" dur="10">Second line of text</div>
</t:par>
. . .
```

In this example, two lines of text will appear on the screen at the same time and disappear 10 seconds later.

The <par> element supports all element timing attributes except for one. You cannot apply a timeContainer attribute to a <par>, because this attribute is a type of time container itself.

But, as with <seq>, you can use timeContainer to attach <par> characteristics to any XML component. This allows you to bring SMIL to languages such as XHTML. In Internet Explorer, using timeContainer for a <par> would look like this, which makes three graphics play on the screen at the same time:

```
. . .
<span class="time" timeContainer="par">
    <img class="time" dur="5" src="bannerad1.gif">
    <img class="time" dur="5" src="bannerad2.gif">
    <img class="time" dur="5" src="bannerad3.gif">
</span>
. . .
```

Although you can use <par> to have multiple media elements running at the same time, you might not want to. What I mean by this is that <par> makes it very easy to overload the available bandwidth. An audio file running here, a movie running at the same time over there, and suddenly you have a presentation that may use more bandwidth than you have available. When using <par>, keep a tight eye on the total bandwidth that each media object consumes.

Throughout the SMIL modules, the language offers a number of elements and attributes that enable you to determine what type of content a viewer receives or tweak the bandwidth-influenced behaviors of that content. You have a number of options to help you manage getting that fat content of yours down a narrow pipe. As you read the specification, keep an eye out for these features and use them whenever helpful.

Element: `<excl>`

- Version Compatibility: SMIL 2.0

- Possible Attributes: `begin, dur, end, endsync, fill, fillDefault, higher, lower, max, min, pauseDisplay, peers, repeat, repeatCount, repeatDur, restart, restartDefault, syncBehavior, syncBehaviorDefault, syncMaster, syncTolerance, syncToleranceDefault, timeAction`

New to SMIL 2.0, `<excl>` offers a unique twist to the Timing and Synchronization elements. `<excl>` allows only one child element to be played at a time. That might sound like the `<seq>` element, but the `<excl>` element imposes no sequential order. Its only concern is that only one element plays at a time. If an element begins to play while another element is playing, the new element takes charge and the old element is paused or stopped.

How might this be useful? Suppose you have supplementary material that supports your main presentation. By using `<excl>`, your viewer could pause the main presentation, branch off to the supplementary material, and then return to pick up where the user left off in the main presentation. In essence, `<excl>` becomes the new interactivity powerhouse in SMIL 2.0. Some interactivity was possible with creative use of SMIL 1.0, but SMIL 2.0 makes it easier.

At its most basic, using `<excl>` in RealPlayer might look something like this:

```
. . .
<excl>
    <img src="myImage1.jpg" begin="5" dur="5" />
    <img src="myImage2.jpg" begin="0" dur="5" />
</excl>
. . .
```

In this example, the second image actually plays (exclusively) before the first image because of the `begin` timing. But this is an overly simplistic sample. A SMIL 2.0 player such as RealPlayer can do so much more. Consider the following example from Internet Explorer. It shows a more complex, but still simple, two-image gallery linked to two buttons. <excl> provides the interactive power:

```
. . .
<button id="first">First Image</button>
<button id="second">Second Image</button>

<t:excl dur="indefinite">

    <t:par begin="first.click">
        <img class="time" dur="indefinite" timeAction="display"
src="first.gif" />
        <div class="time" dur="5" timeAction="display">The first
image</div>
    </t:par>

    <t:par begin="second.click">
        <img class="time" dur="indefinite" timeAction="display"
➥ src="second.jpg" />
        <div class="time" dur="5" timeAction="display">Sunset at an
African Beach</div>
    </t:par>
</t:excl>
. . .
```

With each click of a button on the screen, a corresponding parallel element begins displaying an image and text. This is because each parallel element within the exclusive grouping has a begin value linked to a click of a named button. A lot is going on in this sample, but it shows how a <par> element can be called with a button click if that parallel element is wrapped in a <excl>. With <excl>, SMIL 2.0 gains powerful new interactivity.

The <excl> element can work closely with the <priorityClass> element from the Content Control modules (see Chapter 12, "Optimizing Content Delivery: The Content Control Modules") to control interactivity. The <priorityClass> element groups child elements together and enables you to control the pause, resume, and interruption characteristics of those children as they become active in the timeline.

The <excl> element supports all element timing attributes except for the timeContainer attribute; this attribute is a type of time container itself.

But you can use timeContainer to attach <excl> characteristics to any XML component. This allows you to bring SMIL to languages such as XHTML. A timeContainer for <excl> in Internet Explorer would look like something like this:

```
. . .
<span class="time" timeContainer="par">
    <img class="time" begin="ad1.click" dur="5" src="bannerad1.gif">
    <img class="time" begin="ad2.click" dur="5" src="bannerad2.gif">
    <img class="time" begin="ad3.click" dur="5" src="bannerad3.gif">
</span>
. . .
```

A user clicking a button (created elsewhere in the markup) could choose one of three potential images.

Element: `<priorityClass>`

- Version Compatibility: SMIL 2.0
- Possible Attributes: `peers`, `lower`, `higher`

`<priorityClass>` adds power to the `<excl>` element by enabling the SMIL author to control the specific behavior of supporting objects when a given object is chosen. This control can be forced upon a `peer`, a `lower` element, or a `higher` element. Typical behaviors offered by these attributes allow the author to pause or stop the playback of supporting elements when a new element is chosen. In some uses of `<priorityClass>`, the new element choice will be ignored until the previous element finishes its playback.

`<priorityClass>` is put to work by making it a child of an existing `<excl>` element. For example, in RealPlayer, `<priorityClass>` and a `peers` attribute can be used to pause one clip when another begins playing:

```
. . .
<excl>
    <priorityClass peers="pause">
        <video id="first" src="first.rm" />
        <video id="second" src="second.rm" />
    </priorityClass>
</excl>
. . .
```

Because the video clips are peers of each other, running one clip will pause the other.

Using `<priorityClass>` within Internet Explorer is pretty much the same. In the following example, activation of the second line of text forces the first one to pause in the timeline:

```
. . .
<t:excl>
    <t:priorityClass peers="pause">
        <span class="time" begin="0" dur="15">
            First line of text displayed.
        </span>
        <span class="time" begin="5" dur="10">
            Second line of text is displayed, interrupting the first.
        </span>
    </t:priorityClass>
</t:excl>
. . .
```

The Timing and Synchronization Module Attributes

If <seq>, <par>, and <excl> elements group the elements of your content, the Timing and Synchronization attributes provide much of the control over when those groups play. Much of this work is done by the critical begin and end attributes. However, you will also find attributes that allow you to tweak your presentation for varying bandwidth conditions. Finally, timeContainer and timeAction give you attributes for use in other environments, allowing new SMIL power for languages such as XHTML.

Attribute: begin and end

- Version Compatibility: SMIL 1.0, SMIL 2.0

- Possible Values: See the following for basic descriptions. begin and end support a wide range of options, including begin-value-list, offset-value, syncbase-value, event-value, repeat-value, accesskey-value, media-marker-value, wallclock-sync-value, indefinite

If the <seq>, <par>, and <excl> elements are the building blocks of SMIL timing, the begin, dur, and end attributes are the workers helping to put it all together. Because the values of begin and end are identical, I have combined the two attributes in this one section.

To those new to SMIL, all the possible values I list here will seem a bit intimidating. Don't let the options scare you. If you're new to SMIL, a begin can be as easy as saying begin="2s"—if you want to begin your element at 2 seconds into the timeline. But begin and end attributes can also mean so much more. What if you wanted an element to begin only when another element ends? Or what if you want an element to begin when a mouse click occurs? These attributes offer just that kind of power.

My coverage of `begin` and `end` values starts simply enough: with basic SMIL 1.0 legal clock values. These might be reflected in full clock, partial clock, or time-count values. An example of a full clock value might be 01:15:03 (as in `begin="01:15:03"`); the element will begin playing at 1 hour, 15 minutes, and 3 seconds. With a partial clock value, unneeded time components such as hours are hidden. For example, `begin="00:30.25"` will cause the element to play at 30.25 seconds. For many SMIL authors, timecount values are probably the most convenient to use. An example would be an `end="25s"` declaration. This would end the element at 25 seconds. In their abbreviated form, timecounts are easy to figure out quickly and enter in as a value in an attribute. Most people understand 25 seconds as 25s more easily than 00:00:25.0.

Implementations can vary in preferred ways of representing time values. That is not to say that one player cannot understand the time value used by another. But it is important to keep an eye on these issues. For example, a `begin` in QuickTime would look like this:

```
<video src="myMovie.mov" begin="10sec" />
```

In RealPlayer, a `begin` attribute would look like the following:

```
<video src="myMovie.rm" begin="10s" />
```

Finally, an Internet Explorer `begin` attribute would appear as follows:

```
<div class="time" begin="10">My Text</div>
```

You can also use offset values with `begin` and `end`. An offset is simply the negative or positive space off of the given time. Thus, a `begin="+5s"` means that the element should begin 5 seconds after the parent element begins. In a grouping with other media objects, this might mean your audio starts 5 seconds after the first image appears.

With SMIL 2.0, more interactivity enters the fray with the use of the `accesskey` value for `begin` and `end`. This looks for the user to press a specific key. `end="accesskey(y)"` tells the player or browser to end the element when the "y" key is pressed.

Both SMIL 1.0 and 2.0 support extensive use of `id` to relate `begin` and `end` times to identified elements. Before we get too far, some review of `id` is in order. `id`, an attribute of the Structure module, can be attached to any element in a SMIL document. As covered earlier, it requires a "valid XML identifier," but that can really

mean nothing more than a short, text-based name. Therefore, attaching id="1",
or id="first", or even id="firstSection" to a time container or media object
will identify that element with that name. After something is named, it can called
by name for use in other elements and attributes.

The use of id has changed a little from SMIL 1.0 to SMIL 2.0, but the end goal
is basically the same. Let's take a quick look at the differences. In the following
generic example of SMIL 1.0, an id of "fred" is given to the first clip in the
<par> block:

```
<par>
   <audio src="myaudio" id="fred" />
   <animation src="myanimation" begin="id(fred)(5s)" />
</par>
```

In this example of SMIL 1.0, the <animation> element references the <audio>
element called "fred" in its begin value and tells "myanimation" to begin 5 seconds after "fred" begins. In SMIL 2.0, this reference might be rewritten to look
like this:

```
<par>
   <audio src="myaudio" id="fred" />
   <animation src="myanimation" begin="fred.begin+5s" />
</par>
```

The end result is the same, but the first example is deprecated in SMIL 2.0. That
means that the SMIL 1.0 approach can be used, but the W3C does not recommend it.

So what can id do for you? You are probably beginning to get just a taste
already. Suppose that you want to synchronize the actions of one element to the
status of another. begin="fred.begin" sounds redundant, but it really means that
the current element will begin when the element identified as "fred" begins. You
also might use begin="fred.end" to start the new active element in motion after
"fred" ends. And I'm just getting started with the possibilities. Suppose you
wanted the current element to end="fred.end+5s". This would end the element 5
seconds after "fred" ends; or why not try end="fred.begin-5s" to end the element 5 seconds before "fred" begins. Notice that I'm using the same values for
both the begin and end attributes. Likewise, you can mix and match in your work
as well.

An example of this kind of timing with an Internet Explorer `begin` attribute would appear as follows:

```
<div class="time" begin="jane.begin+10">My Text</div>
```

Now that you have some `id` basics down, let's look for more options. SMIL 2.0 supports additional teaming of `id` with `media-marker` values or `wallclock-sync` values. If you use a media type that supports markers, you might embed the value `"sally"` somewhere within the timeline of that media object. Now by identifying that media object as `"fred"`, you have opened the door to accessing that marker. `begin="fred.marker(sally)"` will begin the current element when the media object called `"fred"` hits its internal marker labeled as `"sally"`.

Wallclock values allow the `begin` or `end` attributes to make the connection with the outside world. Several time formats represent global and local time approaches. For example, `end="wallclock ( 2002-01-01T12:00-08:00 )"` would force the element to end on January 1, 2002 at 12 p.m. in the U.S. Pacific time zone. `wallclock-sync` values create the path for live SMIL-driven events.

One of the most important aspects of SMIL 2.0 `id` use is in connecting `begin` and `end` to events. What is an event? An event is an occurrence that the computer can recognize and acknowledge. It could be the playing of a media clip, or with a user action event, it could be the click of a mouse.

This provides powerful interactivity without the need for using a scripting language. When implemented in a Web browser that supports SMIL, the result can feel a lot like JavaScript. In a Web multimedia SMIL player, event-driven use of `begin` and `end` makes SMIL 2.0 a vast improvement over SMIL 1.0. Event-driven `begin` and `end` is especially handy when used with the `<excl>` element.

SMIL 2.0 defines three events: `beginEvent`, `endEvent`, and `repeat`. `beginEvent` occurs when the local element timeline begins to play. `endEvent` occurs when the active element ends in the local timeline. `repeat` looks for the local timeline repeating. Coupled with other events that `begin` or `end` other elements in the timeline, `beginEvent`, `endEvent`, and `repeat` can kick in to move the presentation on to its next step.

The `repeat` event offers additional hooks to get at what is happening in the timeline. The form uses the `id`, followed by a dot and the keyword `repeat`, followed by an iteration (or loop) value in parentheses. Therefore, `end="fred.repeat(2)"` means that the element will `end` when `"fred"` begins its second iteration (loop).

Additional action events are defined by the environment in which the player or browser exists. Click your mouse and you have just created an occurrence that the computer can recognize and acknowledge. This could be described as a "click" action. Depending on the environment, other occurrences could be rolling the mouse point over an object (a "mouseover") or even a dragging one object on top of another.

An example of an event-driven use of begin is begin="fred.click" or begin="fred.activateEvent". The first example is from HTML+TIME support in Internet Explorer. The second is from SMIL 2.0 support in RealPlayer. Both use a familiar dot syntax approach in which the event is tied to an object that is labeled with an id attribute. In the case of both examples, this happens to be some type of media object to which the author as added the id="fred" attribute. In the case of Internet Explorer, the user event of clicking the mouse is known as a click. Clicking the mouse in RealPlayer is known as an activateEvent. Despite the minor syntax differences, both look for a mouse click happening to "fred" and force the element to begin.

As with other value options with begin and end, events can also pick up clock-value offsets. These are times added to or subtracted from the timing of the event. Again, we see the familiar dot syntax. begin="fred.click+2s" will delay the begin by 2 seconds when "fred" is clicked. end="fred.repeat(2)-5s" will likewise end the element 5 seconds before "fred" begins its second iteration (loop) in a repeat.

One additional power of begin and end that might not be immediately obvious is that you can specify multiple begin and end times, although begin="5s" might delay the element by 5 seconds, you could also double up the work of that statement by converting it to begin="5s; fred.click". A semicolon separates the two (or more) events. In this example, the element will begin after 5 seconds and/or after "fred" is clicked.

Both begin and end support a set value of indefinite. Depending on whether the provided attribute is begin or end, using indefinite means that a subset of methods will determine the beginning or ending value. With begin, the methods beginElement() and beginElementAt() can begin the active duration of an element. This will also begin the active duration of an element with a hyperlink targeted to the element. With end, the methods endElement() and endElementAt() can determine the active duration of the element. How can this be used? In HTML+TIME implementations of Internet Explorer for example, an endElement() method linked to a Web page button can be used to shut down a continuously repeating object. Following is a HTML+TIME markup sample that shows just that in action:

```
. . .
<t:excl id="myText" repeatDur="indefinite">
    <div class="time" begin="0" dur="4">It was a dark and stormy
➥ night.</div>
    <div class="time" begin="4" dur="5">The Captain turned to me and asked me
➥ to tell a story. And so I began. . .</div>
</t:excl>
<br>
<button onclick="myText.endElement()">Stop It!</button>
. . .
```

In this example, my attempt at a short story will loop indefinitely. But with the endElement() method attached to "myText" in the onClick statement in the last line of the code snippet, I have a way out. I can click the button and make it all end.

Attribute: dur

- Version Compatibility: SMIL 1.0, SMIL 2.0
- Possible Values: A legal clock value greater than or equal to 0, media, or indefinite

After you have a beginning for an element established with begin, it is time to give the element a duration. SMIL incorporates two types of duration terminology. A *simple duration* is the basic presentation length of a single element. An *active duration* is the sum of simple duration and any repeated events of that simple duration.

The dur attribute establishes the simple duration of a media element. It supports clock values greater than 0. You can also use the value media to set the duration of a media object to the inherent duration of the media itself. A value of indefinite sets the value at an indefinite duration in time.

How the element is impacted by the dur value is based on the nature of the element itself. For media that have built-in durations (such as video or audio), specifying a shorter duration would potentially chop short that media object. Specifying a longer than normal duration might mean that the viewer is left with "dead air." This would not be true for an object that has no predefined duration.

For example, a slide show of images would follow the lead of whatever durations you specify in your markup.

In QuickTime, a simple duration would use the following form:

```
<img src="myImage.gif" dur="10sec" />
```

Similarly, RealPlayer appears almost identical in use

```
<img src="myImage.gif" dur="10s" />
```

In Internet Explorer, a duration value would appear as

```
<div class="time" dur="10">My text</div>
```

Attribute: min

- Version Compatibility: SMIL 2.0
- Possible Values: A legal clock value greater than or equal to 0 or media

As stated earlier, within SMIL timing, the author makes use of two types of duration: simple and active. Playing an element through from beginning to end would be the simple duration. Playing that element through three times would create an active duration.

The min attribute defines what the minimum active duration of an element will be. If a clock value is given, the element will play at least that much material before moving on. Even if the user makes an interactive choice, the min attribute will lock that user into the presentation until that minimum active duration is reached. If you are using a media element, the media value locks the active duration down to the duration of that media element.

Attribute: max

- Version Compatibility: SMIL 2.0
- Possible Values: A legal clock value greater than or equal to 0, media, or indefinite

The max attribute picks up as the opposite of what the previously discussed min attribute sets out to do. In this case, the element cannot play longer than the specified clock value. If media is the set value for a media element, the element cannot play longer than the media itself. If indefinite is specified, no limitation on the element is made.

Attribute: `endsync`

- Version Compatibility: SMIL 1.0, SMIL 2.0
- Possible Values: `first`, `last`, `all`, `media`, or a legal XML Id value

endsync first appeared in SMIL 1.0. This attribute allows the author to end the children of <par> or <excl> elements on the basis of one of the children reaching the end of its duration. This is handy for objects that do not have a readily defined or known duration.

In SMIL 1.0, endsync offers the `first`, `last`, and Id-value options. Using a `first` value tells the element to end its group along with the very first child to reach the end of its duration. Using `last` means that the element group will end when the very last child reaches its complete duration. If you think about it, this essentially means that everything will end in its own time. So you will find that `last` is the default value for endsync. You can also endsync with a legal XML Id value. For example, if endsync=`"id(fred)"`, the group will end when the clip labeled as `fred` ends. The Id-value approach has been updated slightly in SMIL 2.0, although most authors will barely notice the difference in the syntax between the two uses.

Newer implementations of SMIL in QuickTime support the SMIL 1.0 approach to endsync. In that environment, you might see endsync used with `first`, `last`, or as shown below, `id`:

```
. . .
<par endsync="id(myAudio)">
    <audio id="myAudio" src="narration.mov" />
    <video src="theVideo.mov" />
</par>
. . .
```

In SMIL 2.0, the additional values of `all` and `media` are added to the mix. `all` means that the grouping of children ends when all of them have reached the end of their durations. The value of `media` is meant for media objects. Using `media` as an endsync value means that the time container itself will end with the end of the media object in that time container.

Attribute: `repeat`

- Version Compatibility: SMIL 1.0, SMIL 2.0
- Possible Values: Integers greater than `0` and `indefinite`

SMIL 1.0 introduced the `repeat` attribute to allow for an element to repeat a specified number of times. The value for the number of iterations of the repeat can be specified as an integer greater than 0. For continuously repeating elements, a value of `indefinite` can also be used.

SMIL 2.0 lists `repeat` but deprecates the usage in favor of the more flexible `repeatCount` and `repeatDur` attributes.

Currently, Apple QuickTime prefers the `repeat` form of the language:

```
<video src=""myMovie.mov"" repeat=""2"" />
```

Attribute: `repeatCount`

- Version Compatibility: SMIL 2.0
- Possible Values: A floating-point numeric value or `indefinite`

`repeatCount` specifies how many iterations (or loops) of the simple duration of the element.

In the following sample of SMIL from RealPlayer, the video clip will repeat 3 times:

```
<video src=""myMovie.rm"" repeatCount=""3"" />""
```

Using a fractional value will cause a fractional portion of the duration. In the following example of a fractional value used in Internet Explorer, the sequence of images within the time container will display two and a half times:

```
. . .
<span class="time" timeContainer="seq" repeatCount="2.5">
    <img class="time" dur="5" src="bannerad1.gif">
    <img class="time" dur="5" src="bannerad2.gif">
    <img class="time" dur="5" src="bannerad3.gif">
</span>
. . .
```

If you want the element to repeat continuously, use `indefinite` as the value.

Attribute: `repeatDur`

- Version Compatibility: SMIL 2.0
- Possible Values: A legal clock value or `indefinite`

While `repeatCount` controls how many iterations or partial iterations of the simple duration of an element appear in the timeline, `repeatDur` takes a time-based approach. In other words, you might ask yourself how much time you want to fill with the element repeating. Then, by your specifying a clock value, the element will repeat as many times as necessary to fill that amount of time. Like `repeatCount`, using `indefinite` as a value will cause the element to repeat continuously.

In this sample of SMIL from RealPlayer, the video clip will repeat for a duration of 2 minutes:

```
<video src="myMovie.rm" repeatDur="2min" />
```

Attribute: `fill`

- Version Compatibility: SMIL 1.0, SMIL 2.0
- Possible Values: `remove, freeze, hold, transition, auto, default`

`fill` allows Web multimedia authors to provide a smoother presentation by accounting for different duration times in various elements on a timeline. The `fill` attribute first appeared in SMIL 1.0. Possible values in SMIL 1.0 include `remove` and `freeze`. If the `remove` value is used, the element will disappear after its simple duration is finished. If the `freeze` value is used, the element will freeze when its simple duration is finished. For example, a video clip might freeze on the last frame of the video.

SMIL 2.0 adds the additional attribute values of `hold, transition, auto`, and `default`. `hold` has the same effect as `freeze` with one important difference. Using `hold` means that the element will stay frozen only until the parent group of elements is finished. With `transition`, the element will stay frozen at the end of its duration until a transition effect is finished. The `auto` value creates a variable result depending on other conditions. If you have specified a value or values for an attribute such as `dur, end, repeatCount`, or `repeatDur`, the `fill` value will automatically set itself to `freeze`. But if you have not specified a value for any of those attributes, the `fill` value will automatically behave as a `remove`.

SMIL 2.0 also offers a `default` attribute value. This value forces the element to take its lead from the `fillDefault` value specified in the parent element.

In the following sample from RealPlayer, fill keeps text on the screen even as the movie clip ends:

```
. . .
<par>
    <video src=""myMovie.rm"" region=""movie"" />
    <textstream src=""myText.rt"" region=""credits"" fill=""freeze"" />
</par>
. . .
```

Attribute: `fillDefault`

- Version Compatibility: SMIL 2.0
- Possible Values: `remove, freeze, hold, transition, auto, inherit`

SMIL 2.0 adds the `fillDefault` attribute to the Timing and Synchronization bag of tricks. `fillDefault` offers the same `remove, freeze, hold, transition,` and `auto` values of `fill`. With `fillDefault`, an entire block of elements can be set with one attribute value. `remove` causes the element to disappear after its simple duration has ended. `freeze` causes the element to end as frozen after it has completed its duration. `hold` keeps the element frozen until the other elements in the group are finished. `transition` waits until a scheduled transition is finished before removing the element. Like the `fill` attribute, `auto` determines a `freeze` or `remove` behavior depending on whether a `dur, end, repeatCount,` or `repeatDur` value is specified.

`fillDefault` adds one other attribute value to the set offered by `fill`. If a value of `inherit` is used, `fillDefault` will look to the `fillDefault` of a parent element to determine what its value should be.

In the following sample from RealPlayer, `fill` is set to `"freeze"` across all the objects in the time container:

```
. . .
<par fillDefault=""freeze"">
    <video src="myMovie.rm" region="movie" />
    <textstream src="myText.rt" region="credits" />
</par>
. . .
```

Attribute: `higher`

- Version Compatibility: SMIL 2.0
- Possible Values: `stop, pause`

The `higher` attribute extends the previously listed `peers` attribute by allowing elements with a higher priority to affect the children elements. With `stop` specified, after a higher priority element becomes active, it forces the child elements to stop in the timeline. `pause` forces the child elements to pause when the higher priority element becomes active. When the higher priority element is finished, the child elements resume.

The following sample shows how higher can be used in RealPlayer:

```
. . .
<excl>
    <priorityClass id="first">
        <video id="clip1" src="first.rm" />
        <video id="clip2" src="second.rm" />
    </priorityClass>
    <priorityClass id="second" higher="pause">
        <video id="clip3" src="third.rm" />
    </priorityClass>

</excl>
. . .
```

The first block of video clips is a higher class than the second block containing the third clip. If a clip in the first block begins to play while clip3 is playing, higher="pause" means that clip3 will immediately pause.

The markup for higher in Internet has the same result:

```
. . .
<t:excl>
    <t:priorityClass>
        <span id="first" class="time" begin="5" dur="15">
            This line of text interrupts the following line.
        </span>
    </t:priorityClass>
    <t:priorityClass higher="pause">
        <span id="second" class="time" begin="0" dur="10">
            This line of text displays first.
        </span>
    </t:priorityClass>
</t:excl>
. . .
```

Here, the second line of text will display at the beginning. But at 5 seconds into the timeline, the higher class will pause the second line of text.

Attribute: lower

- Version Compatibility: SMIL 2.0
- Possible Values: defer, never

Much like the previously listed higher attribute, the lower attribute enables the author to control the child elements, depending on how the lower priority elements behave. If a lower-priority element becomes active in the timeline, a value of defer will force that element to wait until the active child elements are completed. If the never value is used, the lower priority element will never become active if the child elements are currently active.

The following sample from RealNetworks shows lower in action:

```
. . .
<excl>
    <priorityClass id="first">
        <video id="clip1" src="first.rm" lower="never" />
    </priorityClass>
    <priorityClass id="second">
        <video id="clip2" src="second.rm" />
    </priorityClass>

</excl>
. . .
```

In this example, if clip2 attempts to play, it could potentially interrupt clip1. lower="never" tells the player not to let that happen. clip2 cannot play until clip1 is done.

Internet Explorer markup follows a similar approach:

```
. . .
<t:excl>
    <t:priorityClass lower="never">
        <span id="first" class="time" begin="0" dur="15">
            This line of text interrupts the following line.
        </span>
    </t:priorityClass>
    <t:priorityClass>
        <span id="second" class="time" begin="5" dur="10">
            This text will never appear while the first line is active.
        </span>
    </t:priorityClass>
</t:excl>
. . .
```

The first line of text will appear immediately and display until the 15-second mark. At 5 seconds, however, the second line attempts to interrupt the show. lower="never" means that it cannot happen.

Attribute: pauseDisplay

- Version Compatibility: SMIL 2.0
- Possible Values: disable, hide, show

Suppose you have taken control of elements by use of the <excl> and
<priorityClass> elements. You may have paused their presentation in the time-
line, but what about their actual display? To fill this need, SMIL 2.0 offers the
pauseDisplay attribute. When a child element of <priorityClass> is paused, a
value of disable will cause the element to become disabled. This will vary
depending on the SMIL implementation of the player or browser. But an example
of a disabled element might be one that is "grayed out." hide will cause the element to disappear from view. show, the default value for pauseDisplay, will
cause the element to show normally.

In RealPlayer, use of pauseDisplay with peers is shown next:

```
. . .
<excl>
    <priorityClass peers="pause" pauseDisplay="show">
        <video id="first" src="first.rm" />
        <video id="second" src="second.rm" />
    </priorityClass>
</excl>
. . .
```

If the second video clip becomes active, the first clip will pause. pauseDisplay
reinforces the effect of peers="pause" by keeping the paused clip showing in the
player.

Attribute: peers

- Version Compatibility: SMIL 2.0
- Possible Values: stop, pause, defer, never

If the <priorityClass> element is used as a child of a <excl> element, a set of
attributes becomes available to help control the behavior of the grouped elements. This allows for presentation control as the user branches among the elements bundled together by <excl> and <priorityClass>. In essence, these
attributes act like traffic lights directing the flow of the presentation.

Children elements of a <priorityClass> element are referred to as peers. The
peers attribute controls how its siblings function when one of the children
becomes active. stop is the default value for peers. If stop is specified, an active
element is stopped as the newly active element begins. If pause is declared, an
active element is paused as the newly active element begins. When the new element finishes or stops, the old active element resumes again. With defer, the

newly active element waits until the currently active element is finished. If never is specified, a newly active element does not begin if another element is already active.

In RealPlayer, peers is used in the following manner:

```
. . .
<excl>
    <priorityClass peers="pause">
        <video id="first" src="first.rm" />
        <video id="second" src="second.rm" />
    </priorityClass>
</excl>
. . .
```

Suppose the second video clip becomes active. Its peer, the first clip, will pause.

The markup for peers in Internet Explorer looks much the same:

```
. . .
<t:excl>
    <t:priorityClass peers="pause">
        <span class="time" begin="0" dur="15">
            First line of text displayed.
        </span>
        <span class="time" begin="5" dur="10">
            Second line of text is displayed, interrupting the first.
        </span>
    </t:priorityClass>
</t:excl>
. . .
```

The first line of text will appear immediately and display until the 5-second mark. At that point, the second line appears. As a peer of the second line of text, the first line pauses. In the case of this example, the first line of text disappears from the browser screen. After 10 seconds have elapsed, the second text line will disappear and the first will resume its count toward its 15-second duration.

Attribute: restart

- Version Compatibility: SMIL 2.0
- Possible Values: always, whenNotActive, never, default

If an element is to be restarted in the timeline, the restart attribute controls the behavior of that function. An always value means that the element can be restarted at any time. As it sounds, whenNotActive means the element cannot be restarted until its active role in the timeline ends. never means the element can never be restarted. default means the element will grab its behavior from the restartDefault attribute defined for the block of grouped elements. The default value of the restart attribute, as you might expect, is default. If no restartDefault is specified, the result is that the restart attribute functions with a value of always.

Attribute: restartDefault

- Version Compatibility: SMIL 2.0
- Possible Values: always, whenNotActive, never, inherit

For a group of elements in a parent element, restartDefault sets the overall behavior for a restart in the timeline. Like the restart attribute, an always value means the associated element can be restarted at any time. whenNotActive allows the element to be restarted when it is not actively functioning in the timeline. And never means the element can never be restarted. inherit allows the restartDefault attribute to snag the value from the parent element's restartDefault. The default value of restartDefault is inherit.

Attribute: syncBehavior

- Version Compatibility: SMIL 2.0
- Possible Values: canSlip, locked, independent, default

If you have media objects playing at the same time, you also have the potential for synchronization issues. What happens if one media object loads smoothly and another stream does not? syncBehavior offers the author a set of behaviors that address this.

The canSlip value allows the timing of the element to slip in relation to other grouped elements. locked forces the element to keep in step with the other elements. With independent, the element runs on its own timeline. Even if other elements in the grouping stop or seek to a new location in the timeline, independent makes sure the associated element keeps on its own merry way. default matches syncBehavior to the value established for a group of elements by the syncBehaviorDefault attribute.

To use syncBehavior with RealPlayer, tuck the attribute in with the media object or time container:

```
<video src="myVideo.rm" syncBehavior="canSlip" />
```

It is important to note that the implementation of the SMIL player or browser can have a great deal to do with how these attributes are followed. A player using canSlip might just let the timeline slip or it might try to catch up by skipping ahead in the playback. You may need to do further research or experimentation to get a result that successfully matches your presentation.

Attribute: syncBehaviorDefault

- Version Compatibility: SMIL 2.0
- Possible Values: canSlip, locked, independent, inherit

If you have a lot of media objects playing at the same time, you have a need for a syncBehavior that is more global. SyncBehaviorDefault fulfills this mission. Attached to an element, syncBehaviorDefault establishes the default synchronization behavior for all children of that element. You can override this default behavior by specifying a syncBehavior in a given element. This is ideal for that one errant element that seems to need something different.

As with syncBehavior, the canSlip value will allow the element to slip in the timeline. locked forces the element to keep in step with the timeline. With independent, the element runs on its own timeline. Even if other elements in the grouping stop or seek to a new location in the timeline, independent makes sure the associated element keeps on its own merry way. syncBehaviorDefault swaps the default value for inherit. This value tells syncBehaviorDefault to inherit the syncBehaviorDefault value from a parent element.

To use syncBehaviorDefault with RealPlayer, place the attribute in with the time container that holds the media objects:

```
. . .
<par syncBehaviorDefault="locked">
    <video src="myVideo.rm" />
    <audio src="myAudio.rm" />
</par>
. . .
```

Attribute: syncTolerance

- Version Compatibility: SMIL 2.0
- Possible Values: An acceptable clock value or default

If you set your syncBehavior or syncBehaviorDefault with the locked value, you might want to hedge your bets by saying just how locked the locked value really is. For example, you might set syncTolerance to a clock value of 3s, meaning 3 seconds. As long as the offending element stays timed within 3 seconds of the other elements, everything proceeds normally. If the errant element falls outside of that 3-second range, the player might drop data to catch the presentation up, or it might halt the presentation until the late element comes back up to speed. Like syncBehavior, a default value for syncTolerance reaches back to find out what the syncToleranceDefault value is.

syncTolerance in RealPlayer is applied to the time container that groups the elements:

```
. . .
<par syncTolerance="3s">
    <video src="myVideo.rm" syncBehavior="locked" />
    <audio src="myAudio.rm" syncBehavior="locked" />
</par>
. . .
```

Attribute: syncToleranceDefault

- Version Compatibility: SMIL 2.0
- Possible Values: An acceptable clock value or inherit

If you have a number of elements that you want to lock the synchronization to, syncToleranceDefault makes it easy to establish the tolerance across the entire group. Like syncTolerance, you can use an acceptable clock value to represent hours, minutes, seconds, or milliseconds, and like syncBehaviorDefault, syncToleranceDefault offers an inherit value to follow the guidance of syncToleranceDefault in a parent element.

Just like syncTolerance, SyncToleranceDefault in RealPlayer is used on the time container that groups the elements:

```
. . .
<par syncToleranceDefault="3s">
    <video src="myVideo.rm" syncBehavior="locked" />
    <audio src="myAudio.rm" syncBehavior="locked" />
</par>
. . .
```

Attribute: syncMaster

- Version Compatibility: SMIL 2.0
- Possible Values: true, false

If all you want to do is synchronize your elements to one master element, syncMaster is your choice. syncMaster is attached to the media element or time container to which you want the timeline locked. With a lead element identified, all other elements within that time container will follow its direction. But syncMaster is ignored if the element is paused.

Attribute: timeContainer

- Version Compatibility: SMIL 2.0 (Integration Set)
- Possible Values: par, seq, excl, none

With SMIL 2.0, Web multimedia authors now have the capability to incorporate SMIL into other XML languages. A great example of this is the HTML+TIME implementation of SMIL 2.0 in the Internet Explorer Web browser. With Internet Explorer, SMIL behavior appears right within the Web browser.

timeContainer attaches timing capability to XML elements. The attributes are the expected par (parallel), seq (sequential), and excl (exclusive) methods of grouping and timing elements that you would find in more traditional implementations of SMIL. timeContainer also offers a none value. This default value turns off the timeContainer function.

Obviously, you cannot use timeContainer as an attribute for an existing <par>, <seq>, or <excl> element. Beyond that restriction, it is up to the XML language author as to what elements timeContainer can be attached.

On first glance, timeContainer might seem a bit redundant. For example, you could use the following markup in Internet Explorer to display three banner ads in sequence:

```
. . .
<span class="time" timeContainer="seq">
    <img class="time" dur="5" src="bannerad1.gif">
    <img class="time" dur="5" src="bannerad2.gif">
    <img class="time" dur="5" src="bannerad3.gif">
</span>
. . .
```

Of course, you could also use a more traditional approach with normal use of a
<seq> element. So why is `timeContainer` so handy? At times, you might want to
leverage the time container aspects of SMIL against the power already built in to
the host environment. For example, Internet Explorer supports a <marquee> element intended for scrolling text. With `timeContainer` attached, it is possible to
scroll images across the screen while they change every few seconds:

```
. . .
<marquee class="time" timeContainer="seq" repeatCount="indefinite">
    <img class="time" dur="5" src="bannerad1.gif">
    <img class="time" dur="5" src="bannerad2.gif">
    <img class="time" dur="5" src="bannerad3.gif">
</marquee>
. . .
```

Now, an image will scroll across the Web page; every 5 seconds, the image will
change to the next image in the sequence. The result is subject to your interpretation of taste. But it does quickly demonstrate the power available in a SMIL
Integration Set.

Attribute: `timeAction`

- Version Compatibility: SMIL 2.0 (Integration Set)
- Possible Values: `intrinsic`, `display`, `visibility`, `style`,
  `class:classname`, `none`

The purpose of `timeAction`, as the name suggests, is to specify what action is
taken on an element while it is active in the timeline.

`intrinsic` is the default value for `timeAction`. It basically tells the element that
it should do its natural thing, whatever that may be, when the timing is applied.

When used with the `style` value, `timeAction` controls the application of a style
as set by an inline `style` attribute. As shown in the following markup sample
from Internet Explorer, you could set text to appear temporarily bold for a few
seconds after the Web page loads:

```
. . .
<span class="time" style="Font-Weight:bold;" begin="0" dur="10"
➥ timeAction="style">
    <p>This text will be bold for the first ten seconds of display before
➥ reverting to normal.</p>
</span>
. . .
```

After the duration of 10 seconds has elapsed, the text returns to a normal nonbold style.

Similarly, `class` controls the application of a classname to the element during the associated timeline. The form for the `class` value is to specify the appropriate classname after `class` and a colon (as in `class:`*classname*). none turns off any timing effect on the element.

Finally, the `display` and `visibility` values of `timeAction` have very similar functions with slightly different flavors. Both `display` and `visibility` cause the element to appear while the timeline is active. Both `display` and `visibility` also cause the element to disappear when the timeline is finished. So what is the difference? With `display`, the element is not a part of the presentation until it is displayed. So what the user might see with `display` is a SMIL-based Web page that dynamically changes to make room for the element as it appears. When the element is no longer displayed, the Web page may dynamically change back to its old layout. With `visibility`, the element is a part of the presentation, but it is hidden until it is made visible. Therefore, the Web page layout would stay the same, but the element would appear in the position already set aside for it.

If you are used to Web pages sitting still on the screen, all this dynamic reformatting might seem a foreign concept. So let's look at a markup example that uses both values. Again, we'll use a sample from Internet Explorer. Suppose you had a two lines of text displayed on the screen:

```
. . .
<span class=time begin="0" dur="10" timeAction="visibility">
    <p>This first line of text will disappear after ten seconds.</p>
</span>
<p>This second line of text will stay in its original place on the
screen.</p>
. . .
```

Both lines of text will appear on the screen when the Web page loads. The first line of text will disappear from the screen after 10 seconds. But with `timeAction="visibility"` the second line will stay anchored to its original position on the screen.

Now let's try something a little different:

```
. . .
<span class=time begin="0" dur="10" timeAction="display">
    <p>This first line of text will disappear after ten seconds.</p>
</span>
```

```
<p>This second line of text will shift up to occupy the space of the first
➥ line.</p>
. . .
```

Once again, both lines of text will appear on the screen when the Web page
loads. And as with the previous example, the first line of text will disappear from
the screen after 10 seconds. But now things change. With timeAction="display"
the second line of text will jump up to fill the vacant hole left behind as the first
line disappears. The Web page dynamically changes.

These two examples are pretty simple. You can imagine how drastic the changes
would be if an entire paragraph of text or large graphic disappeared. With
timeAction="display" the other page objects will reshuffle on the page as if the
old elements never existed. In a strange way, timeAction="display" creates a
kind of SMIL-based quicksand.

The Timing and Synchronization Module Summarized

Even in SMIL 1.0, Timing and Synchronization did the bulk of the work for the
SMIL Web multimedia author. SMIL 2.0 greatly expands the earlier <seq> and
<par> time containers with the highly interactive <excl> and a whole new set of
attributes that allows for a great deal of fine-tuning of the presentation. Attributes
take the power of SMIL time containers right into other XML languages, meaning you can now flavor your XHTML with SMIL. SMIL 2.0 authors will find
that the language has now earned the Synchronized Multimedia portion of its
title.

8

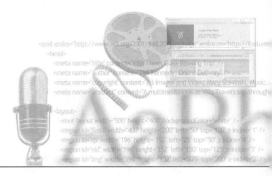

Bring on the Media: The SMIL Media Object Modules

From the previous chapters, you know that a SMIL document does not contain any media on its own. Instead, it references the source for a media element and activates the retrieval of the file contents. The SMIL document also informs the player as to how, where, and when to play back the media source file that has been retrieved. These source files, which can contain audio, video, text, streaming text, animations, still images, or even other SMIL files, are commonly referred to as *media objects*. Therefore, the Media Object modules provide the elements and attributes used to integrate these media files into a SMIL presentation.

SMIL 2.0 has slightly expanded the methods for handling media content that were available in SMIL 1.0, but in many ways, the new specification continues with what worked well previously. The BasicMedia module retains much of the functionality found in SMIL 1.0, and most of what is now reorganized into the other Media Object modules (such as MediaClipping, MediaClipMarkers, MediaAccessibility, and MediaDescription modules) also hails from the SMIL 1.0 specification. However, the MediaParam module and the BrushMedia module introduce two new elements: one that assists with attaching media-specific attributes to objects (param) and one that allows the painting of a single color in place of a media object (brush).

Although a few timing attributes are included with the Media Object modules, almost all timing and control in SMIL 2.0 is achieved through the use of the elements and attributes found in the Timing and Synchronization modules, which are covered in depth in Chapter 7, "Grouping Your Content: The Timing and Synchronization Module." Although a presentation's interactivity and hyperlinking is often carried out in association with media object elements and attributes, those functions are not discussed here; instead, they are discussed in Chapter 11, "Making It Interactive: The Linking Modules," which focuses on SMIL 2.0's Linking modules.

Conformance Profiles and the Media Object Modules

The naming and retrieving of media elements is essential to a SMIL presentation, and without the functionality of the BasicMedia module, there would be no media in the multimedia presentation. Therefore, it is not surprising to find that the SMIL 2.0 Language Profile and SMIL 2.0 Basic Language Profiles support all the Media Object modules in full.

Integration-set conformant language profiles, should they choose to make use of the MediaParam or BrushMedia modules, must support the elements of the BasicMedia module and define several of the terms describing attributes of the new brush and param elements as well. Otherwise, most of the attributes and values that have been supported since SMIL 1.0 will most likely continue to follow the syntax used to implement them using that earlier specification.

The Media Object Module Elements

The elements that make up the Media Object modules provide the means for introducing media files into a SMIL presentation. Without these essential elements and the attributes that describe them, there would be no visuals, soundtracks, narrations, HTML documents, or the capability to link to other related presentations. In addition, the new param element allows for a set of modifying attributes to be attached to a media object. These attributes are activated when the media file is called for in the presentation. We'll go into each of the elements in the following section and then proceed to the attributes that work with them.

Element: `<animation>`, `<audio>`, `<img>`, `<ref>`, `<text>`, `<textstream>`, `<video>`

- Version Compatibility: SMIL 1.0, SMIL 2.0
- Possible Attributes: `clipBegin, clip-begin, clipEnd, clip-end, erase, mediaRepeat, sensitivity, src, type`

These elements are the basis of how a SMIL document references and retrieves the media files that make up the presentation and, as such, create the backbone of the Media Objects modules. It is important to note that although these appear to be distinct types of media, this is not the manner by which the player determines which type of media is contained in the file. The player will instead determine the type of a media object from the `type` attribute or from the MIME-type information communicated by the server or the viewer's operating system.

In spite of this, the author of a SMIL presentation should attempt to use the element that most closely resembles the media object in question, and if in doubt, use the generic `ref` element to identify a media object. This increases the readability of the SMIL document and, in turn, increases the chance that the viewer will experience a media-rich presentation without delays, holes, or stoppages.

The `animation` element that is in this module is used to reference an animation such as a scalable vector graphics animation or an animated GIF. In contrast, the Animation modules discussed in Chapter 10, "Bringing Graphics to Life: The Animation Modules," allow for the control of specific attributes and elements of an animation in a more in-depth manner. Be sure to read through Chapter 10 to incorporate these capabilities and fully make use of SMIL 2.0's new functionality concerning animation.

As mentioned in this chapter's overview, anchors and links can be attached to visual media objects that are rendered onscreen. This is covered in depth in Chapter 11, which details the functionality of the SMIL 2.0 Linking modules.

Element: `<brush>`

- Version Compatibility: SMIL 2.0
- Possible Attributes: `color`, `clipBegin`, `clipEnd`, `erase`, `mediaRepeat`, `sensitivity`, `type`

The `brush` element, new to SMIL 2.0, gives the author the option of using a solid color in place of a media object. All the attributes of the regular media objects are supported, with the exception of the `src` attribute, which is ignored because there is no media object to be retrieved. However, a separate `color` attribute is added for this element because it is necessary for the implementation of this effect. In brief, the `brush` element paints a solid color on the screen and can be used to create a succession of color changes between media clips.

Element: `<param>`

- Version Compatibility: SMIL 2.0
- Parent Element: `animation`, `audio`, `img`, `ref`, `text`, `textstream`, `video`
- Possible Attributes: `name`, `value`, `valuetype`

Also new to SMIL 2.0 is the `param` element, which allows authors to attach a set of modifying attributes and values to a media object, which is then accessed as the media file is pulled into play. This is accomplished by enclosing one or more `param` elements inside a particular media object element (for instance, a `video` element). The `param` element attributes are then used to augment or modify the media object. The bare bones structure of this process follows, with the `param` element at hand to modify the media object with an `id` of poem. Note that the media object element is not closed until after the `param` element has been closed.

```
<ref id="poem" . . . >
   <param . . . />
</ref>
```

Some sample uses of the `param` element include attaching design parameters that are instance-specific to an object (such as adding a cloud to an animated sky for only that particular instance of the sky animation), providing a link to a resource that stores player-specific runtime values, or calling by name in media elements found elsewhere in the presentation.

The information provided by the param element and its attributes are intended
only for a specific media object and its subsequent implementation in a player or
browser. Therefore, it is outside the scope of the SMIL specification to define the
syntax used to interpret the modifying information by that media file or its
player. In fact, the names and values delivered by the param element are assumed
to be understood by the media object in question, or by its player. No specifics
are given as to how players should retrieve or resolve the data that is supplied by
the param element.

However, the SMIL specification does define several key attributes for the param
element and thus sets the basic methodology for these modifications to take
place. We'll use the animated sky mentioned previously as an example to illustrate this process.

```
<ref src="http://www.whoknows.com/sky.blue">
   <param name="weather" value="cloudy" valuetype="data"/>
</ref>
```

The first attribute in param, name, calls up a modifying or augmenting parameter
by name. This parameter, again, is assumed to be understood by the media object
to which it is attached, or by its player; in other words, either the sky.blue animation itself or its designated player are expected to understand the parameter
passed to it. In this example, suppose that our animated sky can be modified to
display a variety of weather patterns. Our parameter for these possibilities could
be called weather and have several values available to it, each of which would
modify the animated sky in a particular fashion. The value attribute is used to
specify which of a parameter's possible values to call forth. Let's say that two
values are available: one called cloudy and one called snow. Because we want a
cloud, not snow, our example specifies cloudy to be the value paired with
weather. Last, the valuetype attribute is used to specify the type of data that will
be supplied by the name-value pair. In our case, cloudy is evaluated and passed
to the player as a string, which is then implemented. Any number of param elements can be attached to a media object, in any order, but they must come at the
start of the media object element and be enclosed by it. More information on the
attributes of the param element is provided in the attributes section of this
chapter.

The Media Object Module Attributes

The Media Object modules attributes provide definition and information about the media objects included in a SMIL presentation. Some of the attributes are used to supply information for viewers who are visually or hearing impaired; other attributes supply information about the content itself, and others assist with the way the media objects are handled.

Attribute: abstract

- Version Compatibility: SMIL 1.0, SMIL 2.0 (deprecated)
- Parent Elements: animation, audio, img, ref, text, textstream, video
- Possible Values: author-generated text

The abstract attribute is described under the MediaDescription portion of the Media Objects module and is meant to describe, briefly, the content contained in the media element. In contrast to the information contained by the alt attribute, this information is not displayed as alternate content, but is used for media content descriptions when a table of contents is generated from a SMIL presentation.

Although supported, this attribute is deprecated in favor of the use of the informational attributes found in and supported by the Metainformation modules (see Chapter 5, "Data About Data: The Metainformation Module").

Attribute: alt

- Version Compatibility: SMIL 1.0, SMIL 2.0
- Parent Elements: animation, audio, brush, img, ref, text, textstream, video
- Possible Values: author-generated text

Defined within the MediaAccessibility module, the alt attribute specifies alternate text to be displayed when the viewer's player cannot display a particular media object or if a player has had its preferences set so as not to display the given media type. alt text can also be displayed along with the media object, although this is implementation dependent and is often used by assistive devices for viewers with disabilities. The alt description of the media object should be brief and meaningful so that it indicates what it is that the viewer is not seeing. It is strongly recommended that the author always include the alt attribute for a

given media element because viewer environments and support for the display of
media types are widely variable.

In the example that follows, the alt value of `photo of cat` will be read to a
viewer using an assistive device or be displayed as text if the image itself is not
rendered because of viewer preferences or system limitations.

```
<img src="cat.jpg" alt="photo of cat" . . . />
```

Attribute: author

- Version Compatibility: SMIL 1.0, SMIL 2.0
- Parent Elements: `animation, audio, img, ref, text, textstream, video`
- Possible Values: author-generated text

The `author` attribute identifies the name of the author of the media element itself.
To identify the author of the entire presentation, use the `author` attribute found in
the Metainformation modules.

In the example that follows, Jane Doe is identified as the author of the media clip
with the `id` of `wildthing`; if she is also the author of the presentation, that information should be included in the `head` section using the metainformation elements and attributes.

```
<ref id="wildthing" author="jane doe" . . . />
```

Attribute: clipBegin, clip-begin, clipEnd, clip-end

- Version Compatibility: SMIL 1.0 (`clip-begin` and `clip-end`), SMIL 2.0
- Parent Elements: `animation, audio, brush, img, ref, text, textstream, video`
- Possible Values: `npt, smpte, smpte-30-drop, smpte-25, marker`

As mentioned in the introduction to this chapter, the MediaObject modules are
primarily concerned with the basic handling of media objects, whereas the timing
and synchronization of media elements is principally done by the elements and
attributes found in the Timing and Synchronization modules (discussed in
Chapter 7). The attributes defined in this section, which is formally identified as
the MediaClipping module, are the exception, and provide SMIL authors with the
tools to begin and end playback of a continuous media object from starting and

stopping points along its internal timeline. When used in conjunction with the Timing module, these attributes are applied first.

The smaller portions of the continuous media object that are created by these starts and stops are commonly referred to as *sub-clips*. clipBegin specifies the beginning of a subclip offset from the start of the media object, whereas clipEnd designates the point at which the subclip will stop playing, again measured from the start of the media object. clip-begin and clip-end offer the same functionality, but are deprecated in favor of the non-hyphenated attributes. In the following example, playback of the video object begins 10 seconds after the start of the clip and ends 25 seconds from the start of the clip.

```
<video src="movie.rm" clipBegin="10s" clipEnd="25s"/>
```

The values available for defining these attributes are designated as "a metric specifier followed by a related time value;" in the preceding example, the timing syntax is making use of the default time measurement of npt, or *normal playing time*, which represents SMIL clock values. The inclusion of s indicates seconds in this case. The metric specifiers available for defining time values are described in detail in the Timing and Snychronization modules (covered in Chapter 7) and include smpte, smpte-30-drop, smpte-25, npt (the default value) or marker. SMPTE timecode can be used for frame-level access and is measured in units that are specified as hours:minutes:seconds:frames.subframes, in which *subframes* are measured in one-hundredths of a frame. smpte-30-drop corresponds to the NTSC drop-frame timecode of 29.97 frames per second and smpte-25 corresponds to the PAL standard of 25 frames per second. Again, for more information on time measurement, be sure to reference Chapter 7.

The use of the marker value is defined in the MediaClipMarkers module and allows for the use of named time points in a media object, if that media format supports the creation of marked time points. The value is expressed using the syntax marker=#URI, where the link is relative to the src attribute of the media object. In the following example, a video file in a format that supports marked time points has had a particular point marked as "night". The clipBegin attribute expresses that the video object should begin at that named marker.

```
<video src="zoo.mov" clipBegin="marker=#night/>
```

The SMIL 2.0 Language Profile includes support for all four attributes, whereas SMIL 1.0 recognizes only the hyphenated clip-begin and clip-end. On the

other hand, integration-set conformant language profiles that implement only
the BasicMedia and MediaClipping modules recognize only the non-hyphenated
`clipBegin` and `clipEnd`. Because SMIL 1.0 implementations will not recognize
the non-hyphenated attributes, and profiles supporting only the SMIL 2.0
MediaClipping module may not recognize the hyphenated ones, you should
include both styles of attributes when using any one of them. In addition,
`clipBegin` and `clipEnd` take precedence over `clip-begin` and `clip-end`, respectively. In the following example, a SMIL 1.0 implementation will begin the video
clip at 10 seconds after the start of the clip and ignore the `clipBegin` attribute
entirely. A SMIL 2.0 Language Profile implementation and any language profile
that supports the MediaClipping module will begin the video at 15 seconds and
ignore the `clip-begin` attribute.

```
<video src="zoo.mov" clip-begin="10s" clipBegin="15s"/>
```

As an alternative to including both styles of attributes, the `switch` element outlined in the ContentControl modules can be employed. See Chapter 12,
"Optimizing Content Delivery: The Content Control Modules," for more information regarding this functionality.

Attribute: `color`

- Version Compatibility: SMIL 2.0
- Parent Elements: `brush`
- Possible Values: hexadecimal colors or keyword colors

Defines the color that fills the screen when using the `brush` element.

Attribute: `copyright`

- Version Compatibility: SMIL 1.0, 2.0
- Parent Element: `animation, audio, img, ref, text, textstream, video`
- Possible Values: author-generated text

The `copyright` attribute contains the copyright notice for the content of the
media element or object. To state the copyright notice for the entire SMIL presentation, use the `copyright` attribute found in the Metainformation modules.

Attribute: `erase`

- Version Compatibility: SMIL 2.0
- Parent Element: `animation, audio, brush, img, ref, text, textstream, video`
- Possible Values: `whenDone, never`

Used with any media element, the `erase` attribute controls whether a media object will stay onscreen after the effects of any timing have been completed. The default value of `whenDone` has the effect of removing the media after any applied timing is completed. Use of the value `never` will keep the media displayed in its last state until the region is reused or until the media is restarted. Any linking behavior will stay active as long as the links are displayed. In the following example, two media elements are displayed sequentially and kept onscreen until the presentation ends.

```
<seq>
   <video src="video1.mov" region="one" fill="freeze" erase="never"/>
   <img src="clown.jpg" region="two" fill="freeze" erase="never"/>
</seq>
```

Attribute: `longdesc`

- Version Compatibility: SMIL 2.0
- Parent Element: `animation, audio, brush, img, ref, text, textstream, video`
- Possible Values: URI link

Another attribute found in the MediaAccessibility module, the `longdesc` attribute is a URI that links to a long text description describing the media object. The description should be supplementary to the information provided in the object's `alt` and `abstract` attributes, and if the object contains hyperlinks, it should also provide information about the linked content. In the following example, the `longdesc` attribute identifies the resource `wordy.html` as the document that describes the content of `fox` in detail.

```
<video id="fox" longdesc="wordy.html" alt="video of our fox" abstract="a
➥short film about the daily life of a fox". . . />
```

Attribute: `mediaRepeat`

- Version Compatibility: SMIL 2.0
- Parent Element: `animation, audio, brush, img, ref, text, textstream, video`
- Possible Values: `preserve, strip`

Used with media types for which a distinct repeat value is found in their specification, such as animated GIFs or looped video sequences, the `mediaRepeat` attribute allows the SMIL author to override the repeat behavior intrinsic to the media type as the object is referenced. The default value of `preserve` leaves the repeat value of the media object intact. In this case, an animated GIF that has been intrinsically defined to repeat indefinitely would do so until it leaves the screen. A value of `strip` would remove the repeat behavior of a media object. In the example of the animated GIF used previously, the GIF would display only once in spite of its intrinsic indefinite repeat value. The following code indicates that the animated GIF `repeatme.gif` will be stripped of its indefinite loop and play only once.

```
<animation src="repeatme.gif" mediaRepeat="strip" . . ./>
```

To use this attribute, a media type must have a formal specification of the exact repeat value to which the `mediaRepeat` attribute will apply, or the media type viewer must provide an interface for controlling the repeat value of the media. When using `mediaRepeat` with the SMIL Timing module attributes of `repeatCount` and `repeatDur`, `mediaRepeat` will be applied first with the Timing attributes controlling the repeat behaviors subsequently.

Attribute: `name`

- Version Compatibility: SMIL 2.0
- Parent Element: `param`
- Possible Values: implementation-specific (or player- specific) values

The `name` attribute declares the name of a runtime parameter for a media object and is expected to be understood by the object's player. The `name` attribute is paired with the other `param` attributes of `value` and `valuetype`. The following example calls up the parameter `weather`, pairs it with a value of `cloudy`, and identifies that the information will be passed to the player as data.

```
<param name="weather" value="cloudy" valuetype="data"/>
```

Attribute: readIndex

- Version Compatibility: SMIL 2.0
- Parent Elements: animation, audio, brush, img, ref, text, textstream, video
- Possible Values: positive integers

The readIndex attribute presents the order in which assistive devices read aloud the content of any longdesc, alt, and title attributes of a given media element in relation to other media elements that are being presented simultaneously. The media object with the lowest readIndex value will have its description(s) read first, followed sequentially by objects with higher readIndex values. The default value of zero results in an element's descriptions being read last. The numbers assigned for readIndex values need not be sequential and can be randomly assigned. If two elements have identical readIndex values, their descriptions will be read in the order that they appear in the SMIL document.

In the following example, assistive devices will read aloud any accompanying alt, longdesc, or title values of the media object cow first because its readIndex value is the lowest. The values of those attributes for the audio object moo will be read next. In the case of field and captions, which have identical readIndex values, any descriptive values would be read in the order in which they appear in the document; in this case, field would be dealt with first, followed by captions.

```
<par>
   <ref id="cow" readIndex="2" . . . />
   <audio id="moo" readIndex="3" . . . />
   <video id="field" readIndex="7" . . ./>
   <text id="captions" readIndex="7" . . . />
</par>
```

Attribute: src

- Version Compatibility: SMIL 1.0, SMIL 2.0
- Parent Element: animation, audio, img, ref, text, textstream, video
- Possible Values: URI link

The src attribute provides the address of the media object that is being called up by the SMIL document. The URI provided, whether relative or absolute, is used

to locate and retrieve the media clip and present it for playback. This attribute is
not required, but no media will be retrieved or presented for a media element that
does not have a src value; however, the object will be given an intrinsic duration
of zero and calculated into any timing that occurs in the presentation. In the
example below, the media object moon is retrieved from a source external to the
presentation using absolute addressing, whereas sun is retrieved using relative
addressing from a file that exists locally to the presentation in a directory named
images.

```
<par>
   <img id="moon" src="http://www.nasa.org/images/themoon.jpg . . ./>
   <video id="sun" src="images/sun.mov" . . . />
</par>
```

Attribute: sensitivity

- Version Compatibility: SMIL 2.0
- Parent Element: animation, audio, brush, img, ref, text, textstream,
  video
- Possible Values: opaque, transparent, percentage value

The sensitivity attribute allows the SMIL author control over whether a particular media object is sensitive to user-interface selection events, such as hyperlink
activation, or whether the user event is passed onto media objects that are lower
in the display hierarchy. The default value of opaque indicates that the entire area
of the media object is sensitive to user interactivity. A value of transparent
passes an event down to media on layers that are beneath the top-layer media.

In the following example, the region onTop has a z-index value higher than the z-
index of the region behind, which results in behind being displayed behind the
region onTop. If picture, which is a media object displayed in onTop, was given
(or left with) the default sensitivity value of opaque, it would be sensitive to
user interaction. However, because it has been assigned a value of transparent,
any links or clickable regions in links (displayed in behind) will be available
for the viewer to activate.

```
<layout . . . />
   <region id="onTop" z-index="7" . . . />
   <region id="behind" z-index="1" . . . />
</layout>
. . .
```

```
<body>
   <img src="picture" region="onTop" sensitivity="transparent". . . />
   <ref src="links" region="behind" . . . />
</body>
```

If the rendered media supports an alpha channel, and the opacity of the media is less than the value declared using the `sensitivity` attribute, the media element is considered as if it were declared `transparent` and passes the event down to media lower in the display hierarchy. In other words, if the media object is only 30% opaque, and the `sensitivity` value is set lower than 30%, the object is considered transparent. If the alpha channel sets the opacity of the object at more than the percentage declared using the `sensitivity` attribute, the media object is considered `opaque` and is available for user interaction.

Attribute: `title`

- Version Compatibility: SMIL 1.0, SMIL 2.0
- Parent Elements: `animation, audio, brush, img, ref, text, textstream, video`
- Possible Values: author-defined text

The `title` attribute is intended to inform about the element to which it is attached and should include information that is brief, yet meaningful. Implementation depends on the player or browser; for example, the information may be displayed in a title bar or viewed as a mouse is rolled over an element.

How this information is displayed varies not only on the player, but also on the browser version and the operating system of the user. For example, on a Mac using RealPlayer, after a media object is activated, the `title` is displayed in a rolling title bar. In Internet Explorer on a Mac, the title is displayed in the top of the window.

Attribute: `type`

- Version Compatibility: SMIL 1.0, SMIL 2.0
- Parent Element: `animation, audio, brush, img, ref, text, textstream, video`
- Possible Values: depends on the protocol of the `src` attribute for the media element (see the following)

The type attribute, although not required, identifies the content type of the media
object referenced by the src attribute. Very similar to MIME types, this attribute
can directly influence the type of helper application that is used to play back
media. Although SMIL allows authors to use a variety of elements, such as
animation, audio, or video, to introduce media to the presentation, the element
an author uses to enclose the media does not really declare the kind of media the
media object contains. The type attribute specifies the kind of media that the
media object contains, as well as what helper application may be used to play
back the file.

The way this is done depends on the protocol used to deliver the file or the src
value of the media object. In the following example, the media object newsvideo
is delivered using RTSP (for more information on transfer protocols, see Chapter
2, "SMIL Authoring"). Because it uses this protocol for delivery, the type attribute is used to declare that the content be selected and, if the type is unknown to
the current playback engine, that it be played back using the playback engine
declared by the type attribute. In this case, application/x-pn-realmedia
declares that if the viewer's media player doesn't know what to do with a file
with the extension .rm, the playback engine to use is RealPlayer.

```
<par>
   <video id="newsvideo" src="rtsp://realserver.wherever.com/video.rm"
      type="application/x-pn-realmedia"  . . . />
   <audio id="headlines" src=http://www.mydomain.com/captions.mov"
      type="audio/quicktime"  . . . />
</par>
```

The media object headlines is delivered using HTTP as its delivery protocol; in
this case, the type attribute influences the selection of the helper application to
play back the file. Although the viewer's browser may have its preferences set to
launch another audio tool to play back .mov files, the type attribute will force the
file to play back using QuickTime.

In the case where the content is available in multiple formats, implementations
may use the type attribute to influence which format is used.

Attribute: value

- Version Compatibility: SMIL 2.0
- Parent Element: param

- Possible Values: author-defined text, a URI link or the `id` attribute of another media element

The `param` element sets up parameters for a given media object that are pulled into play when a media object is called by a presentation. The `param`, `name`, `value`, and `valuetype` attributes are used to modify or augment the media object. The parameter is called by name by the media object, and the `value` attribute is used to select from a list of possible values to pair with the named parameter. The values, in turn, are used to modify the media object. In the following example, the `param` attributes describe a runtime parameter with the name of `weather` that is used to modify the media object `sky.blue`, whose paired value of `cloudy` dictates that a cloud be included in the `sky.blue animation`.

```
<ref src="http://www.whoknows.com/sky.blue">
   <param name="weather" value="cloudy" valuetype="data"/>
</ref>
```

Attribute: `valuetype`

- Version Compatibility: SMIL 2.0
- Parent Element: `param`
- Possible Values: `data`, `object`, `ref`

The attribute `valuetype` defines the type of information that will be passed on to a media element's player when a named parameter is called up using the `param` element. The default value for the `valuetype` attribute is `data`, which means that the information specified by the `value` attribute will be evaluated and passed to the media object's player as a string. The preceding example (under the attribute `value`) is an example of such a `valuetype`.

If the `value` attribute of the `param` element is the `id` attribute of another media object within the SMIL document, `valuetype` is assigned the value of `object`. In the following example, a media object has previously been assigned the `id` of `musik` and is called up in the runtime parameter named `sound`.

```
<param name="sound" value="musik" valuetype="object"/>
```

When the `valuetype` attribute is given a `ref` value, this specifies a URI or link to a resource where runtime values are stored. This URI must be passed unresolved and also necessitates the use of an additional attribute called `type`, which

specifies the type of content found in the named resource. In the example that
follows, a set of runtime parameters are stored at `http://www.surlygrrl.com/`
`params.txt`. The parameter with the `name` of `betsy` and the `valuetype` of `ref`
links the media object specified in the `video` element to these parameters. The
`type` attribute is used to identify the resource as having the content type (or
MIME type) of `text/plain`.

```
<video . . .>
   <param name="betsy" value="http://www.surlygrrl.com/params.txt"
➥valuetype="ref"  type="text/plain"/>
</video>
```

Attribute: `xml:lang`

- Version Compatibility: SMIL 2.0

- Parent Element: `animation`, `audio`, `img`, `ref`, `text`, `textstream`, `video`

- Possible Values: valid language codes (with options from Ami to English
  to Klingon to Xiang)

Included in the MediaDescription module and as covered in the XML specification, this attribute identifies the natural or formal language of the media element.
The information provided by this attribute concerns the media object's language
and is independent of what SMIL players may do with the information. It is not
to be confused with the `test` attribute of `systemLanguage`, which tests for the
viewer's language preference. In the following code snippet, the language spoken
in the audio clip `speech.aiff` is identified as German (`de` being the language
code for deutsch, or German).

```
<audio src="speech.aiff" xml:lang="de" . . . />
```

The Media Object Modules Summarized

The best multimedia presentations tend to offer media-rich experiences for the
viewer by combining a variety of media elements with interactivity, often over
time. To effectively create such a presentation, media objects must first be referenced, retrieved, and readied for playback. The Media Object modules in SMIL
2.0 and the media resourcing functionality found in the SMIL 1.0 specification
provide the tools to do just that. When the Media Object modules are combined
with others, such as the Timing and Synchronization modules or the Linking
modules, the SMIL author is well on the way to creating a media-rich experience
for the viewer.

9

From This to That: The Transition Effects Module

The SMIL 2.0 Transition Effects module defines new elements and attributes that can be used to create transitions between displayed objects in a presentation. This new capability allows for media to be artfully ushered on or off the presentation stage. It also enables authors to apply transitions such as dissolves, fades, and wipes to media objects that are displayed visually or aurally (although the specification does not address how audio transitions should behave).

In SMIL 1.0, no such capability existed; by sequencing the appearance of the media objects, the visual effect of simple cuts could be evoked, but no provision to execute true transitions existed. In response to the limitations of SMIL 1.0, RealNetworks developed RealPix, a SMIL-based proprietary language that allowed a variety of transitions to be applied to still images (Chapter 14, "SMIL That Isn't SMIL: RealNetworks's RealPix and RealText," provides detailed information on RealPix). Files using this syntax are given the extension of .rp, and are displayed by conventional SMIL presentations the same as any other media element is displayed. The downside of these .rp files is that they are playable only by the RealPlayer and thus are limited to audiences with this player or plug-in installed. However, with the introduction of the following elements and attributes, the functionality found in RealPix is now available for any SMIL player whose language profile includes the Transition Effects module. In short, these modules mark a new beginning for SMIL authors.

Before we proceed to the specific elements and attributes of the Transition Effects modules, let's first take a moment to clarify and understand the working model used by the SMIL 2.0 specification in regard to transitions.

The first concept is that a transition behavior is a property of the media object to which it is applied. When the Transition Effects module is included in a SMIL 2.0 language profile, a "transition filter behavior" is automatically added to all media objects that contain content that is visually displayed. Although the elements and attributes found in the Transition Effects module can be used to specify and control the effect of a transition on the object, this transition behavior has no direct effect whatsoever on the media object itself. The media object to which a transition is applied dictates the space in which the transition will occur (its own stated display region). Likewise, transitions do not alter the duration of the media object because that is either intrinsic to the media file or designated using other attributes.

Next, it is important to understand that three inputs are used to create transition effects. One of those three inputs is the progress of the transition, which will be considered in the next section. The other two inputs declare the displayed media that will be transitioned to and from. Whatever is currently visible in the region where the transition will occur is referred to as the *background*, or *source element*, input for the transition. The background can be actively changing media, frozen media, or a solid background color. This is the element that will become less visible as a transition progresses. The other input is the element that will become more visible as the transition progresses, or the *destination element*. So the destination media object is transitioned to, whereas the background element is transitioned from.

The concept of transition "progress," or the progression of a transition effect through its simple duration, is the third foundation of the working model employed by SMIL 2.0 to specify and control transitions. A transition's progress through its effect can be represented by a number between 0.0 and 1.0, in which 0.0 indicates that only the background is displayed and 1.0 indicates that only the destination media object is displayed. From this we can see that a value of 0.5 would represent a combination of equal parts of the background and destination object displays. Progress is a parameter that is common to all transitions and should be thought of as an animation of the effect, much like the animateMotion element (see Chapter 10, "Bringing Graphics to Life: The Animation Modules") animates the position of an element. More on the potential of animating transitions is discussed later in this chapter.

In summary, a transition can be thought of as a filter or effect applied to a media object. Three inputs are considered when a transition is rendered: the background, the destination element or media object, and the progress value of the transition. These inputs dictate how an effect is rendered and can be controlled directly by the SMIL 2.0 author.

Now that we've gained an understanding of the transition model, let's briefly touch on how a transition is applied before we proceed to the elements and attributes of these modules. To apply a transition, one of two methods are employed. Using the first method, the author establishes a transition and its identifier in the <head> section of the SMIL document and then calls it by name using an attribute attached to the targeted media object. The second method, which provides a finer degree of author control, applies transitions at the time the object is called up by the presentation and allows for the progress through a transition effect to be controlled by the author. Both of these methods and their outcomes will be discussed later in this chapter.

The transitions that are available to SMIL authors were drawn from an existing set of transitions referred to collectively as *SMPTE wipes* (pronounced "simptee" wipes), which were defined and classified by the Society of Motion Picture Engineers years ago. The SMIL 2.0 specification has organized these transitions into two levels: types and subtypes. Each type describes a closely related set of transitions and each subtype usually determines the direction and/or origin of the transition. The names assigned to these transition types and subtypes can be used as values for the type and subtype attributes of the <transition> and <transitionFilter> elements. (These predefined transitions, of which there are many, are presented along with their SMIL names in table form at the end of this chapter.) In addition, the Transition Effects module provides authors with the power to create their own transitions outside of the predefined ones.

Now that we have a basic understanding of the transition model, let's take a look at the elements and attributes that make up this segment of the SMIL 2.0 specification. The BasicTransitions module defines the <transition> element, which is used to assign an identifier to a transition, and the transIn and transOut attributes, which are used in the body of the presentation to apply the named transition to media objects. The InlineTransitions module features the <transitionFilter> element. This enables authors either to attach a transition directly to an element or to target an element, usually a media object, and to fine-tune the progress of that transition over time. The TransitionModifiers module gives additional control over the visual effect of a transition.

Conformance Profiles and the Transition Effects Module

The SMIL 2.0 Language Profile and Basic Language Profile support all three of the Transition Effects modules. Integretion-set conformant profiles and any other created language profiles will have to decide whether to support the modules, which of the modules to support, and may decide to create proprietary syntax to describe and implement transitions for playback in their specific media player.

One important note for language designers is that for profiles to include the TransitionModifiers module, they must also include either the BasicTransitions or InlineTransitions module as it forms the basis on which the modifications are made. Additional support for the <transition> element and the capability to use XML identifiers with this element are also required of host-conformant language profiles that include the BasicTransitions module. Profiles integrating the InlineTransitions module must also provide a means of declaring an XML identifier on <transitionFilter> elements, as well as choose whether to support the targetElement attribute (see the targetElement attributes section of this chapter for more details).

The text and examples of code in this chapter are based on the SMIL 2.0 Language Profile. Be aware that language developers may choose to define their own syntax for declaring and implementing transitions and may use the extensibility of the <param> element in conjunction with either the <transition> or <transitionFilter> elements to define new types of transitions that are specific to their chosen player. A language profile can also determine the elements, outside of media objects, to which a <transitionFilter> may be applied. If this is the case, the syntax used by the developer may vary from this chapter.

The Transition Effects Module Elements

As mentioned previously, you can incorporate transitions into a SMIL 2.0 presentation in two basic ways. The first involves the use of the <transition> element in the <head> section of a document, along with an identifier for that transition. The assigned identifier is later used to apply the transition to media objects in the body of the presentation; one benefit of this method is that transitions that are named can be applied to multiple media objects in a presentation.

The other method of applying transitions is done inline, or when the media object is presented in the SMIL document. This method makes use of the

`<transitionFilter>` element along with its attributes and provides full author control over the progress through a transition effect.

Element: `<transition>`

- Parent Elements: `<head>`
- Child Elements: `<param>`
- Possible Attributes: `id`, `type`, `subtype`, `dur`, `startProgress`, `endProgress`, `direction`, `fadeColor`, `horzRepeat`, `vertRepeat`, `borderWidth`, `borderColor`

The `<transition>` element defines a single transition in the `<head>` of a SMIL document. The `id` and `type` attributes are required when using a `<transition>` element. The `id` attribute assigns an identifier to the transition and `type` declares the type of transition, based on an existing set of values. The rest of the attributes define how the transition effect is rendered, but they are optional. Figure 9.1 illustrates a simple transition commonly called a bar wipe, which has been assigned a SMIL 2.0 `type` value of `barWipe`. In this transition, the white area represents the destination media, which will increase in width from left to right across the display area until the entire display space is filled with the destination media.

Figure 9.1   *A barWipe transition.*

A simple example of the use of this transition in SMIL 2.0 follows. In this case, the transition `trans1` is applied to the media object `joe`, which will "push" across the background object `sam` until `joe` fills the display area.

```
<head>
   <transition id="trans1" type="barWipe" />
</head>
. . .
<body>
   <seq>
      <ref id="sam" . . . />
      <ref id="joe" transIn="trans1" . . . />
   </seq>
</body>
```

Multiple transition elements can be defined in the <head> section of a document, but each one is used to define a single identifiable transition.

Element: <transitionFilter>

- Parent Elements: Any media object with renderable content

- Child Elements: <param>

- Possible Attributes: type, subtype, mode, fadeColor, begin, dur, end, repeatCount, repeatDur, from, to, by, values, calcMode, targetElement, href

The <transitionFilter> element is used to apply transitions directly to a targeted element. This can be done either by including it as a child element of a media object or by referring to the targeted element through the use of the targetElement or href attributes. As is true for the <transition> element, the <transitionFilter> element is not a time container and cannot be used to alter the timing of a media object, and the type attribute is required for the transition to be rendered. However, unlike the <transition> element, the id attribute is not required for the <transitionFilter> element. The timing support found in the BasicInlineTiming module (see Chapter 7, "Grouping Your Content: The Timing and Synchronization Module," for more information on this module) and the BasicAnimation module (covered in depth in Chapter 10, "Bringing Graphics to Life: The Animation Modules") are integrated into this element.

The following example uses simple <transitionFilter> syntax to apply a bar wipe (as illustrated previously) to the media object cat.

```
<body>
. . .
<ref id="cat" . . . >
   <transitionFilter type="barWipe" . . . />
</ref>
. . .
</body>
```

The Transition Module Attributes

Many of the attributes in this module apply to both the <transition> and <transitionFilter> elements. However, some belong distinctly to one or the other. In almost all cases, the attributes are optional and are used to fine-tune the effect the transition has on the targeted element.

Attribute: `begin, end`

- Parent Element: `<transitionFilter>`
- Possible Values: Time values as defined in the Timing and Synchronization module (see Chapter 7)

These attributes can be used to declare when a transition begins or ends, if the transition is being applied using the inline syntax of the `<transitionFilter>` element. A full description of the timing values that are valid for use by these attributes is included in Chapter 7. In the example that follows, simple clock-values are used to designate that a bar wipe transition be applied to the media object `field` 5 seconds after it is begins its display. The `end` attribute declares that the transition will end at 7 seconds. Therefore, the duration of the transition will be 2 seconds.

```
<ref id="field" . . . >
     <transitionFilter type="barWipe" begin="5s" end="7s" />
</ref>
```

Attribute: `borderColor`

- Parent Elements: `<transition>`, `<transitionFilter>`
- Possible Values: color name or hexadecimal color, `blend`

The `borderColor` attribute determines the content of the border that is generated along the edge of a wipe. If the value is a color, the edge of the transition will be filled with this color. If `blend` is the value specified, the border is filled with a blending of the elements involved in the transition. The effect of `blend` is an additive blur of the two media sources. This can be applied to all transitions with the exception of `fade`, in which case no leading edge is generated. The default value of this attribute is `black`.

Attribute: `borderWidth`

- Parent Elements: `<transition>`, `<transitionFilter>`
- Possible Values: integers greater than or equal to zero

The `borderWidth` attribute specifies the width of a border generated along the leading edge of a wipe. The default value is `zero`, in which case no border is rendered. In the following example, the bar wipe transition is given a red leading-edge border 1 pixel wide.

```
<transitionFilter type="barWipe" borderWidth="1" borderColor="red">
```

Attribute: by

- Parent Element: <transitionFilter>
- Possible Values: numbers between 0.0 and 1.0

This attribute establishes a relative offset value for the progress of a transition effect. For example, if the by attribute is set to 0.5, the accompanying attributes defined in the parent <transitionFilter> element will be fully executed at the halfway point of the transition. This attribute is ignored if the values attribute is specified.

Attribute: calcMode

- Parent Element: <transitionFilter>
- Possible Values: discrete, linear

Used with the values attribute, which contains a list of values that specify the progress of a transition, the calcMode determines how the movement from one value to another is accomplished. A value of discrete specifies that the transition will jump from one value to the next. A value of linear, which is the default value, indicates that the movement between the values is accomplished using a simple linear interpolation. In the example that follows, the bar wipe transition progresses in four distinct steps as it moves through the values list. The calcMode value of discrete specifies that the progress through the values list is executed as a series of four "jumps" to the next assigned progress value.

```
<transitionFilter type="barWipe" values="0.25; 0.50; 0.75; 1.00"
➥ calcMode="discrete" />
```

The calcMode attribute, when used with the elements found in the BasicAnimation module, can also take a value of paced or spline. These are ignored when the calcMode attribute is used with transitions and are replaced with the value of linear.

Attribute: direction

- Parent Elements: <transition>
- Possible Values: forward, reverse

The direction attribute specifies the direction the transition in which will run. This will not affect which element is considered the background and which is considered the destination media, but only the execution of the transition itself. Figure 9.2 illustrates a transition with the SMIL 2.0 name of irisWipe that begins as a fully black area, which represents the background element. A white area, representing the destination media, expands from the center of the display space until it replaces all the background (black) and reveals all the destination media object (white).

Figure 9.2   *An irisWipe transition.*

If the direction attribute were set to reverse, the iris wipe would appear as illustrated in Figure 9.3, again with the white area representing the destination media.

Figure 9.3   *The effect of the attribute direction="reverse" when applied to an irisWipe transition.*

The transition would begin as before with black, which represents the background media, fully filling the display space. The white area (representing the destination media) would appear around the edges of the display space and "close in" on the black until the black area was completely replaced by white. The use of the direction attribute is limited to transitions that contain a directional progression; a crossfade between two elements, for example, does not move in a direction across the display area and therefore would not be affected by the direction value.

Attribute: `dur`

- Parent Elements: `<transition>`, `<transitionFilter>`
- Possible Values: clock-values

This attribute specifies the duration of the transition. The default value of all transitions defined by the SMIL 2.0 specification is a duration of one second.

Attribute: `endProgress`, `startProgress`

- Parent Elements: `<transition>`
- Possible Values: numbers between 0.0 and 1.0

These two attributes work with the `<transition>` element only and specify the amount of progress through a transition at which to begin or end execution. The `<transitionFilter>` element uses the `to` and `from` attributes to accomplish similar controls. Keep in mind that a value of 0.0 indicates that the background is fully displayed, and a value of 1.0 indicates that the destination media is fully displayed. In the example that follows, the transition `column` begins with the destination media displayed over half of the display space and ends when it is displayed over three-quarters of the background. This will be accomplished over the duration of three seconds.

```
<transition id="column" type="barWipe" startProgress="0.5"
    endProgress="0.75" dur="3s" />
```

The default value for `startProgress` is 0.0, and the default value for `endProgress` is 1.0.

Attribute: `fadeColor`

- Parent Elements: transition, `<transitionFilter>`
- Possible Values: color names or hexadecimal colors

If the value of the `type` attribute is set to `fade` and the `subtype` is set to `fadeToColor` or `fadeFromColor`, this attribute specifies the color that is either faded to or faded from. If the `type` or `subtype` values are other than those just mentioned, this attribute is ignored. The default value is `black`.

Attribute: `from, to`

- Parent Element: <transitionFilter>
- Possible Values: real numbers between 0.0 and 1.0

Similar to the `startProgress` and `endProgress` attributes used by the <transition> element, these attributes specify the amount of progress through a <transitionFilter> at which to begin or end execution. The default value of `from` is 0.0 and indicates that the background is fully displayed. The default value of `to` is 1.0 and indicates that the target element or destination media is fully displayed.

Attribute: `href`

- Parent Element: <transitionFilter>
- Possible Values: an XLink locator

The `href` attribute is used by the <transitionFilter> element to determine the media object to which the transition should be applied. Values must be an XLink locator that refers to the targeted media object. The advantages of targeting destination media in this manner, in contrast to using the `targetElement` attribute, is that the XLink locator syntax is fully extensible for future versions of SMIL and also is more flexible. In the case where both `href` and `targetElement` attributes are specified, the XLink-based `href` will take precedence. The following example first gives an XLink locator for the media object cow and then targets it using the `href` syntax.

```
<cow xmlns:xlink="http://www.domain.com/cow">
   <transitionFilter xlink:href="#cow" . . . />
</cow>
```

Attribute: `horzRepeat, vertRepeat`

- Parent Elements: <transition>, <transitionFilter>
- Possible Values: an integer greater than zero

These attributes specify the number of times a transition pattern is repeated along the horizontal or vertical axis of the display area. The area is divided up evenly using the value of these attributes, and identical transitions are performed with one occurring in each section. The media object is not repeated or tiled, only the transition is, and the result can be described as two or more "smaller" transitions. For example, an iris wipe with a `horzRepeat` value of 2 would divide the display space into two equal horizontal areas, with each area executing an iris wipe simultaneously. Figure 9.4 illustrates this difference.

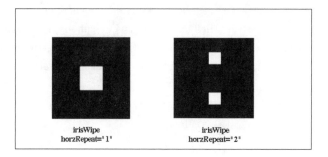

Figure 9.4 *The effect of `horzRepeat` on an `irisWipe`.*

The visual display of some transitions will not be affected by the use of these attributes; a bar wipe, for example, will not look any different if it is assigned a `horzRepeat` value of 2 or more because it will still occur from the left edge of the display space and progress to the right, no matter how many times it is repeated horizontally. `horzRepeat` and `vertRepeat` attributes can be combined to create multiple areas in which replications of the given transition can occur. The following code breaks a display into four quadrants in which four small iris wipes occur simultaneously. Figure 9.5 illustrates the outcome of this code with the white sections indicating the media element that is being transitioned to, and the black representing the background media.

```
<transition . . . type="irisWipe" horzRepeat="2" vertRepeat="2" . . . />
```

Figure 9.5 *Two vertical repetitions and two horizontal repetitions of an iris wipe (the thin lines indicate guidelines only).*

Attribute: id

- Parent Elements: `<transition>`, `<transitionFilter>`
- Possible Values: an author-defined XML identifier

Within the Transition Effects module, the `id` attribute is required by the `<transition>` element so that this identifier can be used to call for the defined transition to be applied to a media object. The `<transitionFilter>` element does not require this attribute.

Attribute: mode

- Parent Element: `<transitionFilter>`
- Possible Values: `in, out`

This attribute specifies whether the targeted media object will transition in or out. The default value of `in` dictates that the media object that acts as the parent element for the `<transitionFilter>` element will become more visible as the transition progresses. A value of `out` specifies that the parent media element will become less visible as the transition progresses. It is important to note that the `mode` attribute does not implicitly tie the start or stop of a transition with the media object begin or end (as is true with the `transIn` and `transOut` attributes); the use of the `begin` attribute is recommended.

Attribute: repeatCount

- Parent Element: `<transitionFilter>`
- Possible Values: a floating-point numeric value or `indefinite`

The `repeatCount` attribute specifies how many times the simple duration of a `<transitionFilter>` is repeated. A whole or fractional number (specified as .25 or .75, and so on) dictates the number of times the transition is repeated. A value of `indefinite` specifies that the transition is repeated until the targeted media element ends. Transitions specified by the `<transition>` element do not repeat.

Attribute: repeatDur

- Parent Element: `<transitionFilter>`
- Possible Values: clock-values or `indefinite`

The repeatDur attribute specifies a time period during which the <transitionFilter> is repeated. If the value of this attribute is a clock-value, the transition will repeat as many times as necessary to fill that amount of time. A value of indefinite will have the effect of repeating the transition until the targeted media element ends. To reiterate: Transitions specified by the <transition> element do not repeat.

Attribute: targetElement

- Parent Element: <transitionFilter>
- Possible Values: the XML identifier of an element

The targetElement attribute is used by the <transitionFilter> element to determine the media object to which the transition should be applied by using the identifier of the media object. Values must be the id value of a media element within the same document. The advantage of targeting destination media in this manner, in contrast to using the href attribute, is that the syntax is much more simple and direct. In the case where both href and targetElement attributes are specified, the XLink-based href will take precedence. The following example targets the media object cow using the targetElement syntax.

```
<transitionFilter targetElement="cow" . . . />
```

Attribute: transIn, transOut

- Parent Elements: any media object with renderable content
- Possible Values: the identifier of a transition or a semicolon-separated list of transition identifiers

These attributes call up the transition, defined in the <head> section of the document using the <transition> element, that is to be applied to a media object by using its identifier as a value. Alternatively, these attributes can be used to provide a list of possible transitions, of which the first one recognized by the specific SMIL player will be executed. As mentioned previously, to be applied to the media object, transitions need to be declared and named with an identifier in the head portion of the SMIL document.

In the following example, the transition black will be applied to the media object flag when it begins its display, unless the SMIL player does not recognize the transition type value of black. If that is the case, the transition red will be applied if it is supported by the player. If neither of the first two transition types are understood by the media player, the next value in the transIn attribute will be checked and applied, if supported. In the case that none of the transition types are supported, flag will play the length of its active duration without a transition effect taking place.

```
<head>
   <transition id="black" type="bowTieWipe" . . .  />
   <transition id="red" type="ellipseWipe". . . />
   <transition id="yellow" type="spiralWipe" . . ./>
</head>
. . .
<body>
   <ref id="flag" transIn="black; red; yellow" . . . />
</body>
```

The transition specified by the transIn attribute will be applied at the beginning of a media object's active duration and progress through the transition effect during its active duration. The transOut transition will end at the end of the media object's active duration or at the end of its fill state. Let's look a little more closely at how the fill state of a media object impacts the visual display of a transition.

When a media object has a fill value of freeze, the last image of the media object is frozen until its parent ends. This allows for the object to act as the background input for the transition. An even better choice of a fill value for a media object, however, is transition. In this case, the background media will remain on display, as is true when the fill attribute is set to freeze, but will remain displayed until the transition to the next media object is completed rather than have its duration tied to the duration of its parent.

If the fill value is implicitly or explicitly set to the default value of remove, the media object will disappear from the display space as soon as its active duration is complete. If the destination media object has not yet filled the display area, whatever is behind the media file that has been removed will be considered the background for the transition. Care should be taken to carefully craft the layout and region attributes so that when the media object departs, the transition effect is not lost or compromised.

Here is an example of the `fill` attribute at work. In the first code sample, the sequence of images are sequential and each "leaves" the stage prior to the next arriving image.

```
<seq>
   <img id="tom" dur="3s" . . . />
   <img id="harry" dur="3s" . . . />
   <img id="sally" dur="3s" . . . />
</seq>
```

If we want to transition between these images using our simple bar wipe, no overlap would occur between them, and the destination media would enter over the background of the region, whatever that may be. However, if we use the `fill` attribute and keep the exiting image on the display area using a `fill` value of `transition`, the "exiting" media will remain in place until the transition between it and the targeted element is completed. Here's the code:

```
<head>
   <transition id="bar" type="barWipe" . . ./>
</head>
<body>
. . .
   <seq>
      <img id="tom" dur="3s" fill="transition". . . />
      <img id="harry" dur="3s" fill="transition" transIn="bar". . . />
      <img id="sally" dur="3s" transIn="bar". . . />
   </seq>
</body>
```

The image identified as `tom` remains displayed until `harry` is fully displayed, which in turn stays displayed until `sally` is fully displayed. There is no reason to correct the default `fill` value of `remove` on the media object `sally`; it occurs last in the sequence and can be removed at the end of its active duration. Transitions can also be applied to the media elements contained in an `excl` element using the same method.

If both a `transIn` and `transOut` attribute are specified for a given media object and the times overlap, the `transIn` takes precedence and the `transOut` is ignored. If a media element repeats or loops, the transition applied by either `transIn` or `transOut` will play only once at the beginning or ending of the total active duration of the media object.

Attribute: `type, subtype`

- Parent Elements: `<transition>`, `<transitionFilter>`
- Possible Values: See the tables at the end of this chapter.

As mentioned previously, the SMIL 2.0 specification has organized a large body of transitions into a two-level catalog of named types and subtypes. Each of the type groups defines a closely related set of transitions; the subtypes usually determine the direction and/or point of origin for the transition. The names that have been assigned to these transition types, which are fairly descriptive, can be used to call up a particular style of transition. The `type` attribute is required by both the `<transition>` and `<transitionFilter>` elements.

The names assigned to the subtypes can be used as values for the `subtype` attribute as long as the transition `type` recognizes the specified subtype as its own. If not, the `subtype` attribute will be ignored. The `subtype` attribute is not required; when it is not specified, the default subtype for the given transition type will be enacted.

The list of available transition types and subtypes is quite extensive; for complete tables detailing each of them, turn to the end of this chapter. Specific SMIL players can choose not to support all the available transitions; however, four transition types with set default subtypes are required by all SMIL players and host-language conformant profiles. These four are `barWipe`, `irisWipe`, `clockWipe`, and `snakeWipe`. The default subtype value for each can be found in the tables at the end of this chapter.

One last note: a SMIL media player may decide to define transitions that are not included in the specification's list of transitions. When this is the case, the `param` element may be employed as a child of the `<transition>` element to set any additional parameters needed to modify any proprietary transitions.

Attribute: `values`

- Parent Element: `<transitionFilter>`
- Possible Values: numbers between 0.0 and 1.0 in a semicolon-separated list

The `values` attribute, which contains one or more numerical values separated by semicolons, is used to step a transition through its progression from the background element to the destination element. Again, keep in mind that a progress value of 0.0 indicates that the background element is fully displayed, whereas a value of 1.0 indicates that the destination element is fully displayed. The value assigned to the accompanying `calcMode` attribute (described earlier in this chapter) determines how the movement from one value to another in the `values` list is accomplished; either a jump will occur from one value to the next, or a linear interpolation will be applied that smoothes the movement from value to value. In the example that follows, the iris wipe transition progresses in four distinct steps as it moves through the `values` list, but it never fully completes the transition (because of the final progress value of 0.90).

```
<transitionFilter type="irisWipe" values="0.15; 0.30; 0.45; 0.60; 0.75;
➡ 0.90" />
```

The Transitions Effects Module Summarized

Finally, the elements and attributes are in place that will allow SMIL 2.0 authors to artfully transition between displayed objects. The extensive list of possible transitions, should an implementation choose to support them all, and the multiple means for applying them to elements and media objects should serve as ample fuel for creative, interesting, and arresting presentations.

Transition Types and Subtypes

In Table 9.1, the white area represents the element being revealed by the transition.

Table 9.1   Edge Wipes

Transition type	Subtype	Example	Transition type	Subtype	Example
barWipe	leftToRight (default)		diagonalWipe	topRight	
	topToBottom		bowTieWipe	vertical (default)	
boxWipe	topLeft (default)			horizontal	
	topRight		miscDiagonalWipe	doubleBarnDoor (default)	
	bottomRight			doubleDiamond	
	bottomLeft		veeWipe	down (default)	
	topCenter			left	
	rightCenter			up	
	bottomCenter			right	
	leftCenter		barnVeeWipe	down (default)	
fourBoxWipe	cornersIn (default)			left	
	cornersOut			up	
barnDoorWipe	Vertical (default)			right	
	horizontal		zigZagWipe	leftToRight (default)	
	diagonalBottomLeft			topToBottom	
	diagonalTopLeft		barnZigZagWipe	vertical (default)	
diagonalWipe	topLeft (default)			horizontal	

In Table 9.2, the white area represents the element being revealed by the transition.

Table 9.2   **Iris Wipes**

Transition type	Subtype	Example	Transition type	Subtype	Example
irisWipe	rectangle (default)	■	hexagonWipe	vertical	⬡
	diamond	◆	ellipseWipe	circle (default)	●
triangleWipe	up (default)	▲		horizontal	⬭
	right	▶		vertical	⬮
	down	▼	eyeWipe	horizontal (default)	◆
	left	◀		vertical	◆
arrowHeadWipe	up (default)	▲	roundRectWipe	horizontal (default)	▭
	right	▶		vertical	▯
	down	▼	starWipe	fourPoint (default)	✦
	left	◀		fivePoint	★
pentagonWipe	up (default)	⬠		sixPoint	✶
	down	⬠	miscShapeWipe	heart (default)	♥
hexagonWipe	horizontal (default)	⬡		keyhole	⚷

In Table 9.3, the white area represents the element being revealed by the transition.

Table 9.3 Clock Wipes

Transition type	Subtype	Example	Transition type	Subtype	Example
clockWipe	clockwiseTwelve (default)		singleSweepWipe	clockwiseRight	
	clockwiseThree			clockwiseTopLeft	
	clockwiseSix			clockwiseBottomRight	
	clockwiseNine			counterClockwiseTopRight	
fanWipe	centerTop (default)			counterClockwiseBottomLeft	
	centerRight		doubleSweepWipe	parallelVertical (default)	
	top			parallelDiagonal	
	right			oppositeVertical	
	bottom			oppositeHorizontal	
	left			parallelDiagonalTopLeft	
doubleFanWipe	fanOutVertical (default)			parallelDiagonalBottomLeft	
	fanOutHorizontal		saloonDoorWipe	top (default)	
	fanInVertical			left	
	fanInHorizontal			bottom	
pinWheelWipe	twoBladeVertical (default)			right	
	twoBladeHorizontal		windshieldWipe	right (default)	
	fourBlade			up	
singleSweepWipe	clockwiseTop (default)			vertical	
	clockwiseBottom			horizontal	
	clockwiseLeft				

In Table 9.4, the direction of the transition and its path are represented by the directional arrows.

Table 9.4 Matrix Wipes

Transition type	Subtype	Example	Transition type	Subtype	Example
snakeWipe	topLeftHorizontal (default)		parallelSnakeWipes		
				verticalBottomLeftOpposite	
	topLeftVertical			horizontalLeftSame	
	topLeftDiagonal			horizontalRightSame	
	topRightDiagonal			horizontalTopLeftOpposite	
	bottomRightDiagonal			horizontalTopRightOpposite	
	bottomLeftDiagonal			diagonalBottomLeftOpposite	
spiralWipe	topLeftClockwise (default)			diagonalTopLeftOpposite	
	topRightClockwise		boxSnakesWipe	twoBoxTop (default)	
	bottomRightClockwise			twoBoxBottom	
	bottomLeftClockwise			twoBoxLeft	
	topLeftCounterClockwise			twoBoxRight	
	topRightCounterClockwise			fourBoxVertical	
	bottomRightCounterClockwise			fourBoxHorizontal	
	bottomLeftCounterClockwise		waterfallWipe	verticalLeft (default)	
parallelSnakeWipes	verticalTopSame (default)			verticalRight	
	verticalBottomSame			horizontalLeft	
	verticalTopLeftOpposite			horizontalRight	

Table 9.5 describes several types of wipes. In pushWipe transitions, both the background and destination media are moving, with the effect that the destination media is "pushing" the background off the display space.

In slideWipe transitions, the destination media moves but the background does not, with the effect that the destination media is "sliding" across the background media.

The fade transitions are pixel-by-pixel blends between the destination media and either the background (crossfade) or the specified color.

Table 9.5   Non-SMPTE Wipes

Transition Type	Subtype
pushWipe	fromLeft (default)
	fromTop
	fromRight
	fromBottom
slideWipe	fromLeft (default)
	fromTop
	fromRight
	fromBottom
fade	crossfade (default)
	left
	up

10

Bringing Graphics to Life: The Animation Modules

One multimedia aspect that was noticeably absent from SMIL 1.0 was support for animation. Sure, you could use SMIL to bring together files that contained animation with files that contained other media types. But actual support for animation tricks right in the language was missing. The SMIL 2.0 specification offers up a healthy serving of animation capability throughout the language. As you will see, this dedicated grouping of animation modules is enough to get any animator started.

There are two animation modules in SMIL 2.0. For the most part, the BasicAnimation Module offers the bulk of the language and its power. But for those who like riding the curve, SMIL 2.0 adds to the power of BasicAnimation with the attributes of the SplineAnimation Module. These additions provide a way to create a more natural and organic animation than the original BasicAnimation offers.

Conformance Profiles and the Animation Modules

Neither BasicAnimation nor SplineAnimation are required for SMIL Host Language or Integration Set Language Conformance. That said, both animation modules draw inspiration from other languages, including Scalable Vector Graphics (SVG) and Cascading Style Sheets (CSS). Most likely, you will see animation included in a range of player and browser implementations.

BasicAnimation and SplineAnimation Module Elements

- Module: BasicAnimation

- Conformance: Not Required for either SMIL Host Language or SMIL Integration Set

- Profile Compatibility: SMIL 2.0, XHTML+SMIL

- Possible Elements: `<animate>`, `<set>`, `<animateMotion>`, `<animateColor>`

BasicAnimation provides the foundation module on which the SplineAnimation Module is built. In BasicAnimation, you will find the critical elements to make an object move, change color, or animate a value to provide dynamic change in your media. Unlike SplineAnimation, BasicAnimation offers the `<set>` attribute to temporarily change a property for a given period of time.

As covered later in this chapter, it is important to note that animation can mean more than just moving an object, changing its size, or rotating its color. Depending on the player or browser, you may find other attributes of an object that you can "animate" over time. For example, you might animate audio levels to match the mood of your presentation.

- Module: SplineAnimation

- Conformance: Not Required for either SMIL Host Language or SMIL Integration Set

- Profile Compatibility: SMIL 2.0, XHTML+SMIL

- Possible Elements: `<animate>`, `<animateMotion>`, `<animateColor>`

SplineAnimation borrows heavily from the BasicAnimation Module, ignoring the `<set>` element and adding the critical `path`, `keyTimes`, and `keySplines` attributes to offer precise control over the speed of the animation. This allows serious animators to use easing effects to create animations with a more natural feel.

Element: <animate>

- Version Compatibility: SMIL 2.0

- Possible Attributes: attributeName, attributeType, targetElement, href,
  actuate, show, type, from, to, by, values, calcMode, accumulate,
  additive, keyTimes, keySplines

A dedicated animation module needs a generic element that sets things in
motion. <animate> is just such an element. It supports a variety of attributes that
enable you to control all aspects of the animation. The <animate> element is
used in both BasicAnimation and SplineAnimation.

In Microsoft Internet Explorer, changing values of properties over time is what
animation is all about. In the following markup sample, the <animate> element
changes the value of the left attribute from its original 25 pixels to 500:

```
...
    <div id="moving" class="time" style="position:absolute;left:25px">
    ➡Moving SMIL!</div>
    <t:animate targetElement="moving" attributeName="left" to="500"
    ➡dur="3" />
...
```

In changing the property values, the text element wrapped in the <div> will
appear to move (or animate) from the left side of the screen to the right.

Animation in SMIL can incorporate more than just moving graphics or changing
object sizes. In this sample from a larger RealNetworks RealPlayer SMIL document, the level of the sound is "animated" from off to full volume:

```
...
    <animate targetElement="mySound" attributeName="soundLevel"
    ➡values="0%;100%" dur="5s" />
...
```

Element: <set>

- Version Compatibility: SMIL 2.0

- Possible Attributes: attributeName, attributeType, targetElement, href,
  actuate, show, type

Suppose you needed to change a value of an attribute for a specified period of
time. In time, your attribute would change, creating a temporary effect for the

attribute. This is the basic goal for <set>: a temporary value for an attribute across a defined period of time. The <set> element is used only in BasicAnimation.

In this use of <set> in Internet Explorer, the image immediately jumps from the upper left edge of the screen to coordinates of 300 pixels over. After sitting there for 10 seconds, it jumps back to its home position at 50 pixels from the left edge:

```
...
    <t:img id="gottaMove" src="ODlogo.gif" style="position:absolute;left:50"
    ➡ />
    <t:set targetElement="gottaMove" attributeName="left" to="300"
    ➡dur="10" />
...
```

RealPlayer uses <set> in the same fashion. In this sample, a region previously identified as "myRegion" in the SMIL document is temporarily animated (or moved) from the bottom level (z-index="0") to the top level (z-index="1"):

```
...
    <set targetElement="myRegion" attributeName="z-index" to="1" dur="10s"
    ➡/>
...
```

This type of animation would be a great application for revealing a clip that plays when a button is clicked.

Element: <animateMotion>

- Version Compatibility: SMIL 2.0
- Possible Attributes: targetElement, href, actuate, show, type, from, to, by, values, calcMode, accumulate, additive, origin, keyTimes, keySplines, path

<animateMotion> does just what it sounds like it might do: make an element move. In this case, that motion will be along a path as defined with an x, y coordinate. The <animateMotion> element is used both in the BasicAnimation and the SplineAnimation modules.

In the following use of <animateMotion> in Internet Explorer, the image animates from the upper left corner of the screen to coordinates of 200 pixels over and 300 pixels down:

```
...
    <t:img id="gottaMove" src="ODlogo.gif" style=
  ➥"position:absolute;left:50;top:50" />
    <t:animateMotion targetElement="gottaMove" to="200,300" dur="10" />
...
```

Similarly in RealPlayer, the following SMIL sample makes a region containing an image move from the upper left corner of the player to coordinates 200 pixels over and 300 pixels down:

```
...
        <img src="ODlogo.gif" region="myImages" dur="30s" />
        <animateMotion targetElement="myImages" to="200,300" dur="15s" />
...
```

Element: `<animateColor>`

- Version Compatibility: SMIL 2.0

- Possible Attributes: `attributeName`, `attributeType`, `targetElement`, `href`, `actuate`, `show`, `type`, `from`, `to`, `by`, `values`, `calcMode`, `accumulate`, `additive`, `keyTimes`, `keySplines`

Like the previous element, `<animateColor>` also accomplishes what it sounds like it should do: it animates a color attribute across time. The `<animateColor>` element is used both in the BasicAnimation and the SplineAnimation modules.

Among other possible uses, `<animateColor>` is a quick way to change the color of text or a background over time. The following markup sample from Internet Explorer does just that:

```
...
    <div id="colorMe" class="time" style="color:red">I'm changing
  ➥color!</div>
    <t:animateColor targetElement="colorMe" attributeName="color"
  ➥to="green" dur="10" />
...
```

The `<div>` element places the text "I'm changing color!" on the screen with an initial color of red. `<animateColor>` steps in to animate the color change from red to green over 10 seconds.

The following example from RealPlayer shows the use of <animateColor> to change the background color of a region named "myBkground" as specified elsewhere in the SMIL document:

```
...
<animateColor targetElement="myBkground" attributeName="backgroundColor"
➥ values="red;black" dur="3s" />
...
```

The BasicAnimation and SplineAnimation Module Attributes

Depending on the element and the module, the combined Animation Modules offer control over a wide variety of attributes. Even so, the major implementations make the heaviest use of a common set of attributes. Again and again, the SMIL author will bump into attributeName, targetElement, from, to, by, values, and calcMode. When using SplineAnimation, the additional attributes of keyTimes and keySplines will be used heavily. Other attributes are more obscure and may never be used by the particular browser or player you are authoring for.

Attribute: attributeName

- Version Compatibility: SMIL 2.0

- Possible Values: A name for the target attribute. May use an XMLNS preface to indicate the XML namespace.

attributeName is used by the <animate>, <set>, and <animateColor> elements. This attribute sets up the name of the target attribute. In that fashion, the element knows what the attribute is that will add functionality to the element.

At first this may sound more complex than it really is. In this snippet of markup from a larger Microsoft Internet Explorer page, you can see attributeName doing its job inside an animate element:

```
...
    <div id="moving" class="time" style="position:absolute;left:25px">
    ➥Moving SMIL!</div>
    <t:animate targetElement="moving" attributeName="left" to="500"
    ➥dur="3" />
...
```

The first line in this example creates the text and positions it on the screen. The second line commands that text to animate or move. The goal of the `animate` element is to move the text from its far left position at 25 pixels to a new position of 500 pixels from the left edge. `attributeName="left"` tells the browser that the left position value is the one being changed. With a new left value of 500 pixels, the text object will move from left to right across the screen.

The following example from RealPlayer shows a very similar use of `attributeName`:

```
...
    <animate targetElement="mySound" attributeName="soundLevel"
    ➡values="0%;100%" dur="5s" />
...
```

What is interesting to note from this sample is that it animates the sound level from one value to another. You might automatically think of the Animation Modules as moving graphic objects across the screen or making graphic objects change size. But depending on the implementation, many attributes in SMIL are capable of being animated.

Attribute: `attributeType`

- Version Compatibility: SMIL 2.0
- Possible Values: `CSS`, `XML`, `auto`

`attributeType` is used by the `<animate>`, `<set>`, and `<animateColor>` elements. Whereas `attributeName` establishes the name of the attribute, `attributeType` establishes the type of attribute that named attribute is. If you use `attributeType="CSS"`, the named attribute is a Cascading Style Sheet property. `XML` sets the attribute as an XML property as defined by the XML namespace.

For `auto`, the default setting, the player or browser will try to find the best type for the named attribute. Starting with `CSS` and then moving on to `XML`, the player or browsers search through the properties for the best match.

Attribute: `targetElement`

- Version Compatibility: SMIL 2.0
- Possible Values: Legal XML identifier

`targetElement` is used by the entire group of `<animate>`, `<set>`, `<animateMotion>`, and `<animateColor>` elements. `targetElement` is the easiest method for linking animation to an element. With `targetElement`, you can tell the player or browser which element you want to apply the animation to. Obviously, you want that element to have been previously named in your SMIL. The value must be the value of an XML identifier attribute.

In the following excerpt of markup from a larger Microsoft Internet Explorer page, you can see `targetElement` is used to target a prior line that creates a block of text:

```
...
    <div id="moving" class="time" style="position:absolute;left:25px">
    ➥Moving SMIL!</div>
    <t:animate targetElement="moving" attributeName="left" to="500"
    ➥dur="3" />
...
```

The first line of markup creates the text and positions it on the screen. It creates an `id` of `"moving"` for that line of text so that it can be referenced later. This is where `targetElement` enters the markup. The second line calls an `animate` function so that the text will move across the screen. `TargetElement="moving"` makes sure that the `animate` element is attached to the correct `id` so it affects the right component.

The following example from RealPlayer shows a very similar use of `targetElement` to change the background opacity of a text region identified elsewhere in the SMIL document:

```
...
    <animate targetElement="myText" attributeName="rn:backgroundOpacity"
    ➥from="0%" to="100%" dur="5s" />
...
```

Attribute: `href`

- Version Compatibility: SMIL 2.0
- Possible Values: Legal Xlink href value. Additional Xlink attributes include `type="simple"`, `actuate="onLoad"`, and `show="embed"`.

`href` is used by the entire group of `<animate>`, `<set>`, `<animateMotion>`, and `<animateColor>` elements. `href` requires the use of the newer Xlink syntax in linking the animation to the element. This is more difficult from an authoring standpoint because the language use is more difficult. But this solution is provided in the specification as more extensible for the SMIL language as it changes and grows.

The specification encourages player and browser implementations to choose between using the `targetElement` attribute or the `href` attributes (which are shown below). Currently, the major players and browsers use `targetElement`.

Attribute: `actuate`

- Version Compatibility: SMIL 2.0
- Possible Values: `onLoad`

`actuate` is used by the entire group of `<animate>`, `<set>`, `<animateMotion>`, and `<animateColor>` elements. Used with `href`, the value of this attribute must be `onLoad`. This declares that the link to the target element is followed automatically.

Attribute: `show`

- Version Compatibility: SMIL 2.0
- Possible Values: `embed`

`show` is used by the entire group of `<animate>`, `<set>`, `<animateMotion>`, and `<animateColor>` elements. Used with `href`, the value of this attribute must be `embed`. According to the specification, this indicates that the reference does not include additional content in the file.

Attribute: `type`

- Version Compatibility: SMIL 2.0
- Possible Values: `simple`

`type` is used by the entire group of `<animate>`, `<set>`, `<animateMotion>`, and `<animateColor>` elements. Used with `href`, the value of this attribute must be `simple`. That identifies the type of Xlink being used in the target function.

Attribute: `from`

- Version Compatibility: SMIL 2.0
- Possible Values: A legal value dependent upon the specified attribute

`from` is used by the <animate>, <animateMotion>, and <animateColor> elements. The `from` attribute declares the starting point for the animation. In `from`-`to` animation, `from` sets up the first value, and the animation progresses from that point to the ending `to` value. For example, `from`-`to` could be used to move the animated object across the screen or change its size. In `from`-`by` animation, `from` sets up the first value and the animation progresses from that point to a new value that equals the sum of both the `from` and `by` values. For example, `from`-`by` could be used to change a graphic `from` its starting size to a new size that is larger by the `by` value. A `from` value is optional if `by` or `to` attributes are specified.

In this first sample from a Microsoft Internet Explorer page, `from` specifies the starting `left` value for the graphic:

```
...
    <t:img id="gottaMove" src="ODlogo.gif"
    ➥style="position:absolute;left:50;top:50" />
    <t:animateMotion targetElement="gottaMove" attributeName="left"
    ➥from="200" to="500" dur="10" />
...
```

Even though the graphic is originally positioned at 50 pixels in from the left margin, the `from` attribute will jump the graphic to 200 pixels before moving it to the 500 pixel mark. The following sample uses the `by` to make the object grow larger:

```
...
    <div id="colorSquare" style="position:absolute;height:100;width:100;
    ➥background-color:blue"></div>
    <t:animate targetElement="colorSquare" attributeName="width"
    ➥from="100" by="600" dur="5" />
...
```

In this example, the object grows by 600 pixels. In both of these examples, the `from` could be left out and the work would completed by the `to` and `by` elements themselves. from will be more adaptable if you wish to use a different value than that which was originally specified.

Like Internet Explorer, from-to animation can be used dynamically to change a range of attributes in RealNetworks RealPlayer. For example, assuming that you had previously declared the RealNetworks alphaControl namespace in the <smil> element, you can vary the backgroundOpacity of an object from one value to another as shown in this markup snippet:

```
...
    <animate targetElement="myText" attributeName="rn:backgroundOpacity"
    ➦from="0%" to="100%" dur="5s" />
...
```

Attribute: to

- Version Compatibility: SMIL 2.0
- Possible Values: A legal value dependent on the specified attribute.

to is used by the <animate>, <animateMotion>, and <animateColor> elements. The to attribute states the ending value for the animation. In from-to animation, the animation progresses from its from starting point to its destination specified by to. In simple to animation, the animation changes from its default starting point to a destination value defined by to. Both have pretty much the same effect, although from-to is more specific in establishing the source value of your animation. You cannot give both a by and a to attribute in the same element, because you would have potentially conflicting instructions between the destination value established by to and the destination value set up with by. In such cases of a conflict, the to value will be used and the by value will be ignored.

The following abbreviated sample from a Microsoft Internet Explorer page shows to in action:

```
...
    <div id="moving" class="time" style="position:absolute;left:25px">
    ➦Moving SMIL!</div>
    <t:animate targetElement="moving" attributeName="left" to="500"
    ➦dur="3" />
...
```

The first line of markup creates text and positions it 25 pixels from the left edge of the screen. The second line of markup animates that text object from its 25 pixel home to a new place equal to 500 pixels from the left edge. The result is that the text appears to move from left to right.

Using to automatically implies motion of an object across the screen. But sometimes an object stays put and the attributes are what really "move." For example, the following sample from RealPlayer uses to to make a change in the background opacity of a text region identified elsewhere in the SMIL document:

```
...
    <animate targetElement="myText" attributeName="rn:backgroundOpacity"
    ➥from="0%" to="100%" dur="5s" />
...
```

Attribute: by

- Version Compatibility: SMIL 2.0
- Possible Values: A legal value dependent on the established attributeType.

by is used by the <animate>, <animateMotion>, and <animateColor> elements. The by attribute specifies the relative offset value of the animation. In from-by animation, the animation changes from the value established with from to a new value that is the sum of the from and by values. In simple by animation, the animated object changes from its default value to a new value that is the sum of the default and the by value. Functionally, this achieves the same goal, although from-by is more specific in setting up the animated object. You cannot give both a by and a to attribute in the same element, because you would potentially have different values between the destination values established by to and by. In such cases of both being specified, the to value will be used and the by value will be ignored.

In this markup snippet from Internet Explorer, the object animates from a width of 100 pixels to 700 pixels because it changes by="600":

```
...
    <div id="colorSquare" style="position:absolute;height:100;width:100;
    ➥background-color:blue"></div>
    <t:animate targetElement="colorSquare" attributeName="width"
    ➥from="100" by="600" dur="5" />
...
```

In this sample from RealPlayer, a region identified as "myRegion" and previously defined in the SMIL document is animated (increased) in height by 50 pixels over a four second period of time:

```
...
  <animate targetElement="myRegion" attributeName="height" by="50"
  ➥dur="4s" />
...
```

So if "myRegion" started out as an area 100 pixels high, the region will now animate to a height of 150 pixels.

Attribute: `values`

- Version Compatibility: SMIL 2.0
- Possible Values: A legal value for the specified supporting attribute. Values are separated by semicolons.

values is used by the <animate>, <animateMotion>, and <animateColor> elements. The values attribute is used for establishing values needed by a supporting element or attribute. As such, it varies with the element, attributeType, or attributeName.

In the following sample from Microsoft Internet Explorer, the graphic is linked to an animateMotion element through three x,y coordinate pairs specified in the values attribute:

```
...
  <t:img id="timeMe" src="ODlogo.gif" style="position:absolute" />
  </t:animateMotion targetElement="timeMe" values="0,0; 250,200; 500,75"
  ➥dur="6s" />
...
```

The following example from RealNetworks RealPlayer uses values to change the soundLevel attribute. In this case, notice the use of percentages. Once again, values reflect the attribute they are attached to:

```
...
  <animate targetElement="mySound" attributeName="soundLevel" values=
  ➥"0%;100%" dur="5s" />
...
```

Attribute: `calcMode`

- Version Compatibility: SMIL 2.0
- Possible Values: `discrete`, `linear`, `paced`, `spline`

`calcMode` is used by the `<animate>`, `<animateMotion>`, and `<animateColor>` elements. The `calcMode` attribute determines the interpolation approach for the animation. *Interpolation* refers to how intermediate values are determined between two provided values. With `discrete` interpolation, the animation moves from one animation value to the next with no intermediate steps. This makes your animation appear to jump. The default setting, `linear` interpolation, determines linear intermediate values between the provided values. This makes your animation move smoothly, but it allows for changes in pace between different pairs of values in an animation.

For example, you might use the `keyTimes` attribute to cause motion between an initial pair of values to run faster than a second pair. This is in contrast to `paced`, which maintains uniform pacing between all the provided values.

The SplineAnimation Module adds `spline` as a possible value. `spline` interpolation creates values along a Bezier curve. In a real-world application, the animation could be eased in or out of a motion. For example, an animated car graphic appears to pick up speed from a standstill or gradually brake to a stop. Since many objects around us follow similar rules of motion, this creates a smoother and more natural feel to the animation.

In the following sample from Microsoft Internet Explorer, `calcMode` is used to place the graphic on the screen at regular intervals in the animation:

```
...
    <t:img id="timeMe" src="ODlogo.gif" style="position:absolute" />
    </t:animateMotion targetElement="timeMe" values="0,0; 250,200; 500,75"
    ➥calcMode="linear" keyTimes="0;.75;1" dur="6s" />
...
```

As covered later in this chapter, the above sample also shows the use of the animation `keyTimes` attribute to cause a different linear pace between the beginning and ending sections of the animation.

In the SplineAnimation module, `calcMode` uses the `"spline"` value as shown in the following sample from Internet Explorer:

```
...
    <t:img id="timeMe" src="ODlogo.gif" style="position:absolute" />
    </t:animateMotion targetElement="timeMe" values="0,0; 200,200; 500,75"
    ➥ calcMode="spline" keySplines=".9 .1 .1 .75; .75 .2 .75 .4"
    ➥keyTimes="0;.7;1" dur="6s" />
...
```

In this case, where the object is placed on the screen at any moment in time is determined by a calculation based on the various spline properties covered in the values, keyTimes, and keySplines attributes. A closer look at these important features of SplineAnimation are covered later in the chapter.

The following example from RealPlayer shows the use of calcMode to change the width of a targeted region from 100% down to 75% in a linear fashion:

```
...
    <animate targetElement="myRegion" attributeName="width" values=
    ➥"100%;75%" calcMode="linear" dur="5s" />
...
```

I could also pace the calcMode through a set of values so that the changes are always uniform in speed between those values:

```
...
    <animate targetElement="myRegion" attributeName="width" values=
    ➥"35;10;45;90;50" calcMode="paced" dur="5s" />
...
```

Finally, I could jump the width through a set of values by using a calcMode="discrete". In this case, there will be no interpolation (or finding) of intermediate values between the specified values. The object will hop from one value directly to the other:

```
...
    <animate targetElement="myRegion" attributeName="width" values=
    ➥"35;10;45;90;50" calcMode="discrete" dur="5s" />
...
```

Attribute: accumulate

- Version Compatibility: SMIL 2.0
- Possible Values: sum, none

accumulate is used by the <animate>, <animateMotion>, and <animateColor> elements. This attribute controls whether the animation is cumulative. sum builds on each iteration of a repeating animation. none, the default value, means that values will not add upon each other with each repeat of the animation.

Let's take a look at accumulate in action. In the following markup sample from Microsoft Internet Explorer, the <img> graphic is made to bounce up and down using <animateMotion> and following a defined path:

```
...
    <t:img id="bounceLogo" src="ODlogo.gif" style="position:absolute;
    ➥left:10;top:200" />
    <t:animateMotion targetElement="bounceLogo" path="m 0 0 c 25 -200 75
    ➥-125 100 0" repeatCount="4" />
...
```

Don't let your eyes fixate too much on that path attribute and its values. path is covered further along in this chapter. Take my word for it that it describes a parabola trajectory as if you had just thrown the logo up into the sky like a baseball. That motion path is repeated four times because of repeatCount. The problem is that the graphic jumps back to its home position as each iteration (or repeat) begins. The result is a graphic that follows a natural arc up and then down, only to jump back unnaturally to its original starting point as it repeats the process.

I don't know what your personal experience is with throwing a baseball, but I bet the laws of physics means that it will be pretty similar to mine. If I throw a ball up and away from me along a parabolic path, it will hit the ground and bounce up again. The ball will continue to move away from me with each parabolic bounce. There will be no instant transport back to the starting point in my universe. But how do we mimic that natural bounce using the above markup? Use accumulate as shown below:

```
...
    <t:img id="bounceLogo" src="ODlogo.gif" style="position:absolute;
    ➥left:10;top:200" />
    <t:animateMotion targetElement="bounceLogo" path="m 0 0 c 25 -200 75
    ➥-125 100 0" repeatCount="4" accumulate="sum" />
...
```

With the addition of accumulate="sum" I have just told the bouncing logo to add (or sum) its new animation on the end of its old animation with each iteration (repeat). Now at the end of each bounce, the object doesn't jump back to its original home position. Instead it starts the next repeat of the animation where it last left off. The result is that the logo graphic now bounces merrily across the screen.

Like Internet Explorer, RealPlayer offers `accumulate` as well:

```
...
    <t:img id="bounceLogo" src="ODlogo.gif" style="position:absolute;
    ➥left:10;top:200" />
    <t:animateMotion targetElement="bounceLogo" path="m 0 0 c 25 -200 75
    ➥-125 100 0" repeatCount="4" accumulate="sum" />
...
```

In a previous SMIL sample in RealPlayer, I covered how a region in RealPlayer could be animated from one size to another using the by attribute:

```
...
    <animate targetElement="myRegion" attributeName="height" by="50"
    ➥dur="4s"/>
...
```

Suppose you wanted that region to grow repeatedly with each iteration of a looping animation. The following markup will do just that with `accumulate`:

```
...
    <animate targetElement="myRegion" attributeName="height" by="50"
    ➥dur="4s" accumulate="sum" repeatCount="3" />
...
```

Now with each repeat of the animation, the `height` of `"myRegion"` will grow by 50 pixels.

Attribute: `additive`

- Version Compatibility: SMIL 2.0
- Possible Values: `sum`, `replace`

`additive` is used by the `<animate>`, `<animateMotion>`, and `<animateColor>` elements. This attribute controls whether the animation is additive. `sum` adds to the value of the attribute. `replace`, the default value, replaces the value of the attribute.

Suppose you had created a blue square using a <div> element in Microsoft Internet Explorer:

```
...
    <div id="colorSquare" style="position:absolute;height:100;width:100;
    ➥background-color:blue"></div>
    <t:animate targetElement="colorSquare" attributeName="width"
    ➥from="100" by="600" dur="5" />
...
```

This <animate> element will grow the square from its 100 pixel width to 600. This matches the unspecified default value of additive="replace". However, you could use additive="sum" as shown below:

```
...
    <div id="colorSquare" style="position:absolute;height:100;width:100;
    ➥background-color:blue"></div>
    <t:animate targetElement="colorSquare" attributeName="width"
    ➥from="100" by="600" additive="sum" dur="5" />
...
```

Now the square will grow as before, but the browser will add the from value of 100 with the previous width of 100. So instead of growing from 100 to 600 pixels, the square will grow from 200 to 600.

The additive attribute is also available in RealPlayer. Suppose you had the following SMIL sample:

```
...
    <animate targetElement="myRegion" attributeName="height"
    ➥values="150;200;250" dur="6s" />
...
```

If the initial height value for the region called "myRegion" is set at 100 pixels, the height will grow to the specified values of 150, 200, and 250 pixels over the course of 6 seconds. But by using the additive attribute, you could get the same effect in RealPlayer by using the following SMIL:

```
...
    <animate targetElement="myRegion" attributeName="height" values=
    ➥"50;100;150" additive="sum" dur="6s" />
...
```

In this example, each value is added on to the initial value specified in the original definition of the region. So if the region is set at 100 pixels tall, it will grow to 150 (100+50), 200 (100+100), and 250 (100+150) over 6 seconds. As with many things in life, there are usually multiple methods to reach the same goal. Choose the method that works best for you.

Attribute: origin

- Version Compatibility: SMIL 2.0
- Possible Values: Subject to the implementation of the player or browser

origin is an additional attribute available for use by the <animateMotion> element. It declares the origin of motion for the animation. In some implementations, this allows for the motion to be described as relative to a container element.

Attribute: path

- Version Compatibility: SMIL 2.0
- Possible Values: Coordinate values supported by the intended player or browser.

Used in the SplineAnimation Module under the <animateMotion> element, path describes a curve and follows the approach established in the SVG.

The SVG approach uses x,y coordinate pairs and several single letter switches to create a path of motion. Those switches provide the following commands:

Move To commands

M	absolute move to
m	relative move to

Line To commands

L	absolute line to
l	relative line to

Horizontal Line To commands

H	absolute horizontal line to
h	relative horizontal line to

Vertical Line To commands

V	absolute vertical line to
v	relative vertical line to

Closepath commands

Z	absolute closepath
z	relative closepath

Cubic Bezier Curve To commands

C	absolute cubic Bezier curve to
c	relative cubic Bezier curve to

A quick glance shows that the path commands are broken into absolute and relative options. These options apply to the path itself. An absolute command provides the absolute coordinates for the object. A relative command specifies the new point as an offset of the previous coordinates. What does this type of path value look like? In the following sample of markup from Microsoft Internet Explorer, the path attribute creates a parabolic curve for a "bouncing" logo graphic:

```
...
    <t:img id="bounceLogo" src="ODlogo.gif"
    ➥style="position:absolute;left:10;top:200" />
    <t:animateMotion targetElement="bounceLogo" path="m 0 0 c 25 -200 75
    ➥-125 100 0 z" />
...
```

All paths must begin with the absolute or relative Move To command (m or M). In this case, a pair of relative zero values means that the path will begin where it left off. The relative Cubic Bezier Curve To (c) command that follows defines a Bezier curve, which allows our graphic to follow a smooth parabola. The following coordinates, in x,y pairs, establish the general shape of the curve relative to prior coordinates. The Closepath command returns the graphic to its original location.

Attribute: `keyTimes`

- Version Compatibility: SMIL 2.0

- Possible Values: A list of values, separated by a semicolon, from 0 up to and including 1. Each time value needs to be greater than or equal to the preceding value. Each value in `keyTimes` must correspond to a value listed in the `values` attribute list.

`keyTimes` is used by the `<animate>`, `<animateMotion>`, and `<animateColor>` elements. This list of values helps to control the pacing of the animation.

So how does this work? Technically, `keyTimes` could apply to a wide variety of animated attributes. It depends on the implementation of the SMIL player or browser. But let's keep it simple. I'll start with a basic animated motion graphic in Internet Explorer and then add `keyTimes` into the equation. In the following Web page, the logo animates in a rough v shape over six seconds:

```
<html xmlns:t ="urn:schemas-microsoft-com:time">
    <head>
        <style>
            .time {behavior:url(#default#time2);}
        </style>
        <?IMPORT namespace="t" implementation="#default#time2">
    </head>
    <body>
        <t:img id="timeMe" src="ODlogo.gif" style="position:absolute" />
        </t:animateMotion targetElement="timeMe" values="0,0; 250,200;
        ➡500,75" dur="6s" />
    </body>
</html>
```

The `values` attribute helps to define the path of the animated motion, starting at the upper left hand corner, moving over 250 pixels and down 200 pixels, and moving over to 500 pixels and back up to 75 pixels before ending. Three pairs of values define three distinct points in that motion path.

What `keyTimes` offers is the ability to specify how long it will take for the animation to reach each distinct point. Each `keyTime` value will correspond directly to a coordinate pair specified in values. `keyTimes` range between 0 and 1 but it is probably easiest to think of value range as a percentage between 0 and 100. If I take our previous example and add `keyTimes`, it will look something like this:

```
...
    <t:img id="timeMe" src="ODlogo.gif" style="position:absolute" />
    </t:animateMotion targetElement="timeMe" values="0,0; 250,200; 500,75"
    ➡calcMode="linear" keyTimes="0;.75;1" dur="6s" />
...
```

On first glance, you can think of the 0 and 1 keyTimes values as bookends. That is, the 0 stands for 0% into the timeline for the coordinate pair of 0,0. The 1 stands for 100% into the timeline for the coordinate pair of 500,75. So in this example, the real magic happens with the middle value. The value .75 means that the animation will reach the coordinates of 250,200 at 75% of the animation timeline. To the eye, the animation will start slowly and then speed up. That's because 75% of the time will be spent moving the graphic between the first values pair and the second. Because only 25% of the remaining time is left, the graphic will speed up as it closes the distance between the second values pair and the third. You could quickly reverse the effect with the following code:

```
...
    <t:img id="timeMe" src="ODlogo.gif" style="position:absolute" />
    </t:animateMotion targetElement="timeMe" values="0,0; 250,200; 500,75"
    ➥calcMode="linear" keyTimes="0;.25;1" dur="6s" />
...
```

By changing the middle keyTimes value from .75 to .25, I have now told the graphic to spend 25% of its time moving from 0,0 to 250,200. It will run more slowly as it takes the remaining 75% of its time to move from 250,200 to 500,75.

It is important to mention the calcMode attribute in the above code sample. keyTimes is not compatible with calcMode="paced". In this simple example, a value of "linear" allows the keyTimes to function by interpolating (or figuring out) equally spaced locations between each coordinate pair. For a more complex spline animation using keySplines, the calcmode value would need to be set to "spline". This allows for variable spacing between the coordinate pairs.

Attribute: keySplines

- Version Compatibility: SMIL 2.0

- Possible Values: Bezier control points associated with keyTimes. The list of values is from 0 up to and including 1. keySplines values correspond to keyTimes values.

keySplines is used by the <animate>, <animateMotion>, and <animateColor> elements. This list of values helps to control the speed of the animation.

keySplines is one of those attributes that can make your head hurt just trying to figure it out. The basic concept involves graphing a curve using Bezier control points. For those who use vector illustration tools like Adobe Illustrator, these control points are the same as handles that allow you to shape the curve of a line. But if you are thinking that these curves will determine the path of the object, you might be confused by this concept. In keySplines, the shape of the curve helps determine the speed of your animation at any moment in the time of animation. So if you were to figure out the mathematics and plot the curve visually, you would actually be graphing the changes in speed.

This may seem odd at first, but this approach does offer a great deal of power. You could set the speed of an object at any given point in a path on the screen. But the results will be a bit robotic or mechanical. What if you want the speed of an object to change gradually? To graph that many points and speed changes would take forever—but not if you use keySplines. By just using a few values, keySplines will make your object adjust speed gradually.

In a way, it is almost like putting a little person inside your object. Tell that little person to step on the gas and the object will gain speed. Tell him to hit the brake and the object will begin to slow. If you were to graph those changes in speed, you would have a curve. keySplines allows you to quickly define the shape of that curve and, therefore, the changes in speed your object follows.

keySplines values are linked to keyTimes. Together, the two attributes and their corresponding values provide a powerful means to control the speed of the animated object. You can get quite detailed in your values but initially you will probably want keep your keyTimes values simple to cut down on the confusion.

Remember, with keyTimes you need a value that corresponds to each set of values established in the values attribute. That is because keyTimes is directly linked to each set of values. keySplines, in contrast, lives in the spaces between the keyTimes. So, as you can see in Figure 10.1, you will always have one less set of values for keySplines than keyTimes.

Once you have determined how many keySplines values you need, you must determine what those values should be. This gets tricky because you need to visually "see" or imagine what the values will mean in relation to the curve they generate. keySplines are expressed in pairs of x,y coordinates, so you need four values for each set of keySplines. These are not really x,y coordinates as you might think of screen placement. That is because we are not plotting the location of the object on the screen. Instead, we are drawing what is called a "motion graph."

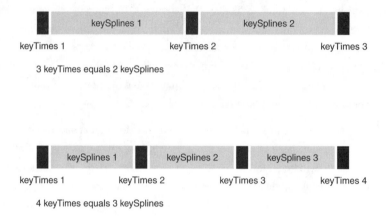

Figure 10.1 *keySplines values control the speed between keyTimes.*

This graph is never meant to be seen by your audience. Instead, a keySplines motion graph is a visual image you can use to get a feel for how the speed of your animation is changing. If you want to sit down and plot one, go right ahead. It might make it easier to plan out your SMIL markup. But it is a better skill to train your brain to imagine the graph as you author SMIL.

As you probably know, it takes two points to draw any line. But with keySplines our graph is already partially plotted. Our first point can be viewed as sitting at 0,0. Our second and last point can be viewed as sitting at 1,1. Draw a line between the two and you get a very straight diagonal line. You can begin to see this visually in Figure 10.2.

keySplines is all about changes in speed. So if this straight line represents changes in speed, what does it do for us? It does absolutely nothing. That is because a straight line represents uniform change. For every move forward on the x axis, we are moving an equal value on the y axis.

If we were to change that straight line to some type of curve, then we would be getting someplace. That is because any deviation from a straight line would mean that one value is changing more rapidly than another. (Or, if you prefer, you could say that one value is changing more slowly than the other.) To keep it simple, we will start with a straight line, but that curve is what we are aiming for in the end.

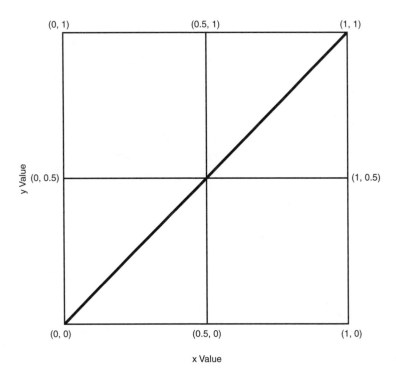

Figure 10.2 *A very boring straight line plotted between two x,y coordinates. The change between the x axis and y axis is uniform.*

So suppose the x axis represents the passage of time and the y axis represents the passage of distance. And suppose I added control points to that graph. Potentially these control points could be used to warp or influence our line. You can think of control points as being like gravity that attracts and pulls on objects in space. For right now, if I set these control points at 0,0 and 1,1, I end up with the same graph as in Figure 10.2. I'm not pulling those control points away from the defined points of my line. Figure 10.3 shows that graph where the object moves forward in time at the same rate that it moves forward in distance.

How does this look in SMIL markup? I can create the graphed effect in Internet Explorer with the following sample:

```
...
   <t:img id="timeMe" src="ODlogo.gif" style="position:absolute" />
   </t:animateMotion targetElement="timeMe" values="0,0; 500,200"
   ↪calcMode="spline" keySplines="0 0 1 1" keyTimes="0;1" dur="6s" />
...
```

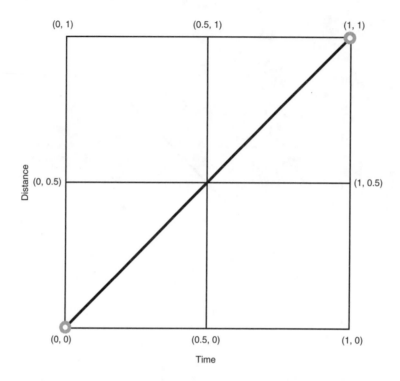

Figure 10.3 *This motion graph illustrates* keySplines *values that do not change the speed of an object. Each moment in time matches a uniform change in distance.*

The keySplines attribute in the markup is the critical detail. The x and y coordinate values always range from 0 to 1 and are separated in the markup by spaces. By saying keySplines="0 0 1 1" I am really saying: Set the control points for the line at coordinates 0,0 and 1,1. Since I'm not pulling the control points away from the defined line, the shape of the line stays straight and the speed of the graphic on the screen stays constant.

Now it is time to play with our line. Let's pull on those control points and watch them exert their gravity on our straight line. In Figure 10.4, I'm plotting the control points at .5,0 and .5,1. This warps the shape of the line along the time axis. The ends of our line are still anchored at 0,0 and 1,1. But you can see the control points pull on the line and reshape it to a curve.

If you trace your finger along the graph, you see that the beginning of the curve uses more of the time axis than the distance axis. The end of the curve does the same. So at both the beginning and the end of the line, the graphic is slower.

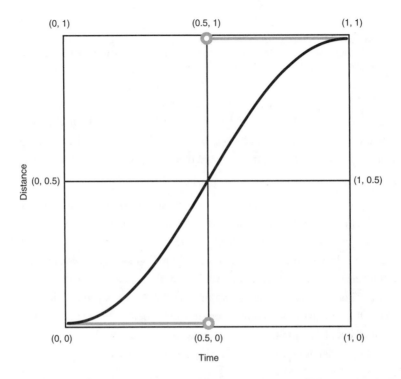

(0, 1)   (0.5, 1)   (1, 1)

(0, 0.5)   (1, 0.5)

Distance

(0, 0)   (0.5, 0)   (1, 0)

Time

Figure 10.4   *keySplines values ease in and ease out the speed of a moving object.*

Why is this? If the object moves farther along the time axis than distance axis, the result is a slower moving object. More time and less distance equals a slower object. If the object moves farther in the distance axis than the time axis, the result is a faster moving object. Less time and more distance equals a faster moving object.

In the middle of Figure 10.4, the graph becomes a diagonal straight line again. Here, the object is travelling as much distance as there is time. This would be full speed since it is the most distance traveled for time anywhere in the curve.

To sum up, Figure 10.4 visually graphs the transitions in speed from stopped to full speed and back down to stopped again. Those transitions are represented by a line that is curved. The shape of the curve is created by the influence or pull of the control points. Those control points are specified as an x,y pair. In creating the same effect in Internet Explorer, the SMIL markup for placing these control points at .5,0 and .5,1 would look like this:

```
...
    <t:img id="timeMe" src="ODlogo.gif" style="position:absolute" />
    </t:animateMotion targetElement="timeMe" values="0,0; 500,200"
  ➥calcMode="spline" keySplines=".5 0 .5 1" keyTimes="0;1" dur="6s" />
...
```

This markup example is a perfect example of why you want to use keySplines.
The graphic accelerates from a stop, reaches speed, and gradually brakes to a
halt. As graphed in Figure 10.4, keySplines gives you a type of variable speed
control.

This is very important because in real life, most objects do not travel at only one
speed. There is some variation as objects begin motion or stop motion. If the
object is coming up from a standstill it typically speeds up until it reaches full
velocity. Likewise, if an object comes to a stop, it gradually slows until it reaches
a full stop. Animators refer to this type of motion as "easing" or "slowing." To
"ease in" or "slow in" is to ease into full speed from a stopped position. An
object that gradually slows down from full speed before coming to a stop is "easing out" or "slowing out." Because easing imitates real life objects more closely,
animators often use it to make animation seem more natural.

Now, before I go on with more examples, I need to disclose an important detail.
This example of moving a graphic across a screen is an over-simplification. As
we have seen in other areas of this chapter, animation does not always mean a
moving object. It is possible that there may be other attributes you could animate
with keySplines within a given SMIL player. For example, animation could refer
to the change in a sound level or a color. But for the sake of covering the concept, I've kept it simple.

The speed of an object moving across the screen is something most of us understand. I didn't want to throw you off with the possibility of easing out a sound
level or slowing in a background color cycle. Just realize that keySplines is as
powerful as the player or browser makes it. The concept of change compared to
time is the same whether the object is travelling a distance, changing volume, or
rotating colors.

Once you understand how to use the control points in your SMIL, a number of
variations are possible. Suppose the keySplines values are reversed. The animation will start fast, gradually slow down, and then speed up at the end of the

motion. With this, an object could fly on the screen, slow down as the viewer concentrates on it for a moment, and then fly off the screen. In Internet Explorer, the markup would look like this:

```
...
    <t:img id="timeMe" src="ODlogo.gif" style="position:absolute" />
    </t:animateMotion targetElement="timeMe" values="0,0; 500,200"
    ➥calcMode="spline" keySplines="0 .5 1 .5" keyTimes="0;1" dur="6s" />
...
```

The corresponding motion graph would look something like Figure 10.5. Now look at how the control points have pulled the line in a different direction. Notice that the beginning of the curve covers more distance than time. This makes the object fast. The middle of the graph levels out. This slows the object. Then the curve becomes sharper at the end, once again covering more distance than time.

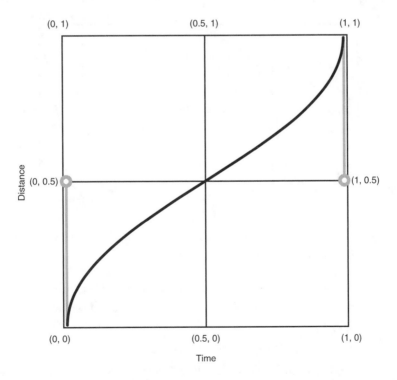

Figure 10.5 *Reversing the* keySplines *to cause the easing to occur in the middle of the animation.*

The following code will create more of a radical motion graph:

```
...
    <t:img id="timeMe" src="ODlogo.gif" style="position:absolute" />
    </t:animateMotion targetElement="timeMe" values="0,0; 200,200; 500,75"
    ➥calcMode="spline" keySplines=".9 .1 .1 .75; .75 .2 .75 .4"
    ➥keyTimes="0;.7;1" dur="6s" />
...
```

Why is the markup suddenly more complex? All I have done is add another set of keySplines to match my extra keyTimes. In this kind of example, it is best to break the numbers down visually in to two motion graphs. The corresponding motion graphs would look something like Figure 10.6.

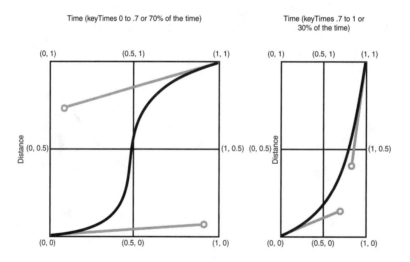

Figure 10.6 *keyTimes and keySplines working together. Notice how the keyTimes shrinks the relative time scale in the second set of values.*

You may also notice that I have weighted the keyTimes toward the beginning of the animation. This will make the first graph longer in time than the second. So I am basically using the keyTimes to further warp the curve defined in the second graph.

In practice, Figure 10.6 looks more radical than the motions you will see on the screen. Between the size of the object, the screen positioning, and the amount of time dedicated to the animation, results will vary greatly. With a small graphic moving slowly in a lot of screen space, the fine speed nuances might just show. With a large graphic in limited space moving quickly, this kind of fiddling will

give little value for the time you put in. So what is the best way to use
`SplineAnimation`? You will want to experiment with your `keySplines` and
`keyTimes` to find the effect you want. For most animations, simple numbers (such
as 0, .5, and 1) will probably do the job.

One last detail to note in the markup is the use of the `calcMode="spline"`:

```
...
    <t:img id="timeMe" src="ODlogo.gif" style="position:absolute" />
    </t:animateMotion targetElement="timeMe" values="0,0; 200,200; 500,75"
    ➥calcMode="spline" keySplines=".9 .1 .1 .75; .75 .2 .75 .4"
    ➥keyTimes="0;.7;1" dur="6s" />
...
```

This is necessary for the animation to determine the placement of the object at
any given time, based on the spline values you have provided. Without `calcMode`
set properly, your SplineAnimation will not function.

The Animation Modules Summarized

Animation is new to SMIL 2.0, so its total impact on the language remains to be
seen. With a range of elements and attributes, the SMIL animation modules offer
a great deal of capability and power to SMIL players and browsers that use it
fully.

11

Making It Interactive: The Linking Modules

- Conformance Profiles and the Linking Modules
- The Linking Module Elements
- The Linking Module Attributes
- The Linking Modules Summarized

The SMIL 2.0 Linking modules, which include the LinkingAttributes module, the BasicLinking module, and the ObjectLinking module, define the elements and attributes used by SMIL 2.0 to create navigational hyperlinks. The links can be activated by user interaction or by other occurrences, such as hitting a mark in time.

Much like HTML, SMIL links have only one source and one destination and can be navigated by clicking an object's entire visible surface or just a portion of it. Unlike HTML, both SMIL 1.0 and 2.0 have the capacity for temporal links as well, which can be activated by time passage and/or given durations for which they are active. In SMIL 1.0, this was done by offsetting the timing of the destination resource from the beginning of the clip or presentation through the use of the deprecated <anchor> element along with begin and end attributes.

In SMIL 2.0 the <area> element takes on these duties, and works with the Timing and Synchronization modules (discussed in Chapter 7, "Grouping Your Content: The Timing and Synchronization Module") to fine-tune the capacity to link to a specific moment in a timed media element. The ObjectLinking module in SMIL 2.0 enables external links to be applied to embedded media and to override internal links in those media elements.

Conformance Profiles and the Linking Modules

Much of the Linking module syntax is similar to HTML hyperlinking syntax. The SMIL linking syntax also conforms as closely as possible to the linking constructs used by XHTML and the XML languages XML Base (XBase), XLink, and XPointer, sharing as many element, attribute, and value names as possible to facilitate learning and writing in these other languages.

In particular, the SMIL 2.0 Language Profile fully supports XML Base, an addendum to XML 1.0, and allows XBase declarations to be applied to the URI attribute values in a SMIL presentation that incorporates this language profile. The support of the other XML languages is a little less direct. SMIL linking constructs are part of a separate namespace from XLink and XHTML, but they do share as much syntax as possible with these XML linking languages. SMIL 2.0 also allows the identifiers found in XPointer, a language that defines expressions for identifying URI fragments, to be placed in the fragment identifier portion of a SMIL URI, but does not require that media players be able to process them.

Language profiles that incorporate the Linking modules use the elements and attributes listed in the following sections for interactivity and linking. Code examples in this chapter will use the SMIL 2.0 Language Profile as their basis; however, if a language profile does not support the Linking modules, another form of linking must be defined, with preference going to one of the linking syntaxes mentioned previously.

The Linking Module Elements

The elements found in the Linking modules enable the author of a SMIL presentation to create links that point to other files within the presentation or to resources that are external to the presentation, including links to materials live on

the Web. The links can be interactive and require the viewer to click them for
activation, or they can be authored in such a way as to be traversed automatically.
Although the entire visual display of a presentation or media object can be clickable, the Linking module elements also enable the author to make only a portion
of the visual surface "hot." Let's take a look at these linking elements first, and
then turn to the attributes that modify and describe them more fully.

Element: `<a>`

- Version Compatibility: SMIL 1.0, SMIL 2.0

- Child Elements: `<animation>`, `<brush>`, `<img>`, `<ref>`, `<text>`,
  `<textstream>`, `<video>`

- Possible Attributes: `href` (required); `accesskey`, `actuate`, `alt`,
  `destinationLevel`, `destinationPlaystate`, `external`, `show`, `sourceLevel`,
  `sourcePlaystate`, `tabindex`, `target`

Similar to the `<a>` element in HTML, the `<a>` element in both SMIL 1.0 and 2.0
forms the backbone for much of SMIL's hyperlinking functionality. It allows a
link to be associated with a media object that has a visual display. Links can lead
to other media objects, HTML pages, XML documents, or other SMIL presentations that are internal or external to the main presentation. They can be triggered
by multiple means: through user interaction; temporal events; the use of a
defined `accesskey`; and/or the event-driven `actuate` attribute (explained later in
this chapter). The following example illustrates a simple use of the `<a>` element.
A link is created to the destination `test.html` and is activated when the user
clicks the media object with the `id` of `mountain`.

```
<a href="test.html">
<ref id="mountain" . . .  />
</a>
```

In SMIL 2.0, new attributes for the `<a>` element have been added that give
authors more flexibility and control over how a link is triggered and what occurs
when the link is traversed or followed. Examples of this include the capability to
trigger a link without user interaction, the power to control whether a presentation continues to play after the viewer follows a link to another file, or even small
details such as controlling the volume level on a background presentation while a
link is followed. We'll cover these new attributes, along with the carryovers from
SMIL 1.0, in depth later in this chapter.

It's important to note that the <a> element is not involved in synchronizing the media it envelopes, nor does it constrain the timing of its child elements, but <a> elements can themselves be time-sensitive. Developers who choose to construct language profiles that apply timing to the <a> element by incorporating support for the Timing and Synchronization modules must make sure to define values for the <a> element's fill attribute.

Element: <anchor>

- Version Compatibility: SMIL 1.0
- Parent Elements: <animation>, <img>, <ref>, <text>, <textstream>, <video>
- Possible Attributes: coords, href, show

The <anchor> element from SMIL 1.0 is deprecated in favor of the SMIL 2.0 <area> element, which carries the same functionality as <anchor>, but expands on it greatly. The <anchor> element can be considered synonymous with the <area> element for the purpose of the SMIL 2.0 specification.

Element: <area>

- Version Compatibility: SMIL 2.0
- Parent Elements: <animation>, <brush>, <img>, <ref>, <text>, <textstream>, <video>
- Possible Attributes: accesskey, actuate, alt, coords, destinationLevel, destinationPlaystate, external, fragment, href, nohref, shape, show, sourceLevel, sourcePlaystate, tabindex, target

Like the <a> element, the <area> element is used to create links that lead to an HTML page, an XML document, another media element, or another SMIL presentation, any of which can be internal or external to the main presentation. As with the <a> element, the <area> element supports multiple methods for activating a link: through user interaction; temporal events; the use of a defined accesskey (defined later in this chapter); or the event-driven actuate attribute (see later in this chapter).

However, unlike the <a> element, which makes the entire display area hot, the <area> element can be used to define a portion of a media object's visual display area as a link. The following code sample illustrates a spatial subdivision with an id of cliclogo, created by the <area> tag. This defines a rectangular area that, when clicked, leads from the <video> element to an HTML document.

```
<video src="ocean.mov" height="200" width="200">
<area id="cliclogo" shape="rect" coords="0,0,100,150"
href="ourpage.html"/>
</video>
```

For language profiles that support the Timing and Synchronization modules (discussed in Chapter 7), the <area> element can be used to create temporal subdivisions that are offset from the start of the media object. In the following code example, which uses the SMIL 2.0 Language Profile, the <area> element is used to create such a temporal subdivision. If users click the <video> element within its first 10 seconds of playing, they will link to the ourpage.html document. If they click the <video> element between 10 and 20 seconds of its start, they are instead linked to ourintro.html.

```
<video src="ocean.mov">
<area href="ourpage.html" begin="0s" end="10s"/>
<area href="ourintro.html" begin="10s" end="20s"/>
</video>
```

For those profiles incorporating support of the Timing and Synchronization modules, links can also be constructed using timing attributes that lead to distinct time points in the referenced media. In the following example, two temporal subdivisions are created in the first presentation (presentationx), with intro beginning with the video and ending 15 seconds later. The subdivision flight starts when the video hits the 15-second mark. If the user clicks the image main in Presentation Y, Presentation X is called and begins playing at the 15-second mark of the video birds.avi.

Presentation X:

```
<smil xmlns="http://www.w3.org/2001/SMIL20/PR/Language">
...
<video src="birds.avi">
   <area id="intro" begin="0s" end="15s"/>
   <area id="flight" begin="15s" />
</video>
```

Presentation Y:

```
<smil xmlns="http://www.w3.org/2001/SMIL20/PR/Language">
...
<a href="presentationx#flight">
   <img id="main" src="birds.jpg" . . . />
</a>
```

An almost endless variety of specifically targeted links with paths that are relative or absolute can be constructed in this manner by making use of the spatial and temporal linking power of the `<area>` element attributes and combining that power with the elements, attributes, and values in the Timing and Synchronization modules.

The Linking Module Attributes

The attributes of the Linking modules give the SMIL author the power to control what happens to a presentation when a link is followed, how resources are treated when they are retrieved using a link, and the capability to define the areas of the display space that is clickable. Attributes are also provided that allow for keyboard access and control of links. Let's take a look at each attribute and the effect each has on a presentation.

Attribute: accesskey

- Version Compatibility: SMIL 2.0
- Parent Elements: `<a>`, `<area>`
- Possible Values: Any keyboard key

The `accesskey` attribute defines a keyboard key that, when pressed by the user, activates the link. Embedded media can be navigated using the defined keypress for the duration of the SMIL presentation. The keystroke links defined in the SMIL document take precedence over the `accesskey` attributes defined in any embedded media. If the chosen language profile supports the Layout Modules and its layering of regions and windows (see Chapter 6, "Placing It on the Page: The Layout Modules"), `accesskey` links placed in the top-level display area will have priority over lower-level objects. If a media object hasn't been assigned to a region, it is assumed to be topmost of the objects that are displayed. In the following code snippet, the link to the HTML document can be activated by clicking the image or by pressing the z key, which is defined as the `accesskey` for that link. Keep in mind that access keys are case sensitive; if the key is defined as a lowercase letter, the uppercase of the same key will not trigger the link.

```
<a href="ourpage.html" accesskey="z">
<img src="image.jpg">
</a>
```

Attribute: `actuate`

- Version Compatibility: SMIL 2.0
- Parent Elements: `<a>`, `<area>`
- Possible Values: `onRequest`, `onLoad`

The `actuate` attribute determines whether a link is triggered by user interaction or automatically followed when the associated media element is made active. The default value of `onRequest` requires an action to trigger link traversal. A value of `onLoad` means the link is followed when the media object becomes active. In the following example, the media object `joe` becomes active when called for in the presentation. At the time it is called, the link that encloses it will be followed as if it had been clicked by the user. Therefore, the link to the sound file `music.aiff` will be followed when `joe` begins.

```
<a href="music.aiff" actuate="onLoad" . . . >
  <ref id="joe" . . . >
</a>
```

In the same manner, a link with its `actuate` attribute set to `onLoad` that is included on the display surface of a media object will be followed when the media object is activated. In the following example, the link opens when the video clip begins to play:

```
<video src="zoo.rm" . . . >
  <area href="details.html" actuate="onLoad".../>
</video>
```

Attribute: `alt`

- Version Compatibility: SMIL 2.0
- Parent Elements: `<a>`, `<area>`
- Possible Values: Author-generated text

Defined within the Media Objects module (covered in Chapter 8, "Bring on the Media: The Media Object Modules"), the `alt` attribute specifies alternative text to be displayed along with a link or in place of it when the viewer's player cannot display the link. How the `alt` text is implemented depends on the SMIL player. The text associated with an `alt` attribute is also used by assistive devices for viewers with disabilities, so the description should be brief, yet informative, and indicate the link's purpose and destination resource.

Attribute: coords

- Version Compatibility: SMIL 1.0 , SMIL 2.0
- Parent Element: <anchor> (SMIL 1.0), <area> (SMIL 2.0)
- Possible Values: Pixel or percentage values

The values assigned by the coords attribute identify a set of spatial coordinates that describe an area on a media object's display space that can trigger a link. In practice, it can be compared to a client-side image map in HTML and, in fact, borrows most of its syntax directly from the HTML 4.0 specification.

If the SMIL document calls for a media object to be rescaled to fit within a display region, measurements for the clickable area will be applied after the scaling occurs. In this case, care should be taken to make sure the display area can accommodate the dimensions of the assigned clickable region. If a media object overflows the bounding box of its assigned region and the SMIL document calls for those overflow areas to be clipped, care should also be taken to ensure that the clickable regions are not discarded.

The order and number of values assigned to the coords attribute is determined by the shape attribute. They are either pixel coordinates of the media display space (rather than the dimensions of its assigned region or the dimensions of the source clip) or percentage values of that display space. The clickable region is offset from the upper-left corner of the media object's display space, using the values assigned by this attribute. Percentage measurements can be substituted for pixel measurements, in which case the clickable area is proportionate to the media object's display space. When using percentage values, the default value of shape is rect.

The following three figures illustrate the coordinate values necessary to define three types of clickable regions on a media object's visual surface: a rectangle, a circle, and a polygon. Each uses absolute pixel values to carve out a hyperlinked area from the image display space, in contrast to the region or the window display area, but keep in mind that percentage values can also be used.

Figure 11.1 illustrates a defined rectangular or square region. The formula for it is as follows:

```
shape="rect" coords="x1,y1,x2,y2"
```

x1 and *y1* indicate the upper-left corner of the rectangle; *x2* and *y2* indicate the lower-right corner. For Figure 11.1, the code would be:

```
<area shape="rect" coords="50,50,100,70"
```

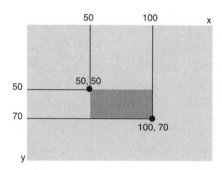

Figure 11.1   *A rectangular or square link region.*

Figure 11.2 illustrates a defined circular region, which uses the following formula:

```
shape="circle" coords="x,y,r" . . . />
```

The x,y coordinate indicates the circle's center point, and r indicates the radius of the circle in pixels. In this case, the code would be:

```
<area shape="circle" coords="100,70,20" . . . />
```

Figure 11.3 illustrates a defined region of any other shape (a polygon with any number of sides). It uses this formula:

```
shape="poly" coords="x1,y1,x2,y2..."
```

Each x,y coordinate indicates a point in the polygon. To create the polygon shown in the figure, the code would be:

```
<area shape="poly" coords="110,10,120,55,80,90,40,65,80,50,70,25" . . . />
```

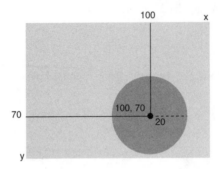

Figure 11.2 *A circular link region.*

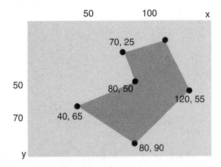

Figure 11.3 *A polygonal link region.*

Attribute: destinationLevel

- Version Compatibility: SMIL 2.0
- Parent Elements: <a>, <area>
- Possible Values: Non-negative percentage values up to 200%

The destinationLevel attribute sets the audio level of a destination resource when a link is followed. The value is set as a percentage of the destination resource's recorded volume, or the volume set in the soundLevel attribute attached to the region where the object is displayed (see Chapter 6). A default value of 100% indicates that the resource will be played at its intended volume. This attribute is useful if the author intends for the originating presentation to continue playing while the secondary resource plays and wants to bring either resource's audio content to the forefront.

In the example that follows, a presentation contains a link that is activated when the viewer clicks the image `guitar.jpg`. After this has occurred, the file `joe.aiff` will play back at 25% of its recorded volume. If the main presentation continues to play, and its audible content is playing at 100% of its recorded volume, `joe.aiff` should appear as if it were playing in the background.

```
<a href="joe.aiff" destinationLevel="25%" . . . />
 <img src="guitar.jpg" . . . />
</a>
```

Attribute: `destinationPlaystate`

- Version Compatibility: SMIL 2.0
- Parent Elements: `<a>`, `<area>`
- Possible Values: `play`, `pause`

When a link's destination resource is a continuous media object, the `destinationPlaystate` attribute determines whether the destination media clip begins playing immediately when the link is followed or is held in a paused state. A default value of `play` causes the destination resource to begin playing when it is reached. A value of `pause` delivers the viewer to the point referenced by the URI in the `<a>` or `<area>` parent element, but the destination media object will remain paused at that point.

Attribute: `external`

- Version Compatibility: SMIL 2.0
- Parent Elements: `<a>`, `<area>`
- Possible Values: `false`, `true`

The `external` attribute identifies whether the destination resource should be opened using the current application or an external one. The default value of `false` causes the SMIL player to attempt to open the destination resource itself. If the media type is not supported, the viewer's operating system should attempt to open it using another external application. A value of `true` indicates that the user's operating system and MIME-type preferences should be used to determine the application in which to open the media object.

Attribute: `fragment`

- Version Compatibility: SMIL 2.0

- Parent Element: `<area>`

- Possible Values: Named anchor (HTML), fragment identifiers (XML), `id` attributes (media objects)

The `fragment` attribute enables a SMIL presentation to attach external links to overlay and override links in embedded media. To use the `fragment` attribute, first a known identifier for the object must be referenced. If the destination resource of the embedded media's link is another media object, the `id` attribute of the object is considered the identifier. If the link's resource is an HTML document, the identifier is the `name` attribute placed in the HTML document itself. If the destination resource is an XML document, the fragment identifier is the part of the link that comes after the # sign.

After the identifier is established and referenced, it is given a new destination. While the SMIL document is active, the links in the embedded media are not active; the SMIL link overrides links in the media. For example, assume that one of the destination resources in the SMIL presentation that follows is an HTML document with links to other HTML pages (`links.html`). For the duration of the SMIL presentation, the author wants to override the links in `links.html` and make them link to other identified elements in the SMIL document. The HTML document has anchor values coded for each link, including an anchor named `link1`. By calling the anchor by name and assigning it a new destination resource value (`#nogo`), a presentation-level link is activated. So for the duration of the SMIL presentation, the `link1` anchor in the HTML document will no longer lead to its link as coded in the HTML document; instead, activating the `link1` link will lead to the `nogo` image.

SMIL presentation:

```
<smil xmlns="http://www.w3.org/2001/SMIL20/PR/Language">
...
<par>
<ref src="links.html" region="links">
   <area fragment="link1" href="#nogo"/>
</ref>
<img id="nogo" src="nogo.jpg"/>
</par>
```

links.html:

```
<html>
. . .
<body>
. . .
<a href="wherever.html" name="link1">
link one
</a>
. . .
</html>
```

Attribute: href

- Version Compatibility: SMIL 1.0, SMIL 2.0
- Parent Elements: <a>, <area>
- Possible Values: URI

The href attribute identifies the URI of the destination resource. A URI, or *Uniform Resource Identifier*, is a generic term for an absolute or relative address of a resource; the term URL, or *Uniform Resource Locator*, is a type of URI. Both essentially point out the pathway to the resource that is being referenced by the linking element. The destination resource can be a media file, an HTML document, an XML document, or another SMIL presentation. If the destination resource is located in the same directory as the SMIL presentation, the addressing can be relative—for example, href="home.html". If the applied language profile supports the Metainformation modules, then a base URI for the entire presentation can be designated and all URI addresses in the presentation will be relative to that base URI. If the destination reference is completely external to the presentation, absolute referencing syntax, such as href="http://www.myhome.com/home.html", should be used.

Identifiers can also be used to target exact starting points in destination resources. Identifiers consist of the object's id attribute if the destination resource is a media object. For links to HTML documents, the fragment identifier is the name attribute placed in the document itself. For XML documents, the fragment identifier is the part of the link that comes after the # sign.

Attribute: nohref

- Version Compatibility: SMIL 2.0
- Parent Element: <area>
- Possible Values: true, false

A value of true for the nohref attribute specifies that the region designated by the <area> element has no associated URI, and hence no link. This attribute overrides links assigned to the region by other <area> elements.

Attribute: shape

- Version Compatibility: SMIL 1.0, SMIL 2.0
- Parent Element: <anchor> (SMIL 1.0), <area> (SMIL 2.0)
- Possible Values: circle, poly, rect

As you saw earlier in Figures 11.1, 11.2, and 11.3, the shape attribute works with the coords attribute to define a portion of a media object's visual display area as a link. This clickable region is first defined as a shape by using the shape attribute and then placed on the object's display surface through pixel coordinates or percentage values assigned by the coords attributes. The pixel coordinates represent x- and y-axis points after the media object has been scaled for the presentation but before any clipping occurs.

In the following example, an area named "hotlink" has been defined first by using the shape attribute to identify it as a rectangular-shaped space. The absolute placement of that rectangular shape is established using pixel values in the coords attribute, which set the rectangle's upper-left corner at 0,0 (or the upper-left corner of the display space) and the lower-right corner at 100 pixels in and 150 pixels down from the display space's upper-left corner.

```
<img src="zoom.jpg" width="200" height="200" >
<area id="hotlink" shape="rect" coords="0,0,100,150" href="cars.html"/>
</img>
```

As shown in the preceding code, the coordinates associated with the rect attribute define a rectangle or square. The circle attribute uses the x,y coordinate of its center point, along with its radius, as values to determine the clickable region. The poly attribute can use an unlimited number of x,y pairs to define the final shape of the media object's clickable portion. poly is very useful when outlining a visual element that is neither round nor rectangular. In SMIL 1.0, this attribute was not available, so the clickable portion was always rectangular.

Attribute: show

- Version Compatibility: SMIL 1.0, SMIL 2.0
- Parent Elements: `<a>`, `<area>`
- Possible Values: `new, pause, replace`

The `show` attribute controls how the display of the source presentation containing the link reacts when the link is followed. Note that, depending on the value assigned to it, the `show` attribute can determine the default value of the `sourcePlaystate` attribute or override its assigned values.

The default value of `show` is `replace`, which pauses the source presentation and replaces it in the display space with the destination resource. Logically, when the `replace` value is used, the `sourcePlaystate` attribute is set to a default value of `pause`, regardless of what value might have been assigned. Depending on the implementation, the user agent can resume playing when the destination resource is complete or the viewer returns to the source presentation. A `show` value of `new` launches the destination resource in a new display container of its own with both presentations or media files playing in parallel. The `pause` value for `show` is deprecated in favor of using a value of `new`, combined with a `sourcePlaystate` value of `pause`. This combination launches a secondary display space for the destination resource and pauses the originating presentation.

Attribute: sourceLevel

- Version Compatibility: SMIL 2.0
- Parent Elements: `<a>`, `<area>`
- Possible Values: Non-negative percentage values

The `sourceLevel` attribute sets the audio level of the presentation containing a link after the link is followed. The value is set as a percentage of the presentation's recorded volume or the volume set in the `soundLevel` attribute attached to the region where the object with the link is displayed (see Chapter 6). A default value of `100%` indicates that the resource will be played at its recorded volume. This attribute is useful if the author intends for the originating presentation to continue playing while the secondary resource plays, and the author wants to bring either resource's audio content to the forefront.

Attribute: `sourcePlaystate`

- Version Compatibility: SMIL 2.0
- Parent Elements: `<a>`, `<area>`
- Possible Values: `pause`, `play`, `stop`

Similar to the `show` attribute, and working with it, the `sourcePlaystate` attribute determines the temporal behavior of the source presentation when a link is followed. A value of `play` indicates that the presentation containing the link will continue to play. A value of `pause` pauses the originating presentation until completion of the destination resource, at which point, depending on the SMIL player, the source presentation resumes playing. A value of `stop` stops the presentation containing the link and resets it to its beginning, without restarting or continuing it when the destination resource is finished. If a link destination is in the same document as the link itself, the destination element's `sourcePlaystate` is ignored and a default value of `stop` is enforced.

Note that the `show` attribute can determine the default value of the `sourcePlaystate` attribute or override its assigned values. If `show` is set to `new`, the `sourcePlaystate` defaults to a value of `play`. This causes the destination resource to open in its own display space and play in parallel to the originating presentation. In the following example, because of the value assigned to `show`, `animi.gif` will play in a separate window as the main presentation continues.

```
<a href="animi.gif" show="new"  . . . />
```

If `show` is set to `replace` or the deprecated `pause`, the value of `sourcePlaystate` becomes `pause`, regardless of what value may be assigned to it.

When the link in the following example is followed, the main presentation is paused while `animi.gif` plays back in the presentation window. The `sourcePlaystate` value of `play` is overridden by the `sourcePlaystate` value associated with `show="replace"`.

```
<a href="animi.gif" show="replace"  . . . />
```

Attribute: `tabindex`

- Version Compatibility: SMIL 2.0
- Parent Elements: `<a>`, `<area>`
- Possible Values: Author-assigned numbers

The tabindex attribute allows the tab order for links to be manually assigned if they are navigated by keyboard. The use of the keyboard to navigate through a tabindex order in a SMIL presentation is limited to active elements, but as elements with tabindex values become active, they too can be navigated. The link with the lowest tabindex value is the first link to receive focus when navigated to by a keyboard. SMIL presentations can include media elements that have their own tabindex values, such as an HTML document that has multiple links; making sure to include them numerically ensures a complete tab list of link starting points.

In the following example, the list of links can be navigated using the Tab key on a keyboard. linkone will be the first link available for activation, followed by linktwo. A user can easily continue using the keyboard Tab key to navigate the links. Any object contained in a linking element can be navigated in this manner, including objects embedded into the main presentation that contain links of their own.

```
<a tabindex="1" href="one.html" id="linkone" . . .>link one</a>
<a tabindex="2" href="two.html" id="linktwo" . . .>link two</a>
<a tabindex="3" href="two.html" id="linkthree" . . .>link three</a>
<a tabindex="4" href="two.html" id="linkfour" . . .>link four</a>
```

Attribute: target

- Version Compatibility: SMIL 2.0
- Parent Elements: <a>, <area>
- Possible Values: The identifier of a display environment

The target attribute, much like the target attribute in HTML, identifies the display environment in which a destination resource should be opened or creates a new display environment with a given identifier. Common display environments include a SMIL region, an HTML frame, or a named window. If the environment called for by name is not currently active, a new environment is launched with the name assigned as the environment's identifier.

In the following example, which uses the SMIL 2.0 Language Profile, clicking the logo image launches the newpres.smil presentation in the region named presenting. Clicking goodbye.jpg launches the HTML document final.html in a new window because the display environment joe is not identified or active.

```
<smil xmlns="http://www.w3.org/2001/SMIL20/PR/Language">
 <head>
  <layout>
    <region id="logo" top="0" height="50"/>
    <region id="presenting" top="50" height="250"/>
    <region id="finish" top="350"/>
  </layout>
 </head>
<body>
  <a href="newpres.smil" target="presenting">
    <img region="logo" src="logo.jpg"/>
  </a>
  <a href="final.html" target="joe">
    <img region="finish" src="goodbye.jpg"/>
  </a>
</body>
</smil>
```

The Linking Modules Summarized

A good portion of the Linking module's syntax is rooted in HTML 4.0, so it is easily learned and familiar. At the same time, much of the new syntax is as close as possible to other available linking languages and takes advantages of the strengths of those newer languages. Because of this, authors working with language profiles that support the Linking modules will find themselves fairly well prepared and certainly well equipped to create interactive and multilinked SMIL presentations.

The new <area> element and the addition of the sourcePlaystate and fragment attributes allow the author to control which portions of the screen are made into links and what happens when they are followed. If the language profile also includes support for the Timing, Synchronization, and Layout modules, a high degree of control can be exercised over when and how elements become links and how they can be activated.

In the next chapter, we'll look into the use of the elements and attributes found in the Content Control modules, which enable authors to optimize the delivery of presentations by considering the viewer's preferences and system limitations.

12

Optimizing Content Delivery: The Content Control Modules

One of the challenges when authoring online content, whether it's a simple Web page or a complex multimedia presentation, is determining how to tailor the content and delivery of your materials to the viewer's system capabilities and preferences. The Content Control modules are SMIL 2.0's answer to this dilemma; they provide the elements and attributes used to optimize content and delivery for a particular viewer's environment.

Four modules are in this section of the SMIL 2.0 specification:

- The BasicContentControl module contains elements and attributes that can be used to evaluate a user's system and/or preference settings and then deliver content that conforms to those findings. It features the <switch> element, the attributes found in SMIL 1.0 that are used to evaluate the user's system, and some new additional attributes.

- The elements and attributes of the CustomTestAttributes module allow authors to customize and define evaluation criteria beyond the predefined test attributes found in the BasicContentControl module.

- The PrefetchControl module enables the author to schedule media files to be preloaded, either in full or in part.

- The SkipContentControl module, which is identical to the skip-content attribute found in SMIL 1.0, allows for the extensibility of future versions of the SMIL language and supports skipping content that is not applicable to the version of the SMIL being employed. We'll go into each in the body of this chapter.

This format of "modules within a module" is seen throughout the SMIL 2.0 specification; in most chapters we note that the submodules then go on to define and describe the attributes and elements as one group. In this chapter, we'll break out the different modules to better explain and understand how customized presentation delivery is accomplished using the hierarchical structure of the modules that make up the Content Control modules.

A critical point to note when discussing the delivery of optimized content is that any given SMIL player is responsible for collecting user data against which to compare attribute values, and also for the delivery of this information from the user to the SMIL player. The SMIL 2.0 specification does not require data to be collected in any specific fashion, nor does it constrain the frequency or schedule of when this evaluation occurs, again leaving it up to the particular player. As the sophistication of the playback engines continues to evolve, data collection will undoubtedly become increasingly automatic, with the resulting comparisons between the user data and test attribute values increasingly instantaneous and reliable. However, at this time, much of the data concerning a user's system and preferences are recorded through direct user action, usually when the player is downloaded or activated for the first time or through the use of a Preferences dialog box. Because of this, data may be entered that does not accurately portray the environment in which the player is operating. This might hamper the capability of the player to deliver truly optimized content.

However, the Content Control modules do indeed provide authoring tools for the delivery of content tailored exactly to the preferences and system environment of a viewer. This capability can add much to a presentation's effectiveness and usability.

Conformance Profiles and the Content Control Modules

The SMIL 2.0 Language Profile and Basic Language Profile support all four of the Content Control modules. Integretion-set conformant profiles and any other created language profiles will have to decide whether to support the modules, which of the modules to support, and might decide to create methods of their own to optimize content and delivery. One important note for language designers is that profiles wanting to implement the CustomTestAttributes module must also implement the BasicContentControl module because it forms the basis on which the custom tests are built.

The text and examples of code in this chapter are based on the SMIL 2.0 Language Profile; be aware that specific players may choose to define their own methods for optimizing content delivery. If this is the case, the syntax for evaluating the user system and preferences may vary from this chapter, especially if a developer chooses to not implement the Content Control modules at all. The tutorial section of this book illustrates implementation in two of the three main SMIL players: RealONE and Microsoft Internet Explorer.

The BasicContentControl Module Element and Attributes

In this first module, the BasicContentControl module, the building blocks for delivering content tailored for the user are established. On a basic level, optimized presentation delivery is accomplished by providing the SMIL player with various content alternatives that are then compared against the user's system and/or preference data. If an alternative matches the user data, the element is activated.

The content alternatives that are presented to the player are presented as test attributes, or evaluation criteria, paired with values. The BasicContentControl module provides predefined test attributes that can check for a user's connection speed, preferred language, operating system information, and more. When a match occurs between a delivery option's test attribute value and a user's system data, a result of true is returned to the player and the element involved is activated. If no match occurs, the element is ignored. When an element is ignored, it is not available for the remainder of the presentation.

These test attributes, or evaluation criteria, can be used within the <switch> element (the BasicContentControl module's only element) or can be attached directly to an object or element through the in-line use of the switch attribute. We'll discuss both next.

Many of the BasicContentControl attributes have been carried forward from SMIL 1.0, but with only one exception, their hyphenated syntax has been deprecated in favor of the camelCase convention of SMIL 2.0. In the following section, the 1.0 hyphenated names are enclosed in parentheses after the preferred syntax. SMIL 2.0 introduces several new attributes as well.

Element: `<switch>`

- Version Compatibility: 2.0 (*1.0 as hyphenated names)
- Parent Elements: `body`, `head`, `par`, `seq`
- Possible Attributes: `systemAudioDesc`, `systemBitrate*`, `systemCaptions*`, `systemCPU`, `systemComponent`, `systemLanguage*`, `systemOperatingSystem`, `systemOverdubOrSubtitle`, `system-overdub-or-caption*`, `systemRequired*`, `systemScreenDepth*`, `systemScreenSize*`

The `<switch>` element is used to select from a list of options based on the user's preferences and system capabilities. For example, an English and Spanish version of a audio file can be placed within a `<switch>`. Depending on the user's stated preferences (Spanish or English), the correct version of the audio file can be activated. Other common uses of the `<switch>` element include providing high and low bandwidth versions of presentations and presentations that are optimized for a given user's screen size. After an option is selected from within a `<switch>` element, all the other options are ignored.

When used within the `head` segment of a SMIL presentation, the `<switch>` element can be paired with `layout` elements to assist with the selection of a screen layout that fits the user's system. If used within the `body` element of a SMIL presentation, a `<switch>` element can be used with media or synchronization elements.

To use the `<switch>` element, you must select test attributes from the preceding list of possible attributes and then pair them with values. These options are then enclosed by the `<switch>` element, which instructs the player to evaluate the test attributes against any system data or preferences to which it has access. Alternatives should be listed in order from the most to the least desirable because this is the order in which the options will be evaluated, and after an alternative is selected, the `<switch>` function is considered completed. Additionally, a relatively fail-safe option should be provided as the last item in the `<switch>`.

Important to note is that in the SMIL 2.0 Language profile, after an element enclosed in a `<switch>` is ignored, the element is not considered present at all; thus, if an ignored element is called by its `id` value elsewhere in the presentation, it will not be retrieved. Timing attributes that reference the `id` of ignored elements will be treated as being indefinite.

Also noteworthy is that players are not allowed to randomly pick an alternative from a <switch> statement. If none of the options in a <switch> statement evaluates to true, all the alternatives will be ignored.

An example of this would be pairing the predefined test attribute systemBitrate with several values, which would then determine the presentation a viewer should receive, based on their stated connection rate. The end result is that the highest quality presentation possible for the viewer's connection speed will be delivered. A value of 56000, or 56000 bits per second, could be paired with systemBitrate as a first option. A second option could pair systemBitrate with 28000. A third option, without a systemBitrate declaration, can be used as a default. This last option will be selected should no information be available or if the user's connectivity rate is less than 28000. The following example shows this in code:

```
<body>
 <switch>
    <par systemBitrate="56000">
      <audio src="fast.aif" . . .   />
      <img src="fast.gif" . . . />
    </par>
    <par systemBitrate="28000">
      <audio src="slow.aif" . . .   />
      <img src="slow.gif" . . . />
    </par>
    <par>
      <audio src="plain.aif" . . .   />
      <img src="plain.gif" . . . />
    </par>
 </switch>
 . . .
</body>
```

In this example, which applies test attributes in conjunction with the synchronization element par, the player would check the preferences or system data of the user against the first test attribute of systemBitrate. If the established value of the user's connection rate is found to be at least 56000 bits per second, an evaluation of true is returned and the first par is activated. If the connection rate is not 56000 or faster, an evaluation of false is returned on the first par; therefore, all the elements it contains are ignored completely. The next test attribute value is then evaluated against the user's data and either a "true" or "false" evaluation is returned. Again, the accompanying attribute is either ignored or applied. Finally, the par that does not have a specified bitrate will be chosen if all other options have evaluated to false. The final par is considered the fail-safe option.

Some network protocols do support content negotiation, in which communication between the server and the client machine are done using the connection protocol. In some cases, this may present an alternative to the use of the <switch> element.

System Test Attribute In-Line Use

- Version Compatibility: 1.0, 2.0

- Parent Elements: media and synchronization elements (if used within the body element); layout elements (if used within the head element)

Test attributes can also be used outside the <switch> element. In this case, the available options are presented along with media, synchronization, or layout objects themselves and are evaluated in-line, or as the objects are called in the presentation. In the following example, if the user's preferences are set to English, the first option would be activated. If the preferences are set to German, the second file would be displayed. If the system language is set to something other than English or German, no audio file will play.

```
<par>
   <audio systemLanguage="en" src="english.aif" . . .  />
   <audio systemLanguage="de" src="german.aif" . . . />
</par>
```

Each element will be evaluated as it is called. If the user's data matches the test attribute value, a true evaluation is returned and the element is run. If the test attribute does not match the user data, the element is ignored. Like the use of the <switch> element, when test attributes are evaluated in-line and none of the options evaluate as true, none of the options are implemented.

Attribute: systemAudioDesc

- Version Compatibility: 2.0

- Possible Values: on, off

This attribute determines whether any closed audio descriptions, or audible captions, in the presentation are rendered. The test attribute evaluates to true if, for example, a viewer indicates that she would like to hear any available audio descriptions included in the presentation. A value of on will render audio only when the user has indicated that she desires audio descriptions. A value of off indicates that the author wants the element's audible descriptions to render even when users declare that they don't want to hear audio descriptions.

Attribute: systemBitrate (system-bitrate)

- Version Compatibility: 2.0 (1.0)
- Possible Values: any integer greater than zero

The calculation of the viewer's available bandwidth depends on the media player that is displaying the SMIL presentation. This calculation can be based on the user's preferences or can be determined by the player itself, depending on the particular media player's capabilities. Measurement is in bits per second and approximates the bandwidth available to the user's system. The test attribute evaluates to true if the viewer's connection speed is equal to or greater than the given value. The evaluation of false is returned if the viewer's bitrate is less than the given value.

In the following example, the <switch> element contains three options; one is chosen if the viewer's bitrate is equal to or greater than 100000 bits per second, or 100Kbps. Another is chosen if the viewer's bitrate is equal to or greater than 56000 bits per second, or 56Kbps. The third option does not specify a bitrate and is chosen if the viewer's connection speed is less than 56000, or 56Kbps.

```
<body>
 <switch>
    <par systemBitrate="100000">
      <audio src="fast.aif" . . . />
      <img src="fast.gif" . . . />
    </par>
    <par systemBitrate="56000">
      <audio src="slow.aif" . . . />
      <img src="slow.gif" . . . />
    </par>
    <par>
      <audio src="basic.aif" . . . />
      <img src="basic.gif" . . . />
    </par>
 </switch>
 . . .
</body>
```

Attribute: systemCaptions (system-captions)

- Version Compatibility: 2.0 (1.0)
- Parent Element: <switch>, media elements
- Possible Values: on, off

This attribute allows the text equivalent of the audio portion of a presentation to be displayed, and works much like the use of on and off values for the systemAudioDesc attribute. The systemCaptions test attribute evaluates to true if the user preference indicates that the viewer would like to view text captions for the audio portion of the presentation. A false evaluation is returned if users specify that they prefer not to see a textual display representing the audio portions of the presentation.

Attribute: systemComponent

- Version Compatibility: 2.0
- Parent Element: <switch>, media elements
- Possible Values: one or more URI resources

This attribute enables the active media player to resource one or more URI addresses, which identify and define a singular component of the playback system. Examples of these component qualifiers may assist a particular player to implement correctly, indicate the number of audio channels used in a presentation, or identify the compression scheme used to compress a video so that the player could decompress the video more efficiently. The URI list is player specific; the implementation and interpretation of returned data is left to the designers of the media player.

One example of this is implemented by the RealPlayer and used to determine which version of RealPlayer the viewer is operating. In the beginning of the SMIL document, a "component version" namespace is defined (designated as cv by RealPlayer), which is then called on by the systemRequired attribute. Following this, the systemComponent attribute declares a URI that is not requested but is instead used to check for a particular feature or component of the RealPlayer. After the correct version of the player is identified, the clips that are appropriate for that player will be rendered. Here is the example in code:

```
<smil xmlns:cv="http://features.real.com/systemComponent">
. . .
<body>
    <switch>
        <seq system-required="cv"
        cv:systemComponent="http://features.real.com/?feature;player=6.0.7.x">
            ...clips to play if RealPlayer is version 6.0.7e...
        </seq>
        <seq system-required="cv"
        cv:systemComponent="http://features.real.com/?feature;player=8.x">
            ...clips to play if RealPlayer is version 8.0...
        </seq>
    . . .
    </switch>
</body>
```

Attribute: systemCPU

- Version Compatibility: 2.0

- Parent Element: <switch>, media elements

- Possible Values: XML NMTOKEN

The evaluation of this test attribute specifies the CPU on which the media player is running. Suggested values have been taken from constants defined by the mozilla project and include m68k (pre-PowerPC Macintosh), ppc (PowerPC Macintosh and Linux), alpha (Compaq alpha processor), vax (DEC VAX running VMS or Unix), x86 (Intel chipset for Windows PCs and servers) and unknown (unknown processor type). These values refer to the processor that the viewer is using to view the presentation and may be useful to speed delivery of the presentation. Values given to this attribute are case sensitive because of the nature of the information being passed. A language profile incorporating this attribute must give the user the opportunity to set this value at unknown for privacy.

Attribute: systemLanguage (system-language)

- Version Compatibility: 2.0 (1.0)

- Parent Element: <switch>, media elements

- Possible Values: predefined language names (RFC1766)

This attribute enables authors to provide alternative content in a variety of languages. The range of available languages is quite wide; in addition to common languages such as English (en), Spanish (es), German (de), French (fr), and Japanese (ja), languages such as Islandic (is), Basque (eu), and Catalan (ca) are included. Subgroups of languages are also available, including Hong Kong Chinese (zh-hk), Australian English (en-au), and Swiss Italian (it-ch). If the viewer has specified a language preference (usually by means of a player-specific preferences dialog box) and the preferred language matches the value attached to this attribute, an evaluation of true is returned and the element is activated. The test will also evaluate to true if the user has specified a language that matches the prefix of the attribute value followed by a hyphen. For example, if the viewer has specified en (generic English) as their language preference, a systemLanguage value of either en or en-gb (British English) will both evaluate as true. The SMIL 2.0 specification recommends that playback engines and authors take care to assist users with correctly setting the system language for their players to ensure maximum compatibility.

Attribute: systemOperatingSystem

- Version Compatibility: 2.0
- Parent Element: <switch>
- Possible Values: player-specific name

This test attribute can be used to identify the operating system on which the playback engine is running and can be used to speed up the interpretation and playback of the presentation. Like most of the test attributes, the acceptable values for this attribute, and the interpretation of that data, are determined by the player itself. The SMIL specification does suggest values that have been taken from constants defined by the mozilla project; examples include aix, beos, linux, macos, ncr, nec, openbsd, os2, palmos, qnx, sinix, rhapsody, solaris, sonly, sunos, unixware, win32, winnt, wince, and unknown, all of which are case sensitive. Important to note is that this attribute does not discriminate between various versions of an operating system. A language profile that supports the use of this attribute must give the user the opportunity to set this value at unknown for privacy. It evaluates to true if a match occurs between the attribute value and the preferences or system data of the viewer.

Attribute: `system-overdub-or-caption`

- Version Compatibility: 1.0, 2.0 (deprecated)
- Parent Element: `<switch>`
- Possible Values: `caption`, `overdub`

Deprecated in favor of `systemOverdubOrSubtitle` and `systemCaptions`. The values indicate a user preference for one or the other: `caption` presents text alternative, `overdub` presents an alternative audio track. Again, the user data must be collected by the playback engine and interpreted by that player.

Attribute: `systemOverdubOrSubtitle`

- Version Compatibility: 2.0
- Parent Element: `<switch>`
- Possible Values: `subtitle`, `overdub`

This attribute specifies whether a user prefers subtitles to be displayed or over-dubbing rendered, usually in cases where the audio content is in a language other than that of the user. This attribute is commonly paired with the `systemLanguage` attribute to assist with the selection of the viewer's language of choice. The value of `overdub` selects for substitution one voice track for another; the value of `subtitle` indicates that the user-preferred text be displayed.

In the following example, a video is displayed with a choice of overdubbed English or German soundtracks, or a default audio track. Subtitles are also available in English and German. The `<switch>` element provides the mechanism for the selection of the correct media objects.

```
<par>
   <video src="themovie.mov" . . . />
   <switch>
     <audio src="en_audio.aiff" systemLanguage="en"
       systemOverdubOrSubtitle="overdub" . . . />
     <audio src="de_audio.aiff" systemLanguage="de"
       systemOverdubOrSubtitle="overdub" . . . />
     <audio src="plain.aiff" . . . />
   </switch>
   <switch>
     <textstream src="en_sub.txt" systemLanguage="en"
       systemOverdubOrSubtitle="subtitle" . . . />
```

```
        <textstream src="de_sub.txt" systemLanguage="de"
          systemOverdubOrSubtitle="subtitle" . . . />
      </switch>
    </par>
```

Attribute: systemRequired (system-required)

- Version Compatibility: 2.0 (1.0)
- Parent Element: <switch>
- Possible Values: a list of namespace prefix language extensions

This attribute provides an extension mechanism for new elements or attributes. If all the XML namespace prefix extensions in the systemRequired value list are supported by the player, it is understood that the player supports the new elements and/or attributes. The test attribute then returns an evaluation of true and the element is rendered. In the following example, the systemRequired attribute calls for the "component version" (designated as cv by Real) used in the namespace called for by the RealPlayer. If the media player being used is a RealPlayer, it will be able to understand and resolve this attribute and play the element.

```
<smil xmlns:cv="http://features.real.com/systemComponent">
. . .
<body>
   <switch>
      <seq system-required="cv"
        cv:systemComponent="http://features.real.com/
        ➡?feature;player=6.0.7.x">
        ...clips to play if RealPlayer is version 6.0.7e...
      </seq>
   . . .
   </switch>
</body>
```

Attribute: systemScreenDepth (system-screen-depth)

- Version Compatibility: 2.0 (1.0)
- Parent Elements: <switch>
- Possible Values: integer greater than zero

This attribute tests for the depth of the viewer's screen color palette in bits and can be used to ensure that the color depth of the presentation is tailored to match the user's system color depth. Typically, values of 8, 16, 24, and 32 are used, although any positive integer can be employed as a test value. An evaluation of true is returned if the playback engine can display the attribute's given color depth. An evaluation of false is returned if the playback engine is capable only of smaller color depth.

Attribute: systemScreenSize (system-screen-size)

- Version Compatibility: 2.0 (1.0)
- Possible Values: screen-height X screen-width (in pixels)

Similar to systemScreenDepth, this attribute tests for the height and width of the viewer's screen size in pixels and is used to select a presentation that is matched to the capabilities of the user's system. Values are expressed by first stating the optimal screen height in pixels, using an "X," and then stating the optimal screen width in pixels. An evaluation of true is returned if the playback engine is capable of displaying a presentation at the given size. An evaluation of false is returned if the playback engine is capable only of smaller-sized presentations.

In the following example, the <switch> element is used to select the presentation that best fits the user's color depth and screen size preference settings. If the viewer's system supports the screen size and color depth in either of the first two par elements, that presentation will be activated. If the user's system or preferences match neither, the last default par element will be made active.

```
<par>
   <switch>
      <par systemScreenSize="1024X1280" systemScreenDepth="24" . . . >
        <. . . >
      </par>
      <par systemScreenSize="600X800" systemScreenDepth="24" . . . >
        <. . . >
      </par>
      <par . . . >
        <. . . >
      </par>
   </switch>
</par>
```

The CustomTestAttributes Module Elements and Attributes

As we've just seen, the BasicContentControl module provides SMIL authors and developers with a number of predefined test attributes that can be used to evaluate a user's system and preferences and then match content delivery to those returned values. The CustomTestAttributes module, for which the BasicContentControl module is a prerequisite, expands on that functionality by enabling SMIL authors to create custom test attributes that are document and player specific. The <customAttributes> and <customTest> elements are used to define the custom tests, whereas the evaluation and implementation of those values are dependent on the media player itself.

As with the predefined test attributes, custom test attributes can be used within timing or media object elements and can be activated either by containing the alternatives within a <switch> element or as in-line test attributes attached to objects themselves. Also, as with the system test attributes, custom tests within a <switch> element will be evaluated in the order in which they appear within the SMIL document, and the inclusion of a final fail-safe element is recommended. Again, any elements whose custom tests evaluate as false are ignored and essentially are rendered invisible for the remainder of the presentation.

Let's take a look at the elements first, and then investigate the attributes that are used to establish settings for those elements.

Element: <customAttributes>

- Version Compatibility: 2.0
- Parent Element: <head>
- Child Element: <customTest>

The <customAttributes> element appears in the header of a SMIL document and contains customTest element and its attributes. The following example illustrates the basic structure of the <customAttributes> element.

```
<head>
  <layout> . . . </layout>
   <customAttributes>
      <customTest id="one" . . .  />
      <customTest id="two" . . .  />
      <customTest id="three" . . .  />
   </customAttributes>
</head>
```

Element: <customTest>

- Version Compatibility: 2.0

- Parent Element: <customAttributes>

- Possible Attributes: defaultState, override, uid, id

The <customTest> element, which is contained by the <customAttributes> element, uses an id attribute to specify the name for a test argument. This identifier is then used to apply the test argument by either including it within the <switch> element or by calling it as an in-line test attribute within media object or timing elements.

A simple example follows that illustrates the use of the <customTest> element, in which the custom tests identified as one and two are enclosed in a <switch> element, and the custom test three is attached to the media object sound.

```
<head>
   <layout> . . . </layout>
      <customAttributes>
        <customTest id="one" . . . />
        <customTest id="two" . . . />
        <customTest id="three" . . . />
      </customAttributes>
</head>
<body>
. . .
   <par>
      <switch>
        <video id="fullscreen" customTest="one" . . . />
        <video id="halfscreen" customTest="two" . . . />
      </switch>
      <audio id="sound" customTest="three" . . . />
   </par>
. . .
</body>
```

Attribute: customTest

- Version Compatibility: 2.0

- Parent Elements: media elements, timing elements

- Possible Values: identifier declared in customTest element

As you can see in the preceding example, the customTest attribute is used to call a custom test that is applied either to a media object or timing element, or used within a <switch> element.

The customTest attribute is only one of the attributes in this section of the ContentControl modules. These additional attributes can be included in the <customTest> element to establish the default or initial state of a custom test, to allow or disallow the user to override this initial state, and to store value settings for the test attribute. Following is a simple example that uses all these attributes. Descriptions of each attribute follow the code sample.

```
<head>
    <customAttributes>
        <customTest id="location" defaultState="false"
            uid="http://www.locations.org/settings/location" override=
            ➥ "visible" />
        <customTest id="allelse" defaultState="true"
            uid="http://www.locations.org/settings/everywhere" override=
            ➥ "hidden" />
    </customAttributes>
</head>
<body . . . />
. . .
    <switch>
        <video id="youarehere" customTest="location" . . . />
        <video id="everywhere" customTest="allelse" . . . />
    </switch>
</body>
```

Attribute: defaultState

- Version Compatibility: 2.0
- Parent Elements: <customTest>
- Possible Values: true, false

This attribute enables the presentation author to establish the initial setting for a custom test. The default value is false, which means that until the custom test is performed and evaluated as true, the element will not play. If the value is set to true, the test automatically evaluates as true and the element is activated. If the uid attribute is included within the element, which identifies a URI where a value setting is stored, the value assigned by the URI will be used in place of the defaultState value.

Any user-specified value will override both the uid attribute value and the defaultState value. For instance, in our previous example, the custom test of allelse is given a defaultState value of true so that it will be activated if the other attributes do not cause the element to be evaluated as true.

Attribute: override

- Version Compatibility: 2.0
- Parent Element: <customTest>
- Possible Values: visible, hidden

This attribute declares whether the capability to override the initial state of a custom test attribute is made available to the user. If the value of override is visible, then the player, in its default configuration, should present to users an interface that allows them to set the value of the test. If the value of override is hidden, the player should not present this interface unless the specific player has allowed the user to declare a preference for this access. The value of override is the final word on the runtime value assigned to the test attribute and overrides both the defaultState and uid values. In the example, the custom test allelse is given an override value of hidden because, as the fail-safe alternative, the author would desire that the user not be able to override the assigned test attribute value.

Attribute: uid

- Version Compatibility: 2.0
- Parent Elements: <customTest>
- Possible Values: a URI resource

This attribute identifies a URI, using either an absolute or relative address in which a value setting for the associated custom test is stored. This is especially useful for storing custom test values that can then be reused in other presentation documents. The value retrieved by the uid attribute replaces any declared defaultState value for the associated test, but can be overridden by user interaction if permitted by the override attribute value.

The PrefetchControl Module Elements and Attributes

The PrefetchControl module allows media to be scheduled for preloading, either in full or in part, by the author. This can eliminate pausing in the presentation if large files need to be available for smooth playback.

Element: `<prefetch>`

- Version Compatibility: 2.0
- Possible Attributes: `bandwidth`, `mediaTime`, `mediaSize`

Normally, media objects are transferred from the server to the player when called for in the SMIL document. The `<prefetch>` element provides authors with a mechanism for scheduling the download of a given media object file, either completely or in part, before it is needed. Preloading large files, or even portions of them, may help prevent the stuttering playback that can occur when a file is unable to download quickly enough for uninterrupted playback. `<prefetch>` can also be used to schedule the downloading of files at times when the available bandwidth is not being consumed by the presentation. In addition, the attributes can be used to define how much of the file is preloaded or the amount of bandwidth dedicated to this function. In the example that follows, `image` is preloaded as `titles` displays. After the entire `image` file is downloaded, the presentation moves beyond that `par` element; when `image` is called for display, it has already been preloaded into the user's cache.

```
<body>
 <seq>
  <par>
   <prefetch id="image" src="animate.gif" />
   <text src="titles.html" />
  </par>
 . . .
  <img src="animate.gif" . . . />
 </seq>
</body>
```

Attribute: `bandwidth`

- Possible Values: number value (bits per second), percentage value

This attribute determines how much available bandwidth is dedicated to prefetching media files. A number value represents the bits per second dedicated to preloading media files; a percentage value represents the percentage of bandwidth used for the task. The default value of 100% uses all available bandwidth to preload the media file. In the following example, 50% of the bandwidth is dedicated to prefetching the "image" source file.

```
<prefetch id="image" src="animate.gif" bandwidth="50%" />
```

Attribute: `mediaSize`

- Possible Values: number value (bytes), percentage value

The `mediaSize` attribute dictates how much of the media object file to preload during the prefetch function. A number value represents the number of bytes of the file that should be preloaded, whereas a percentage value corresponds to the percentage of the entire file that should be fetched. The default value of 100% retrieves the entire file. The following example indicates that 5000 bytes, or 5Kb, of images should be preloaded before the presentation continues.

```
<prefetch id="image" src="animate.gif" mediaSize="5000" />
```

Attribute: `mediaTime`

- Version Compatibility: 2.0
- Possible Values: number value (clock-value), percentage value

Similar to `mediaSize`, this attribute declares how much of the media object file to preload based on the duration of the entire file. Measurement of duration can be done using any of the time-measurement systems outlined in the Timing modules (for more on this, see Chapter 7, "Grouping Your Content: The SMIL Timing and Synchronization Module"); a simple declaration can be made using the syntax "5s," which would indicate the retrieval of the first 5 seconds of a resource. A percentage value dictates the percentage of the entire file's duration to preload. The default value of 100% retrieves the entire file.

The SkipContentControl Module Attribute

This module contains no elements and only one attribute whose functionality is identical in both SMIL 1.0 and 2.0 and whose purpose is to allow for the future extensibility of the language.

Attribute: `skip-content`

- Version Compatibility: 1.0, 2.0
- Possible Values: `true`, `false`

Primarily intended to cover the bases as SMIL evolves, this attribute is used with elements that either allow markup from previous versions of SMIL as content, or that were empty elements in previous SMIL versions and have become nonempty. If either of these statements apply to a given element, a `skip-content` value of `true` will result in the element being skipped. If one of the preceding cases apply, and the value is set to `false`, the content will be processed. The default value of `skip-content` is true. Again, this attribute is primarily intended to control the evaluation of elements used in future versions of the language.

The Content Control Modules Summarized

The Content Control modules supply the elements and attributes that enable authors to tailor presentations that fit the preferences and system restrictions of a given viewer. Keep in mind that user preference and system data collection, and the effect that this information has on the playback of the presentation, is player specific and will continue to evolve as SMIL 2.0 playback engines are developed and refined.

13

Speed Up, Slow Down, and Do It Over Again: The Time Manipulations Module

SMIL 1.0 enabled the Web multimedia author to do pretty much anything with the timeline of the presentation, as long as that timeline went forward with its preordained rate.

What if you could manipulate time itself? No, this is not some sort of treatise on particle physics research. One of the modules tucked neatly away into SMIL 2.0 turns the timeline on its ear. Indeed, the SMIL Time Manipulations module enables the author to add attributes to the elements of the Timing and Synchronization module so that time can speed up, slow down, or even reverse. Now if only you could do that in real life.

Conformance Profiles and the Time Manipulations Module

As a set of element add-on attributes, Time Manipulations is not required for either SMIL Host Language Conformance or Integration Set Language Conformance. Keep an eye out for it in implementations of XHTML+SMIL (also known as HTML+TIME in Microsoft Internet Explorer) and with Scalable Vector Graphics (SVG).

The Time Manipulations Module Attributes

Unlike our coverage of many other modules, Time Manipulations skips the elements and jumps right to the attributes themselves. These attributes control the time behavior of the element they are attached to. It is important to note that support for these attributes is a function of the player implementation and, in some cases, of the media type itself. You should conduct some experimentation and testing with the audience player(s) or browser(s) before the public release of your work.

The biggest beneficiary of the Time Manipulations module is animation. Although other media types offer some promise for this capability, animation is one of the best places for Time Manipulations to do its magic. Is your animation too slow in the player? Speed up its rate. Or perhaps you want to give the animation a smoother feel. Use accelerate to ease the animation from a complete stop into its action. Use decelerate to gracefully bring it to a stop. Take advantage of cycling effects by playing the animation forward and then backward. The Time Manipulations module offers attributes for all these goals.

Attribute: speed

- Version Compatibility: SMIL 2.0
- Possible Values: Floating point values greater than or less than 0

speed is like a scale tool for your timeline. Want to slow down the timeline evenly? Simply scale down its rate with speed. Likewise, you can also scale up the element's playback rate with speed. Applied to the duration of an element or time container, speed can easily make media playback twice as fast. For example, a media element with a 10-second duration would then be 5 seconds in real-time.

Because speed affects the scale of your timeline, a value of 1 is the value for 100% and is considered the default. Every positive value greater than 0 is multiplied by your timeline duration to control its speed up or slow down. A speed value of 5 would play the media 5 times as fast as normal. A speed value of .5 would play the media half as fast as normal. A 0 value, if you wanted to try it, is ignored.

What if you use a negative number? Theoretically, a negative speed value would play the element backward. Of course, as with all the Time Manipulations attributes and their possible values, you would want to test the results to make sure you get what you intended out of your player or browser.

Let's take a look at how speed works with an overly simplified example displayed in Internet Explorer browsers that support HTML+TIME:

```
<html xmlns:t ="urn:schemas-microsoft-com:time">
    <head>
        <style>
            .time {behavior:url(#default#time2);}
        </style>
        <?IMPORT namespace="t" implementation="#default#time2">
    </head>
    <body>
        <t:seq>
            <div class="time" begin="0" dur="5" speed="1" style=
            ➥"color:red">SMIL!</div>
            <div class="time" begin="5" dur="5" speed=".5" style=
            ➥"color:green">SMIL!</div>
            <div class="time" begin="15" dur="5" speed="5" style=
            ➥"color:blue">SMIL!</div>
        </t:seq>
    </body>

</html>
```

As covered in Chapter 4, "First Things First: The SMIL Structure Module,", the first few lines of the markup reference the namespace, import the tag definitions, and set up a means of applying those behaviors to individual elements on the Web page. Within the <body> element we see a sequential time container. Within that <t:seq> element sits three lines of markup that display the text "SMIL!" in red, then green, then blue. Each line of text has its own start time but they all have the same display duration. This is where the attribute speed enters the picture.

The red "SMIL!" text is given a duration of 5 seconds and a speed of 1. Anything scaled by a factor of 1 (100%) doesn't change. This text will display on the screen for 5 seconds. The green "SMIL!" text is given a duration of 5 seconds and a speed of .5. This is represents 50% or half of the normal speed. So the text will display on the screen for 10 seconds. The final blue "SMIL!" text is given a duration of 5 seconds and a speed of 5. This is five times the normal speed. So the blue text will display on the screen for no more than 1 second.

Attribute: accelerate

- Version Compatibility: SMIL 2.0
- Possible Values: Floating point values between 0 and 1

accelerate is applied to the duration of an element or the duration of a time container that holds one or more elements. The value of accelerate falls between 0 and 1, with 0 being the default and 1 being the maximum possible value. The value is proportional to the overall duration. Thus, if you had a 10-second animation and you wanted it to accelerate up from a complete stop for 3 seconds, you would use a value of .3. Likewise, a value of .5 would cause the element to ease in from a stop to full motion halfway through the duration. What if you use a value of 1? Then your animation would be hitting full speed at the end (the 10 second mark). Multiply the accelerate value by the duration and you can quickly determine how long your media element will take to hit full speed.

Why not just start the media at full speed? With some objects, and with animation in particular, easing into the action will appear more natural. That is because most of the world around us does not run at full speed from the moment the switch is thrown. Instead, most action follows a natural arc of time. Does your car instantly go full speed when the light changes to green? We could only wish. Do you run at full speed when the alarm clock goes off in the morning? No, you probably need to ease into the day. Sure, there are exceptions to this rule. You may have already discovered this if you have tried to race the light of a flashlight to the opposite wall.

In this example in Internet Explorer, the text accelerates from a standstill and reaches full speed as it dynamically drops down the Web page:

```
<html xmlns:t ="urn:schemas-microsoft-com:time">
    <head>
        <style>
            .time {behavior:url(#default#time2);}
        </style>
        <?IMPORT namespace="t" implementation="#default#time2">
    </head>
    <body>
        <div id="falling" class="time"
        style="position:absolute;top:25px;left:25px;color:red"
        ➥>Falling SMIL!</div>
        <t:animate targetElement="falling" attributeName="top"
        ➥to="500" dur="3" accelerate="1"/>
```

```
        </body>

</html>
```

The words "Falling SMIL!" are wrapped by a `<div>` element that positions the
text in the top left corner of the browser window and colors it red. The `<div>` element also picks up an `id="falling"`. This allows the animation element in the
following line to target the `<div>` and do its magic. The `<t:animate>` element
tells the `<div>` named "falling" that its `top` value should move from its home
position of 25 pixels to a final position of 500 pixels down the screen in 3 seconds. At this point, `accelerate` steps in. With the given value of 1, the text will
start from a complete stop and hit full speed at about the time it reaches the end
of the animation. The result is an animation where the text seems to drop with
the weight of gravity.

Attribute: decelerate

- Version Compatibility: SMIL 2.0
- Possible Values: Floating point values between 0 and 1

Like `accelerate`, the `decelerate` attribute is attached to the duration of an element or all its children within a time container. Like `accelerate`, `decelerate`
also uses the same proportional value from 0 to 1 to determine the rate of decel-
eration. Therefore, if you wanted your 10-second animation to begin slowing one
quarter of the time from the end of the timeline, use `.25` for the value.

Coupled with the effect of `accelerate`, `decelerate` can help breathe that sense
of real life and gracefulness to an animation. This example in Internet Explorer
plays around with the same approach that my `accelerate` example used. This
time, I move the text from left to right across the screen:

```
<html xmlns:t ="urn:schemas-microsoft-com:time">
    <head>
        <style>
            .time {behavior:url(#default#time2);}
        </style>
        <?IMPORT namespace="t" implementation="#default#time2">
    </head>
    <body>
        <div id="moving" class="time" style="position:absolute;top:
        ➥25px;left:25px;color:red">Moving SMIL!</div>
        ➥<t:animate targetElement="moving" attributeName="left"
        ➥to="500" dur="3" decelerate="1"/>
```

```
    </body>

</html>
```

As before, the words "Falling SMIL!" are wrapped by a `<div>` element that positions the text in the top left corner of the browser window and colors it red. The `<div>` element also picks up an `id="moving"`. Once again, this allows the animation element in the following line to target the `<div>` and do its magic. The `<t:animate>` element tells the `<div>` named "moving" that its `left` value should move from its home position of 25 pixels to a final position of 500 pixels to the right on the screen in 3 seconds. With `decelerate` having a given value of `1`, the text will start at full speed and gradually slow to a stop until it reaches the end of the animation. The result is that `decelerate` helps apply the brakes as the animation ends.

Attribute: `autoReverse`

- Version Compatibility: SMIL 2.0
- Possible Values: `true` or `false`

`autoReverse` effectively doubles the duration of any element it impacts. That is because after the media has played forward to the end, `autoReverse` steps in and runs the media backward. The possible values of `autoReverse` involve a simple on/off switch of `true` or `false`. Switched off with `false` is the natural default for just such an attribute. We cannot have the world running in reverse by default.

With `autoReverse`, a SMIL author could make an animated element move from one side of the display space to another. After the stated duration is complete, the animated element would head for its original home location. Like `speed` and the `accelerate`/`decelerate` pair, `autoReverse` adds a powerful attribute to the SMIL Timing modules. Such a capability allows for the efficiency of animation cycling in which one element can be used again and again in an animation. But it also brings the power to annoy. Too much repeating motion will be quickly tuned out by the viewer. Use `autoReverse` with care.

In the following Internet Explorer example, `autoReverse` causes the text to move from left to right and back again for 5 complete back and forth cycles:

```
<html xmlns:t ="urn:schemas-microsoft-com:time">
    <head>
        <style>
```

```
            .time {behavior:url(#default#time2);}
        </style>
        <?IMPORT namespace="t" implementation="#default#time2">
    </head>
    <body>
        <div id="aroundAgain" class="time" style="position:absolute;top:
        ➥25px;left:25px;color:green">SMIL Back and Forth!</div>
        <t:animatemotion targetElement="aroundAgain" to="400,0" dur="2"
        ➥autoReverse="true" repeatCount="5"/>
    </body>

</html>
```

This time out, the <div> element has been labeled "aroundAgain". The green text
wrapped by the <div> is positioned 25 pixels down from the top and 25 pixels
over from the left edge of the browser window. <t:animatemotion> attaches
itself to the <div> labeled "aroundAgain" and tells it to move that text over 400
pixels (and down zero pixels). With a dur="2" it will take two seconds to move
the text across the screen. At this point, the autoReverse="true" kicks in.
Having just moved the text from the left side of the screen to the right, the text
will now take two seconds to autoReverse and travel back to where it started
from. So the duration is effectively doubled. The repeatCount="5" at the end of
the <t: animatemotion> element will make the whole process happen five times.
The end result will be text that slides back and forth across the screen like the
swinging pendulum of a grandfather clock.

The Time Manipulations Module Summarized

Coupled with the Timing and Synchronization module and the Animation modules, the Time Manipulations module is just what animators need to tweak the
performance of their work in SMIL 2.0. With these attributes attached to the
duration of an element or a time container, SMIL authors can control the behavior of the timeline itself.

14

SMIL That Isn't SMIL: RealNetworks's RealPix and RealText

When SMIL 1.0 first appeared, one of its strengths was its simplicity. By mastering the basic concepts of the <seq> and <par> tags, you were good to go for most SMIL authoring.

That simplicity, however, also revealed a limitation of SMIL 1.0. If you were working with pre-built pieces of animation, video, or audio, SMIL did the job nicely. It synchronized the various media objects into a cohesive presentation. If you had smaller independent building blocks, such as individual images, SMIL offered fewer options. You could certainly add images to a sequential timeline and run them parallel with audio, but SMIL 1.0 lacked the hooks to do much with those images after they were there. In addition, text support in SMIL 1.0 covered the bases, but really did not offer a lot of power beyond its simple role as another media type.

As the most important mainstream Web advocate for SMIL, RealNetworks saw an opportunity and seized it. Not only would the new "G2" version of its player support the upcoming W3C SMIL recommendation, but it would also support two SMIL-based in-house language creations: RealPix and RealText. With RealPix, Web multimedia authors could begin to create the illusion of a high-bandwidth user experience with low-bandwidth streaming images. Rendered locally by the user's machine, images could artfully fade, dissolve, or wipe to transition from one to the next. With full-motion video on the Web, it might seem easier to ignore streaming still images. Done right, though, a good RealPix presentation has a visual poetry to it that is unmatched by video. RealText enables authors to add tricks to the basic text in their presentations. In addition to style changes, text can be made to roll, scroll, and hyperlink.

Although based on SMIL, RealText and RealPix are written into their own text files. Like accessing a complete audio or video clip, your SMIL document does little more than reference files with .rp (RealPix) and .rt (RealText) file extensions. After the RealPix and RealText text files are loaded, RealPlayer renders those instructions in its display area.

Compatibility

Some SMIL purists sneer at RealPix and RealText because these solutions are not true SMIL; rather, they are proprietary RealNetworks solutions. You will not be able to run RealPix or RealText in the QuickTime player or other SMIL players that do not borrow playback support from RealPlayer. Plus, using these languages limits the user to RealPlayer G2 or later. Is that a problem? Not really. RealPlayer G2 (or better) players have been around for a reasonably long time, and RealNetworks has a huge installed user base. Although some Web appliances, such as WebTV, are limited to supporting older versions of RealPlayer, most RealPlayer users today have upgraded to G2.

As a Web multimedia author, you often find yourself living on the far edge of digital voodoo to begin with. RealPlayer version G2 and later attempted to reduce this problem with an auto-update feature. Although this feature still requires the user to wait while new software is downloaded, it does help keep the users relatively up to date.

SMIL 2.0, with its new features and functions, begins a transition that could mean a phasing out of the need for RealPix. Rather than work with a separate .rp file, you will write your image commands directly into the SMIL document. Even with SMIL 2.0, however, RealText still has an ongoing active role to play in RealPlayer.

It is important to take a moment and discuss player version numbers. To RealNetworks, RealPlayer G2 was a major generational change from the previous RealPlayer software. RealPlayer had gradually gained new capabilities, but this second generation player, with SMIL support, began to establish itself as a true multimedia player. Text, pictures, video, and audio capabilities blended together for the first time in the RealPlayer environment.

All that is nice for marketing, but it can make it difficult to understand version numbers. G2 was the first RealPlayer that supported playback of SMIL, RealPix, or RealText documents. But it was part of a larger family of players that started with RealPlayer 1.0. RealPlayer G2 is essentially RealPlayer 6. In the number scheme, G2 is the lowest player you will have to deal with for SMIL, RealPix, and RealText. Subsequent versions are RealPlayer 7 and 8. RealPlayer 9 is, again, a major generational change for the software. As such, it is likely to pick up an additional name that will keep the marketing folks happy. Even so, it is the ninth version of the RealPlayer.

Finally, it is critical to talk about bandwidth. In most RealPlayer formats, the amount of bandwidth consumed by the streaming media is determined by the encoding process. In most cases, that is an established value that doesn't change. However, that is not true in the least with RealPix and RealText. In reality, RealText is an extremely light load on the data stream. In RealPix, you can specify how much bandwidth you want to consume. But that does not guarantee that you can actually stream those images in the bandwidth space you have carved off for them. Be very careful with image sizes and how fast you are requiring those images to load, and test your presentation over conditions that are similar to what your viewing audience will use. If you do not, your viewer might be frustrated by RealPlayer buffering or images that fail to appear in the presentation.

The RealPix Element

After setting up the document, the RealPix elements define the available images (with `<image/>`) and declare the visual effects (with `<fadein/>`, `<fadeout/>`, `<crossfade/>`, `<animate/>`, `<wipe/>`, and `<viewchange/>`).

Element: `<imfl>`

- Version Compatibility: RealPlayer G2 or later
- Child Elements: `<head/>`, `<image/>`, `<fill/>`, `<fadein/>`, `<fadeout/>`, `<crossfade/>`, `<animate/>`, `<wipe/>`, `<viewchange/>`

Remember that your RealPix instructions sit in their own document (with an `.rp` file extension). You reference your RealPix document as a source URL in your SMIL. You could even run them completely separate from any SMIL document. The player will load the file and execute the RealPix instructions directly. Within this separate document, the `<imfl>` and `</imfl>` tag pair set up and surround the RealPix markup, much as `<html>` and `<smil>` set up and surround their respective markup elements. A quick look at a simple RealPix document shows its basic form:

```
<imfl>
    <head width="200" height="200" duration="10000" bitrate="20000" />
    <image handle="1" name="myFirst.jpg" />
    <image handle="2" name="mySecond.jpg" />
    <fill start="0" color="black" />
    <fadein start="1000" duration="3000" target="1" />
    <crossfade start="8000" duration="1500" target="2" />
</imfl>
```

Enough information is in this text file to link a viewer to the document and provide an image-only presentation. But if you want to use RealPix with your SMIL, you simply reference your RealPix document as a source URL. If the preceding streaming-image text file was named `myPictures.rp`, your SMIL page might look something like the following:

```
<smil>
    <head>
        <layout>
            <root-layout height="200" width="200" />
            <region id="myPics" left="0" top="0" height="200" width="200" />
        </layout>
    </head>
    <body>
        <par>
            <img src="myPictures.rp" region="myPics" />
        </par>
    <body>
</smil>
```

Element: `<head/>`

- Version Compatibility: RealPlayer G2 or later
- Possible Attributes: `aspect, author, background-color, bitrate, copyright, duration, height, maxfps, preroll, timeformat, title, url, width`

In a RealPix document, `<head/>` is sandwiched between the `<imfl>` tags. Much like its HTML counterpart, `<head/>` contains information about your presentation. This can range from author and content information to presentation window aspects.

Element: `<image/>`

- Version Compatibility: RealPlayer G2 or later
- Possible Attributes: `handle, name, size, mime`

In a RealPix presentation, each image you access must be identified with an `<image/>` element, which tells RealPlayer where the image is and what it will be called. RealPlayer 7 or later also enables you to attach a `size` and `mime` type to an image if you happen to be serving your content from a traditional Web server. The most critical attributes are `handle` and `name`. These attributes allow the author to identify the images that will be manipulated by other effects elements that perform wipes and fades. `handle` gives a unique number to each image, and `name` tells RealPlayer the path to where the image sits on the server. Shown with a corresponding `<fadein/>` and `<crossfade/>`, a sample of markup would look like the following:

```
. . .
<image handle="1" name="images/myFirst.jpg" />
<image handle="2" name="images/mySecond.jpg" />
. . .
    <fadein start="1" duration="3" target="1" />
    <crossfade start="8" duration="1.5" target="2" />
. . .
```

These `<image/>` attributes reference two images in a directory called "images." The `<fadein/>` and `<crossfade/>` effects `target` the unique number representing the image `handle` for each image.

The range of supported image formats has gradually grown in RealPlayer. Initial support covered only JPEG format files. Shortly after, GIF files were added to the mix. Grayscale JPEG images were first supported in RealPlayer 7. PNG and transparency support for PNG and GIF were added with the first update to RealPlayer 7. Although this covers most of the possible Web graphics formats, newer versions of the player may support additional graphics formats.

Element: `<fill/>`

- Version Compatibility: RealPlayer G2 or later
- Possible Attributes: `color, dsth, dstw, dstx, dsty, start`

The `<fill/>` element places a colored rectangle within the display window. You can use it to create a colored background or to cover the display area at a key moment in the presentation.

The attribute `color`, as the name implies, specifies the color to fill the rectangle with. `start` specifies when that filled rectangle will appear on the timeline. Finally, `dstx`, `dsty`, `dstw`, and `dsth` define the size of the rectangle. The `dst` refers to "destination." `dstx` and `dsty` define the x,y coordinate that sets up the upper-left starting point of the rectangle. After you have defined a starting point, all you need to create a rectangle from that point is a width and height: `dstw` and `dsth`.

Element: `<fadein/>`

- Version Compatibility: RealPlayer G2 or later
- Possible Attributes: `aspect, dsth, dstw, dstx, dsty, duration, maxfps, srch, srcw, srcx, srcy, start, target, url`

The `<fadein/>` element is used to fade an image into the RealPlayer window from a solid color established with the `background-color` attribute or the `<fill/>` element. A duration of `0` seconds makes the image appear without a fade.

Element: `<fadeout/>`

- Version Compatibility: RealPlayer G2 or later
- Possible Attributes: `color, dsth, dstw, dstx, dsty, duration, maxfps, start`

The <fadeout/> element is used to fade the RealPlayer window into a solid color defined by the color attribute. To the viewer, any preceding image will appear to fade away to be replaced by that color. A duration of 0 seconds makes the preceding image disappear without a fade.

Element:

- Version Compatibility: RealPlayer G2 or later
- Possible Attributes: aspect, dsth, dstw, dstx, dsty, duration, maxfps, srch, srcw, srcx, srcy, start, target, url

The element is used to fade from one image to another in the RealPlayer window. A duration of 0 seconds makes the image appear without a crossfade.

Element:

- Version Compatibility: RealPlayer 7 or later
- Possible Attributes: aspect, dsth, dstw, dstx, dsty, duration, maxfps, srch, srcw, srcx, srcy, start, target, url

The element displays the animation of an animated GIF from within the RealPlayer window. The duration attribute establishes the total length of animation cycling.

Element:

- Version Compatibility: RealPlayer G2 or later
- Possible Attributes: aspect, direction, dsth, dstw, dstx, dsty, duration, maxfps, srch, srcw, srcx, srcy, start, target, type, url

The element is used to wipe from one image or colored fill rectangle to another in the RealPlayer window. A wipe creates a hard-edged line between the old image and the new incoming image. That transition can sweep across the screen in one of four directions: up, down, left, or right. You can choose from two types of wipes: normal and push. A duration of 0 seconds makes the transition appear without a wipe.

Element: `<viewchange/>`

- Version Compatibility: RealPlayer G2 or later
- Possible Attributes: `dsth, dstw, dstx, dsty, duration, maxfps, srch, srcw,`
  `srcx, srcy, start`

The `<viewchange/>` element is used to "change the view" of the image in the
RealPlayer window. By using the `source` and `destination` attributes, this element can make the view of the image appear to zoom in, zoom out, tilt up, or pan
across the field of view.

Let's take a look at what playing with the image size will do in some common
situations. Suppose you had an image that's 400 pixels wide by 300 pixels high.
But the only area of that image you want to show is 100 pixels wide by 75 pixels high. Even without `<viewchange/>`, you can zoom in on that area by defining
a source starting point (`srcx` and `srcy`) and the area of 100 pixels by 75 pixels
that you want to use (`srcw` and `srch`).

```
. . .
<fadein start="1" duration="1" srcx="25" srcy="25" srcw="100" srch="75"
➥target="1" />
. . .
```

So far so good. You've zoomed in on a smaller area of the upper-left corner of
the image by adding the size attributes to the `<fadein/>` element. But what if you
wanted to change that view? What if you wanted RealPlayer to pan right and
show an area in the upper-right side of the image? For that you use
`<viewchange/>`:

```
. . .
<fadein start="1" duration="1" srcx="25" srcy="25" srcw="100" srch="75"
➥target="1" />
<viewchange start="2" duration="3" srcx="250" srcy="25" srcw="100"
srch="75" />
. . .
```

Notice that `<viewchange/>` does not need a `target` attribute. It automatically
changes the view of the image targeted in the previous element. In this case,
you're changing the `srcx` and `srcy` attributes, so `<viewchange/>` will move the
view from a 100 by 75 pixel rectangle in the upper-left corner (at coordinate 25
by 25) to the upper-right corner (at coordinate 250 by 25). But you're not done

yet. Now that you have panned across the image to the right, let's zoom out to show the whole image:

```
. . .
<fadein start="1" duration="1" srcx="25" srcy="25" srcw="100" srch="75"
➥target="1" />
<viewchange start="2" duration="3" srcx="250" srcy="25" srcw="100"
srch="75" />
<viewchange start="5" duration="3" />
. . .
```

Is that all there is to zoom out? Yes. The default values for a <viewchange/> will show the whole image. By not specifying srcx, srcy, srcw, and srch in the final <viewchange/>, you have told the player to show the whole image. If you wanted to zoom out and show just a portion of the image, you could just specify new srcx, srcy, srcw, and srch values.

By putting together <viewchange/> with any of the RealPix sizing commands, you can achieve a number of panning, zooming, and shrinking effects in RealPlayer. A still image becomes dynamic and exciting.

But all this power comes with some cautions. First, make sure your images can handle the zoom in. Nothing is worse than a JPEG magnified beyond its comfortable resolution. How do you solve that problem? Simply use a larger image. But now you risk overloading your presentation with an image that will choke your bandwidth.

Second, the RealPlayer will do its best to meet the sizing commands you have given it. Put it through too much and your image might distort. Worse yet, you may get rectangles of background popping in and out of your presentation as it tries to keep your image in proper aspect.

Third, all these <viewchange/> effects are rendered by the viewer's computer, rather than on the server. This cuts down on the bandwidth needs but also puts more of a load on the viewer's computer. Tax the viewer's processor too much and the presentation might act choppy or grind to a halt.

Fourth and finally, use good visual composition. Just because you can move across a larger image doesn't mean that you should. Think like a photographer or videographer. Move from one well-composed view to another. Keep your visual composition pleasing. Provide a good reason for the <viewchange/> in the first place.

The RealPix Attributes

Most of the available RealPix attributes concern themselves with the height and width coordinates because RealPix manipulates images and colored areas with a rectangular shape. By using these attributes, you can define how big that image or colored rectangle appears in the RealPix presentation. Other critical attributes identify the timing of the visual materials, the server location of the images, the metainformation of the presentation, how much bandwidth should be used by the presentation, and the type of wipe transitions.

Attribute: aspect

- Version Compatibility: RealPlayer G2 or getter
- Possible Values: true, false

If the width and height ratio to your source image is different from the width and height ratio of your player window, you have a potential problem with your display. Because of the mismatch, the image will appear squashed or stretched. If aspect="true", RealPlayer scales the actual image size to fit within the destination window. This setting creates bands of background color that appear paired at the top and bottom or left and right sides of the player window. Because most people want their graphics undistorted, aspect="true" is the default value for this attribute. If for some reason you want a graphic to stretch and fill all the available window space, aspect="false" turns the scaling feature off. The aspect attribute may be used in the <head/>, <fadein/>, <crossfade/>, <animate/>, and <wipe/> elements.

Attribute: author

- Version Compatibility: RealPlayer G2 or later
- Possible Values: Text string

Using the author attribute in the <head/> element enables authors to attach their names to a presentation so that it can appear in the RealPlayer window. Just remember that the RealPix author information could be overridden by the author information in other media objects or the SMIL presentation itself.

Attribute: `background-color`

- Version Compatibility: RealPlayer 7 or later
- Possible Values: A 24-bit hexadecimal color value or a predefined color name

Added as a `<head/>` attribute with RealPlayer 7, `background-color` sets up the initial color that appears in the display window. If need be, this color can be changed at any time with the `<fill/>` element. Acceptable values follow the HTML conventions for 24-bit hexadecimal color (for example, white is `#FFFFFF`) or predefined names (black is `black`).

Attribute: `bitrate`

- Version Compatibility: RealPlayer G2 or later
- Possible Values: An integer representing bit rate in bits per second (bps)

Used in the `<head/>` element, this attribute represents the bit rate allocated for the RealPix presentation. For example, setting the bit rate at 12Kbps would mean `bitrate="12000"`. Why would you set the `bitrate`? RealPlayer wants to know how much resources to allocate toward components of a SMIL presentation. By setting the `bitrate`, you tell the player to allow that much bandwidth for that given presentation.

But you aren't safe yet. Just because you have specified a `bitrate` doesn't mean that the images you have placed on your timeline can meet that `bitrate`. That will be a function of how big the images are and how much time they spend on the timeline. Most RealPix authoring tools, such as RealSlideshow, will help you figure out the bandwidth math directly. In the past, RealNetworks has also provided spreadsheets that can be used to help determine whether your images will stream effectively. But even if you don't have these tools, you can figure out the bandwidth math directly.

Suppose you are authoring for a 56Kbps modem. But a 56Kbps modem does not offer a true 56 kilobits of bandwidth. RealNetworks would encourage you to anticipate using no more than 34Kbps. That gives the viewer a healthy safety margin for varying connection speeds and general modem overhead. Now assume that you are using your RealPix for a SMIL presentation. You want to dedicate some of your bandwidth to audio that will play with your slides. After playing with your audio encoding, you come up with a suitable clip that uses a steady 12Kbps stream. That leaves a maximum of 22Kbps left for your RealPix. Therefore, you set your RealPix `bitrate` as follows:

```
<head bitrate="22000" . . . />
```

Now suppose you have five images you want to load in 10 seconds. Each JPEG image is 10KB in size. (That is kilobytes and not kilobits.) You need to convert those image sizes to a measurement that will match up with your kilobits per second. Multiplying the images by 8 will do just that. Each 10KB image will use up 80Kb. Five images in 10 seconds means that each image has roughly 2 seconds of screen time. Therefore, your images will use 40Kbps (80Kb image size/2 seconds). You have just tilted the bandwidth. If you wanted the images to fit in 22Kbps, you are now over the limit by a whopping 18Kbps. A quick solution is to double the time in which you play your five images. At 20 seconds, each image can be on the screen for 4 seconds. That halves their bandwidth needs down to 20Kbps. Now you are safe.

But are you really safe? No. The preceding example assumes that all five JPEGS will be on the screen for an equal amount of time. If you have a creative bone in your body, you will probably want to match the images to music or narration in the audio track. In addition, how likely is it that you would have a set of images that are all the same file size? Now you have a problem because you cannot assume that each image will be on the screen for 4 seconds. With this situation, you will have to figure the bandwidth needs for each image at each moment in time. It can be done. You can run one image longer to bank loading time for an image that runs shorter.

My usual approach to this situation is to cheat. I average my overall bandwidth needs to see how hard I should really compress my images. Next, I look for images that are larger than the norm. Because these are the bottlenecks, I precede them with images smaller in file size or with images that will be on the screen longer. Sometimes I do both. As a last resort, I bank time bandwidth with very small GIF titles that compress down to bytes versus kilobytes. These load quickly and free up the player to begin loading the next images while the title sequence continues to play. Then as a final test, I usually pull out the old dial-up modem and see what I get in a variety of practice runs. At this point, I can quickly see most problem areas and tweak a presentation to suit.

Attribute: color

- Version Compatibility: RealPlayer G2 or later
- Possible Values: A 24-bit hexadecimal color value or a predefined color name

Required as a `<fill/>` or `<fadeout/>` attribute, `color` sets a colored rectangle that appears in the display window. Acceptable values follow the HTML conventions for 24-bit hexadecimal color (for example, white is #FFFFFF) or predefined names (black is `black`).

Attribute: copyright

- Version Compatibility: RealPlayer G2 or later
- Possible Values: Text string

Using the `copyright` attribute in the `<head/>` element allows the author to attach copyright information to a presentation that can appear in the RealPlayer window. Just remember that other media objects and the SMIL presentation itself can also have copyright information that could override your RealPix copyright.

Attribute: direction

- Version Compatibility: RealPlayer G2 or later
- Possible Values: up, down, left, right

Used with the `<wipe/>` effect, the `direction` attribute identifies in which direction the effect should travel across the screen. Possible values include up, down, left, and right.

Envisioning wipe directions usually plays tricks with our minds. The trick is to keep it simple. The following wipe effect (`direction="left"`) travels from the right side of the screen to the left. That means the new image will appear from the right side and the old image will disappear to the left side:

```
<wipe type="normal" direction="left" start="2" duration="2" target="5" />
```

Right side to left side? That can start to sound confusing. Just remember what direction you want the wipe to go, and it gets easier. If you want a wipe to travel toward the left side, you want a `direction="left"`. If you want a wipe to travel toward the upper side, you want a direction="up". Don't even think about where the wipe starts from. Envision the direction of where you want it to go to and use that direction as your value.

Attribute: dstx, dsty, dstw, and dsth

- Version Compatibility: RealPlayer G2 or later
- Possible Values: A valid display coordinate (dstx and dsty) or distance (dstw and dsth) measured in pixels

The dst in the dstx, dsty, dstw, and dsth attributes refers to "destination." When using RealPix, there is no requirement that you use all the display window or region area initially set up by RealPlayer. These attributes determine how much of the RealPlayer window or region space you want to use. dstx is a horizontal coordinate. dsty is a vertical coordinate. The coordinates are measured in pixels from the upper-left corner of the RealPlayer region or window. dstx and dsty work together as a coordinate pair that defines a starting point. So with a 100 pixel by 100 pixel RealPlayer window, 0,0 is the upper-left corner and 100,100 is the lower-right corner.

Therefore, dstx and dsty is the point (or destination) where you want an image or colored fill rectangle to display. Values of dstx="35" and dsty="25" mean that the upper-left corner of your image or rectangle will appear at a point 35 pixels over from the left edge and 25 pixels down from the top edge. Those edges can either be inside the region the RealPix sits in, or the RealPlayer window itself, if the region occupies the whole window.

After you determine the upper-left point, all you need to do is determine how wide and how far down the screen you want the rectangle of your visual material to be. dstw refers to destination width and dsth refers to destination height. Height can be a little counterintuitive because of the coordinate directions in RealPlayer. Vertical values get larger the farther down the window you go, so you might find it helpful to think of the height value as how far down the region or window space the display goes. These two width and height values will help determine the total size of the visual rectangle. Building on the previous example, values of dstw="100" and dsty="100" mean that your overall rectangle or image will go to 135 pixels from the left side of the region or window to 125 pixels from the top of the region or window.

When destination attributes are used with the source size attributes (srcx, srcy, srch, srcw), the author can make an image smaller or larger than normal or display only a selected rectangle of the larger image in RealPlayer.

dstx, dsty, dstw, and dsth can be used as attributes of the <fill/>, <fadein/>, <fadeout/>, <crossfade/>, <animate/>, <wipe/>, and <viewchange/> elements.

Attribute: duration

- Version Compatibility: RealPlayer G2 or later
- Possible Values: A number representing seconds or milliseconds

Required in multiple elements (<head/>, <fadein/>, <fadeout/>, <crossfade/>, <animate/>, <wipe/>, and <viewchange/>) to represent the duration of the presentation or the amount of time specified for a transition. The format for the duration is determined by the timeformat attribute in the <head/> element. Millisecond values are the default if no timeformat is specified.

If your timeformat="dd:hh:mm:ss.xyz", a duration of 5 seconds applied to a <fadein/> element might look like this:

```
<fadein start="10.5" duration="5" target="3" />
```

The same sample with the timeformat left to default to milliseconds would look like this:

```
<fadein start="10500" duration="5000" target="3" />
```

Attribute: handle

- Version Compatibility: RealPlayer G2 or later
- Possible Values: A positive integer

Used with the <image/> element, handle allows the author to attach a unique identifier to each image loaded in a RealPix presentation. In most cases, handle is a sequentially larger positive integer that increments with each <image/> tag. After that number is attached to an image, the image can be displayed or transitioned to by simply calling its number through a target attribute.

The following RealPix sample shows the use of handle and the corresponding use of target:

```
. . .
<image handle="1" name="images/myFirst.jpg" />
<image handle="2" name="images/mySecond.jpg" />
. . .
<fadein start="1000" duration="3000" target="1" />
<crossfade start="8000" duration="1500" target="2" />
. . .
```

In this case, the <fadein/> effect is used on target="1", which happens to be the handle of an image named and located at a path of my images/myFirst.jpg. Although most handles are used sequentially in most situations, there is no requirement to do so. You could just as easily reverse the target usage or use the handles repeatedly out of order:

```
. . .
<image handle="1" name="images/myFirst.jpg" />
<image handle="2" name="images/mySecond.jpg" />
. . .
<fadein start="1000" duration="3000" target="2" />
<crossfade start="8000" duration="1500" target="1" />
. . .
```

Attribute: height **and** width

- Version Compatibility: RealPlayer G2 or later
- Possible Values: An integer representing screen pixels

Used with the <head/> element, height describes the height of the display area measured in pixels. Likewise, width describes the width of the display area measured in pixels. If used with SMIL, RealPix presentations will fit within a region defined by the SMIL. If the region is defined as such, that could be a smaller section of the overall visual content area of the player window, or the height and width could fill the RealPlayer window if the region is set up to do just that.

Attribute: maxfps

- Version Compatibility: RealPlayer G2 or later
- Possible Values: An integer representing the frames per second

For transition effects, the maxfps attribute in the <head/>, <fadein/>, <fadeout/>, <crossfade/>, <animate/>, <wipe/>, and <viewchange/> elements sets the maximum frames per second for transitions in the presentation. Because RealPlayer does the work of determining what the best rate is for the user's CPU, this attribute does not have to be set. If plenty of computer power is available, RealPlayer tops out its transitions at a rate of 30 frames per second. If you find that some other media object is dragging down your presentation and you want finite control of RealPlayer's transition frame rate, you can specify the `maxfps`. Because of choppy performance, RealNetworks does not recommend a rate lower than `maxfps="5"`.

Attribute: `mime`

- Version Compatibility: RealPlayer 7 or later
- Possible Values: `image/gif`, `image/jpeg`, `image/png`

`mime` refers to MIME (multipurpose Internet mail extensions) types, an approach that recalls the early, pre-Web days of e-mailing different kinds of files back and forth. Each distinct type of data file has a MIME type. In the Web environment, MIME information is often communicated from the Web server to the Web browser for the Web browser to successfully handle the file type coming its way. The use in RealPix is similar. In some circumstances, this optional attribute of `<image/>` can be necessary in successfully receiving an image streamed from a Web server. RealServer is already configured to communicate the proper MIME types, so it is needed only if `<image/>` references a file without a `.gif`, `jpeg`, or `.png` file extension and the `size` attribute is used. To play it safe, always use a proper file extension when naming and referencing a named graphic.

Attribute: `name`

- Version Compatibility: RealPlayer G2 or later
- Possible Values: A valid path and filename

The `name` attribute of the `<image/>` element is a source reference to the image file's location. If your RealPix `.rp` file is located in the same server directory as your images, simply state the filename for each `<image/>`. Likewise, if the image is in a folder called `myfolder`, which is one directory down from your `.rp` file, you could reference it with `<image name="myfolder/myimage.jpg" . . . />`. The slash after `myfolder` indicates that "myfolder" is a folder name. The required `handle` reference has been left out in this example, but you get the general idea.

The path format follows the same basic server references also used by HTML or other languages that reference objects with a path.

Attribute: preroll

- Version Compatibility: RealPlayer G2 or later
- Possible Values: An integer representing seconds

This attribute of the `<head/>` element enables the author to specify a longer than normal preroll time for the RealPix clip. Preroll is the buffering time required before a presentation begins playing. During preroll, the player loads images and other resources it will need for the RealPix presentation. RealPlayer automatically calculates preroll time, so this attribute is necessary only if you need to force the player to compensate for a higher bandwidth object farther along in the timeline. Because preroll can leave the viewer impatiently waiting, it is best to use this attribute with a great deal of caution. It is far better to reduce the bandwidth bottleneck at the image file size itself and avoid excessive prerolling.

Attribute: size

- Version Compatibility: RealPlayer 7
- Possible Values: The size of the file in bytes

If you are streaming your RealPix from a Web server, you can use the size attribute of the `<image/>` element to communicate to RealPlayer how big the image is. Potentially, this attribute can speed up your presentation's buffer time, as RealPlayer tries to determine what is about to be displayed. Size="12000" would indicate that an image is 12KB. size is not needed when using RealServer because the server can determine this information directly by opening the files and calculating the optimal streaming characteristics from there.

Attribute: srcx, srcy, srcw, and srch

- Version Compatibility: RealPlayer G2 or later
- Possible Values: A valid source image coordinate (srcx and srcy) or distance (srcw and srch) measured in pixels

The src in the srcx, srcy, srcw, and srch attributes refers to "source." When using RealPix, no requirement specifies that you use all the original source image you are loading. These attributes determine how much of the source image you want to use in your RealPix presentation. srcx and srcy define the starting point (or source) of where you want to start sampling an image from. srcx is a horizontal coordinate. srcy is a vertical coordinate. The coordinates are measured in pixels from the upper-left corner of the image. A convenient means of finding the coordinates you want to use is with the information palette of an image-editing application such as Photoshop. srcx and srcy work together as a coordinate pair that defines a starting point. With a 100 pixel by 100 pixel image, 0,0 is the upper-left corner and 100,100 is the lower-right corner. Values of srcx="45" and srcy="15" mean that you will use the upper-left corner of your image at a point 45 pixels over from the left side and 15 pixels down from the top.

After you have the upper-left point determined, you need to determine how wide and how far down the image you want to use as the rectangle of your shown image. srcw refers to source width and srch refers to source height. Height can be a little counterintuitive—vertical values get larger the farther down the image you go. You might find it helpful to think of the height value as going down the image. Building on the previous example, values of srcw="100" and srcy="100" mean that you will use the image material within an overall rectangle that goes from 45 pixels from the left of the image and continues to 145 pixels, and then begins at 15 pixels from the top of the image to 115 pixels down.

When source size attributes are used with the destination size attributes (dstx, dsty, dsth, dstw), the author can make an image smaller or larger than normal or display only a selected rectangle of the larger image in RealPlayer.

srcx, srcy, srcw and srch can be used as attributes of the <fadein/>, <crossfade/>, <animate/>, <wipe/>, and <viewchange/> elements.

Attribute: start

- Version Compatibility: RealPlayer G2 or later
- Possible Values: An integer representing time in seconds or milliseconds (depending on the timeformat attribute, covered later in this chapter)

A required attribute in the <fill/>, <fadein/>, <fadeout/>, <crossfade/>, <animate/>, <wipe/>, and <viewchange/> elements, start tells RealPlayer when to begin the effect or transition. Assuming that your timeformat attribute in the <head/> element is set to the days, hours, minutes, and seconds format (dd:hh:mm:ss.xyz), start="3" will begin the effect or transition 3 seconds into the timeline of the RealPix presentation. Similarly, a start time of 1 minute, 35 and 1/2 seconds would be `start="1:35.5"`. Millisecond values are the default if no `timeformat` is specified in the `<head/>` element.

If your `timeformat="dd:hh:mm:ss.xyz"`, a start of 5 seconds applied to a `<fadein/>` element might look like this:

```
<fadein start="5" duration="5" target="3" />
```

The same sample with the `timeformat` left to default to milliseconds would look like this:

```
<fadein start="5000" duration="5000" target="3" />
```

Attribute: `target`

- Version Compatibility: RealPlayer G2 or later
- Possible Values: An integer corresponding to a chosen `<image/>` handle attribute

If you are going to use `<fadein/>`, `<crossfade/>`, `<animate/>`, or `<wipe/>` with an incoming image, you need to tell RealPlayer which image you are transitioning into the display window. The `target` attribute uses the number that corresponds with the `handle` used in the `<image/>` element.

The following RealPix sample shows the use of `target` and the corresponding use of `handle`:

```
. . .
<image handle="1" name="images/myFirst.jpg" />
<image handle="2" name="images/mySecond.jpg" />
. . .
<fadein start="1000" duration="3000" target="1" />
<crossfade start="8000" duration="1500" target="2" />
. . .
```

In this case, the `<fadein/>` effect is linked to `target="1"`. This happens to be the `handle` of an image named and located at a path of my `images/myFirst.jpg`. But just because handles are listed in a RealPix document sequentially, it does not mean that you have to target them sequentially. You could just as easily reverse the `target` usage or use the handles repeatedly out of order:

```
. . .
<image handle="1" name="images/myFirst.jpg" />
<image handle="2" name="images/mySecond.jpg" />
```

```
. . .
<fadein start="1000" duration="3000" target="2" />
<crossfade start="8000" duration="1500" target="1" />
. . .
```

Attribute: timeformat

- Version Compatibility: RealPlayer G2 or later
- Possible Values: milliseconds or dd:hh:mm:ss.xyz

timeformat specifies the time format represented in the start and duration values in RealPix markup. Note that early versions of the G2 player recognized times provided only in milliseconds. Milliseconds is the default value if a timeformat is not specified in a newer RealPlayer.

The following sample shows an example of setting the timeformat:

```
<head timeformat="dd:hh:mm:ss.xyz" />
```

Therefore, if you set the preceding timeformat and wanted an image to fade in at the 10 and 1/2 seconds mark for a duration of 5 seconds, your markup might look like the following sample:

```
<fadein start="10.5" duration="5" target="3" />
```

The same sample with timeformat="milliseconds" would look like this:

```
<fadein start="10500" duration="5000" target="3" />
```

Attribute: title

- Version Compatibility: RealPlayer G2 or later
- Possible Values: Text string

Using the title attribute in the <head/> element enables the author to attach a title that can appear in the RealPlayer window. Just remember that other media objects and the SMIL presentation itself can also have titles that could override your RealPix title.

Attribute: type

- Version Compatibility: RealPlayer G2 or later
- Possible Values: normal, push

Used with the `<wipe/>` effect, the `type` attribute identifies the type of wipe effect that appears onscreen. A `normal` wipe travels across the screen, revealing a new image already positioned in place. A `push` wipe makes the new image seem to travel across the screen and into position in the display window, covering the image underneath it. Sample markup using both wipes is shown next:

```
. . .
<wipe type="normal" direction="up" start="10" duration="2" target="3" />
<wipe type="push" direction="right" start="15" duration="2" target="4" />
. . .
```

Attribute: `url`

- Version Compatibility: RealPlayer G2 or later
- Possible Values: A valid URL

With the `url` attribute, the author can specify a URL that is opened when the user clicks the element the `url` is attached to. When used with the `<head/>` element, clicking the display window opens the specified URL. It can also be used on specific images within the timeline when attached to a corresponding `<fadein/>`, `<crossfade/>`, `<animate/>`, or `<wipe/>` element. The `url` function gains a great deal of power in newer versions of RealPlayer. RealPlayer G2 was limited to one presentation open at a time. Following different URLs in RealPlayer was much like changing channels on a television. You may have a lot of channels, but you can watch only one at a time. With RealPlayer 7 or later, you can use multiple RealPlayer windows with the `url` attribute. This is like having multiple televisions; you can turn a new television on with each channel that you want to watch. With each new `url`, you can open a new RealPlayer window.

In RealPix, creating a link to a Web page that opens when the user clicks the image in the element would use the following form:

```
<fadein url="http://www.smilbook.com/" start="10.5" duration="5"
➥target="3" />
```

However, if you wanted to create a link to another SMIL document or media resource (you might see this as a channel) within the same RealPlayer window, you would use the following form:

```
<fadein url="command:openwindow(_current, rtsp://www.smilbook.com/smil/
➥smil.smi)" start="10.5" duration="5" target="3" />
```

This URL assumes that you are using a RealServer and the RTSP protocol. Here, the `command:openwindow` tells the RealPlayer to open a RealPlayer window, whereas `_current` tells the player to play the following URL in the current window. Similarly, if you wanted to create a link to another SMIL document or media resource in a new RealPlayer window (you might see this as turning on a new television each time you want to watch a new channel), you would use the following form:

```
<fadein url="command:openwindow(_new, rtsp://www.smilbook.com/smil/
➥smil.smi)" start="10.5" duration="5" target="3" />
```

The keyword `_new` (you can also use `_blank`) does the magic in opening a new window. But do not open too many new windows or you might confuse and annoy your viewer.

Use of `url` requires a protocol (such as `http://` or `rtsp://`) in the value because relative URLs are not supported.

The RealText Elements

Because the goal of RealText is streaming hypertext, most elements are based on typical HTML elements. Additional elements allow for such capabilities as positioning text, controlling its appearance in a timeline, making sure that the text is streamed effectively, and clearing the screen.

Element: `<window>`

- Version Compatibility: RealPlayer G2 or later
- Child Elements: `<clear/>`, `<pos/>`, `<required>`, `<time/>`, `<tl>`, `<tu>`, `<b>`, `<br/>`, `<center>`, `<hr/>`, `<i>`, `<li>`, `<ol>`, `<p>`, `<pre>`, `<s>`, `<u>`, `<ul>`, `<font, <href>`
- Possible Attributes: `bgcolor`, `crawlrate`, `duration`, `extraspaces`, `height`, `link`, `loop`, `scrollrate`, `type`, `underline_hyperlinks`, `version`, `width`, `wordwrap`

Like the `<imfl>` tag pair in RealPix, the `<window>` and `</window>` tag pair set up and surround the RealText markup. This is the same as using `<html>` and `<smil>` to set up and surround their respective markup elements. Remember that your RealText instructions sit in their own text document (with an `.rt` file extension). A quick look at a simple RealText shows its basic form:

```
<window height="150" width="150" duration="10">
    First line of text.
    <time begin="2" />This line appears two seconds later.
    <time begin="4" />Followed by this line.
    <time begin="6" />And this line.
    <time begin="8" />And finally this line.
</window>
```

To use your RealText with your SMIL, you simply reference your RealText document as a source URL in your SMIL. If the above text document was named myDemo.rt, your SMIL page might look like this:

```
<smil>
    <head>
        <layout>
            <root-layout height="150" width="150" />
            <region id="myText" left="0" top="0" height="150" width="150" />
        </layout>
    </head>
    <body>
        <par>
            <textstream src="myDemo.rt" region="myText" />
        </par>
    <body>
</smil>
```

It is important to note that you do not always need a SMIL document to use RealText. You can always link to and load the RealText directly into the player.

The <window> attributes set up the environment in which the text will appear. width and height set the size of the space in which the text will appear. duration establishes how long the text component will last. bgcolor establishes the background color for the text display. scrollrate and crawlrate describe the simple vertical or horizontal motion of the text. Text can be repeated with the loop attribute. Other attributes address more obscure situations, such as hyperlink appearance and RealPlayer version support.

Element:

- Version Compatibility: RealPlayer G2 or later
- Possible Attributes: none

The element within a block of text content simply clears all preceding text from the window. Therefore, if you wanted to clear a first line of text before the second line appears, the RealText markup would look something like the following:

```
. . .
<time begin="0" />First line of text.
<time begin="5" /><clear/>Second line of text.
. . .
```

Element:

- Version Compatibility: RealPlayer G2 or later
- Possible Attributes: x, y

This element positions the display of a following text block within the RealText window.

For example, the following sample of RealText markup would position the following text block down 5 pixels and over 10.

```
. . .
<pos y="5" x="10" />
This is the text that will be positioned.
. . .
```

Element: <required>

- Version Compatibility: RealPlayer G2 or later
- Possible Attributes: none

Normally, RealPlayer assesses network conditions and makes sure the RealText is displayed properly. If RealPlayer cannot acquire the streaming text, it will display red ellipses (...). Bracketing your text content between a `<required></required>` tag pair ensures that the RealText is displayed no matter what. If necessary, RealPlayer halts the reception of other media objects until the RealText is received.

Element: <time/>

- Version Compatibility: RealPlayer G2 or later
- Possible Attributes: begin, end

Used with `begin` and `end` attributes, the `<time/>` element tells RealPlayer when the text content will appear and disappear from the window.

Element: `<tu>` and `<tl>`

- Version Compatibility: RealPlayer G2 or later
- Possible Attributes: `color`

When used with a RealText `<window/>` set to the `type` of `tickertape` (explained in "The RealText Attributes" section), these elements control where the text is placed in the tickertape. In most stock market tickers, the top line shows the company symbol and the bottom line shows the monetary value or change. Placing your text between `<tu>` and `</tu>` puts the text at the top (upper side) of the `tickertape` window. Placing your text between `<tl>` and `</tl>` puts the text at the bottom (lower side) of the `tickertape` window. The default color for text wrapped by a `<tu>` element is white. The default color for text in a `<tl>` element is green. Adding a color attribute within the opening `<tu>` or `<tl>` tag enables the author to specify a different color than the default colors. An example follows:

```
. . .
<tu>The upper text in default white</tu>
<tl color="red">The lower text in author specified red</tl>
. . .
```

Element: `<b>`

- Version Compatibility: RealPlayer G2 or later
- Possible Attributes: none

Like HTML, this element makes text enclosed between the `<b>` and `</b>` tag pair bold.

Element: `<br/>`

- Version Compatibility: RealPlayer G2 or later
- Possible Attributes: none

Like HTML, this element creates a line break so that text following a `<br/>` is placed one line lower.

Element: `<center>`

- Version Compatibility: RealPlayer G2 or later
- Possible Attributes: none

Like HTML, this element makes text enclosed between the `<center>` and `</center>` tag pair centered in the display area.

Element: `<hr/>`

- Version Compatibility: RealPlayer G2 or later
- Possible Attributes: none

Available for HTML compatibility, this element creates the appearance of two line breaks (`<br/>`) without drawing the implied horizontal rule.

Element: `<i>`

- Version Compatibility: RealPlayer G2 or later
- Possible Attributes: none

Like HTML, this element makes text enclosed between the `<i>` and `</i>` tag pair italicized.

Element: `<li>`

- Version Compatibility: RealPlayer G2 or later
- Possible Attributes: none

Available for HTML compatibility, this element creates the appearance of one line break (`<br/>`) between the `<li>` and `</li>` tag pair.

Examine the following sample from RealText:

```
. . .
<li>This is a of text</li>
This is a line of text<br/>
. . .
```

Each line of text in the preceding sample functions the same way. Both the `<li>` tag pair and the `<br/>` tag create a line return down to the next line.

Element: `<ol>`

- Version Compatibility: RealPlayer G2 or later
- Possible Attributes: none

Available for HTML compatibility, this element indents the text between the `<ol>` and `</ol>` tag pair but does not number it.

Element: `<p>`

- Version Compatibility: RealPlayer G2 or later
- Possible Attributes: none

Like HTML, this element creates a paragraph from text enclosed between the `<p>` and `</p>` tag pair.

Element: `<pre>`

- Version Compatibility: RealPlayer G2 or later
- Possible Attributes: none

Like HTML, text between the `<pre>` and `</pre>` tag pair is displayed in a mono-space font with extra spaces preserved.

Element: `<s>`

- Version Compatibility: RealPlayer G2 or later
- Possible Attributes: none

Like HTML, this element makes text enclosed between the `<s>` and `</s>` tag pair appear with a strikethrough line through it.

Element: `<u>`

- Version Compatibility: RealPlayer G2 or later
- Possible Attributes: none

Like HTML, this element makes text enclosed between the `<u>` and `</u>` tag pair underlined.

Element: `<ul>`

- Version Compatibility: RealPlayer G2 or later
- Possible Attributes: none

Available for HTML compatibility, this element indents the text between the `<ul>` and `</ul>` tag pair but does not show bullets.

Element: `<font>`

- Version Compatibility: RealPlayer G2 or later
- Possible Attributes: `bgcolor`, `charset`, `color`, `face`, `size`

Putting your text content between `<font>` and `</font>` enables you to set font characteristics such as background color, the character set, the font `color`, the font `face`, and its `size`.

Element: `<href>`

- Version Compatibility: RealPlayer G2 or later
- Possible Values: A valid URL, `command:`, `mailto:`, *`protocol:path`*, `target`

Set up like the traditional hyperlinking in HTML, using the `<href>` element enables the author to create a hypertext link to another Web resource. The author can also use `<href>` to pass commands to RealPlayer and target specific RealPlayer windows. The following sections cover the possible `<href>` values.

The RealText Attributes

The Web multimedia author will find the majority of RealText attributes identical to their use in traditional HTML. Notable exceptions are the attributes that control when text appears in the display or how it moves across the display.

Attribute: `begin` **and** `end`

- Version Compatibility: RealPlayer G2 or later
- Possible Values: A time formatted in `hh:mm:ss.xy`

These attributes, used with the `<time/>` element, tell RealPlayer when your text will appear or disappear in the display timeline. It uses the `hh:mm:ss.xy` time format, but you do not have to include every unit of time in your value. For example, to begin showing text at a minute and a half into the timeline, use `begin="1:30"`. To begin at 10 and 1/2 seconds, use `begin="10.5"`.

Attribute: `bgcolor`

- Version Compatibility: RealPlayer G2 or later
- Possible Values: A 24-bit hexadecimal color value, a predefined color name, or `transparent`

Used with the opening `<window>` element and the `<font>` element, the `bgcolor` attribute defines the color for the RealText window. Acceptable values follow the HTML conventions for 24-bit hexadecimal color (for example, white is `#FFFFFF`) or predefined names (black is `black`). A value of `transparent` allows the text to "float" over other material.

Attribute: `charset`

- Version Compatibility: RealPlayer G2 or later (supported set determined by RealText version number and the player itself)
- Possible Values: A supported character set identifier, currently `us-ascii`, `iso-8859-1`, `mac-roman`, `x-sjis`, `gb2312`, `big5`, `iso-2022-kr`

This attribute of the `<font>` element sets the displayed character set for the RealText in RealPlayer. `us-ascii` is a standard U.S.-based ASCII set. `iso-8859-1` is similar to `us-ascii` but supports additional characters used by European languages. `mac-roman` supports those additional European accents on the Macintosh. `x-sjis` supports Kanji and Osaka fonts. `gb2312` supports simplified Chinese, `big5` supports traditional Chinese, and `iso-2022-kr` supports Korean. The current default set for RealPlayer 7 or later is the internationally aligned `iso-8859-1`.

Attribute: `color`

- Version Compatibility: RealPlayer G2 or later
- Possible Values: A 24-bit hexadecimal color value or a predefined color name

Used with the <font> element, color sets the color of the text in the display window. Acceptable values follow the HTML conventions for 24-bit hexadecimal color (for example, white is #FFFFFF) or predefined names (black is black).

Attribute: command:

- Version Compatibility: RealPlayer G2 or later
- Possible Values: pause(), play(), seek(*time*)

When used with <href>, the command: attribute tells the link to issue a command to the targeted RealPlayer window. command:pause() pauses the player when the text link is clicked, and command:play() tells the targeted RealPlayer window to play. command:seek() with a time value inside the parentheses seeks the player to that time. In this use, href="command:seek(02:25)" seeks the player to a point 2 minutes and 25 seconds into the presentation in the targeted RealPlayer window.

Attribute: crawlrate and scrollrate

- Version Compatibility: RealPlayer G2 or later
- Possible Values: A number representing pixels per second

These attributes of the <window/> element set the horizontal or vertical text speed, measured in pixels per second. crawlrate sets the horizontal text speed and scrollrate sets the vertical text speed. The default value for all <window/> types is 0. The exception for the crawlrate of tickertape and marquee are the default values of 20. The exception for the scrollrate of scrollingnews is the default value of 10.

Attribute: duration

- Version Compatibility: RealPlayer G2 or later
- Possible Values: A time represented in hh:mm:ss.xy

This attribute of <window/> tells RealPlayer how long your RealText presentation will be. It uses the hh:mm:ss.xy time format but, like begin, you do not have to use all units of time. For example, a duration of a minute and a half would be duration="1:30", but a duration of 10 and 1/2 seconds would be duration="10.5". The default value is 60 seconds.

Attribute: extraspaces

- Version Compatibility: RealPlayer G2 or later
- Possible Values: use, ignore

The extraspaces attribute of the <window/> element tells RealPlayer to use or ignore any extra spaces that appear in the RealText. Some authors might use extra spaces to help arrange the text display in the RealPlayer window. The default value is use.

Attribute: face

- Version Compatibility: RealPlayer G2 or later
- Possible Values: For the us-ascii and iso-8859-1 character sets, legal fonts include Algerian, Arial, Arial Black, Arial Narrow, Arial Rounded Mt Bold, Book Antiqua, Bookman Old Style, Braggadocio, Britannic Bold, Brush Script, Century Gothic, Century Schoolbook, Colonna Mt, Comic Sans Ms, Courier, Courier New, Desdemona, Fixedsys, Footlight Mt Light, Garamond, Geneva, Haettenschweiler, Helvetica, Impact, Kino Mt, Matura Mt Script Capitals, Modern, Ms Dialog, Ms Dialog Light, Ms Linedraw, Ms Sans Serif, Ms Serif, Ms Systemex, Playbill, Small Fonts, System, Terminal, Times, Times New Roman, Verdana, Wide Latin

Used with the <font> element, face specifies the font face to be used with the given character set. If a font is not available, a suitable fallback of Courier, Geneva, Helvetica, or Times is used by the playback system.

Attribute: height or width

- Version Compatibility: RealPlayer G2 or later
- Possible Values: A valid display height or width as measured in pixels

Used with the opening <window> element, the height and width attributes define the pixel height and width of the display window that the RealText should appear in. This area may or may not be a smaller subsection of the overall player display area.

Attribute: `link`

- Version Compatibility: RealPlayer G2 or later
- Possible Values: A 24-bit hexadecimal color value or a predefined color name

This attribute of `<window/>` sets the color for all hyperlinks in RealText. The default value is `blue`.

Attribute: `loop`

- Version Compatibility: RealPlayer G2 or later
- Possible Values: `true`, `false`

The `loop` attribute of the `<window/>` element turns text looping on and off. With text looping set as `true`, the text repeats in the display window. The default value for the `tickertape` and `marquee` `<window/>` types is `true`. All other types have a default value of `false`.

Attribute: `mailto:`

- Version Compatibility: RealPlayer G2 or later
- Possible Values: A legal e-mail address

Used with an `<href>` hyperlink, `mailto:` plus a legal e-mail address launches an e-mail program with a message intended for the specified address. This attribute is the same as a `mailto:` link in HTML.

Attribute: *protocol:path*

- Version Compatibility: RealPlayer 8 or later
- Possible Values: A legal protocol value followed by a colon and a legal URL path

The *protocol:path* approach is actually a value of an `<href>` link, not an attribute. For RealText presentations set to `version="1.5"` or later, this value format enables the author to link to a specific protocol type and URL path in the link. This attribute can be useful for creating a link to FTP, Telnet, or instant-messaging environments.

An example of a hyperlink that sends an AOL instant message to the screen name of "onlndlvry" is shown next:

```
<a href="aim:goim?screenname=onlndlvry">Send Instant Message</a>
```

Attribute: `size`

- Version Compatibility: RealPlayer G2 or later
- Possible Values: HTML-type font size instructions, such as 1, 2, 3, 4, 5, 6, 7 or -2, -1, +0, +1, +2, +3, +4

This attribute of `<font>` sets the font size using HTML-type conventions. The default value is +0. Font sizes tend to be relative to the viewer because of varying monitor display settings, but you can expect that a relative size of -2 (absolute size of 1) is going to appear as about 12 points in size. +0 (an absolute size of 3) is about 16 pixels in size. At the high extreme, a +4 (absolute size of 7) is about 48 pixels in size.

Attribute: `target`

- Version Compatibility: RealPlayer G2 or later
- Possible Values: `_player`, `_browser`

Used with an `<href>`, `target` tells RealPlayer to open a link in a Web browser or in the player itself. A value of `_player` is used to link to the player. A value of `_browser` will link to the Web browser. If you do not specify a target, RealPlayer opens the link in a Web browser.

Attribute: `type`

- Version Compatibility: RealPlayer G2 or later
- Possible Values: `generic`, `scrollingnews`, `teleprompter`, `marquee`, `tickertape`

Used with the opening `<window>` element, the `type` attribute defines the type of RealText behavior you want displayed. `generic`, the default window type value, displays basic normal text. `scrollingnews` scrolls the text up at an author-specified rate for the length of the presentation. This text first appears at the top of the established text display space before scrolling additional text into the display. `teleprompter` immediately fills the display area with text and then pushes text off the top as new text appears at the bottom. marquee crawls text in a line from right to left. It appears vertically centered within a text display area. tickertape behaves like marquee but places the text at the top or bottom of the display window. By enclosing the text between <tu> or <tl> elements, you can make it appear in the upper or lower portion of the tickertape window.

Attribute: underline_hyperlinks

- Version Compatibility: RealPlayer G2 or later
- Possible Values: true, false

The underline_hyperlinks attribute of the <window/> element specifies whether hyperlinks show an underline. The default setting of true is the setting that underlines hyperlinks.

Attribute: version

- Version Compatibility: RealPlayer 7 or later
- Possible Values: 1.0, 1.2, 1.4, 1.5, 1.6

Starting with RealPlayer 7, the version attribute of the <window/> element made it possible to identify the version of the RealText language the player needed to support. Auto update in RealPlayer can make sure that the correct software is available to make the text appear in its proper form. Versioning is important when dealing with other character sets (especially those with accented characters). With 1.0, the default character set for RealText is us-ascii. With 1.2, the default character set was changed to iso-8859-1, which matches the us-ascii set but adds accented characters used in European languages. Version 1.4 gained the iso-2022-kr Korean character set. Version 1.5 supports hyperlinks using the *protocol:path* format. 1.6 is used when adding RealText to SMIL 2.0 RealPlayer presentations.

Attribute: wordwrap

- Version Compatibility: RealPlayer G2 or later
- Possible Values: true, false

Used with the opening <window> element, wordwrap turns word wrapping on or off in RealText. The default setting is true (which turns word wrapping on).

Attribute: x and y

- Version Compatibility: RealPlayer G2 or later
- Possible Values: A valid x (horizontal) or y (vertical) pixel coordinate within the display area

Both of these attributes are used with the <pos/> element to position the following text block. The value of x is measured from the left side of the window. The y value is measured from the top of the window.

In action, use of the x and y attributes of the <pos/> element would look something like the following markup sample:

```
. . .
<pos x="30" />
<pos y="15" />
    Position this text.
. . .
```

In the preceding example, the text will be positioned 30 pixels from the left of the window and 15 pixels down from the top. You could also combine the attributes in one element, as follows:

```
. . .
<pos x="30" y="15" />
    Position this text.
. . .
```

RealPix and RealText Summarized

Although RealPix and RealText are not true SMIL, they are proprietary SMIL-based streaming picture and text formats that reinforce SMIL presentations in RealPlayer. Should the SMIL author use them? Even though we are firm believers in authoring to a standard, the Web multimedia market is still sorting itself out. If your audience is primarily RealPlayer users—the majority of people using Web multimedia—RealText and RealPix are very useful tools.

All that said, keep an eye on SMIL developments that begin to address the need for RealText and RealPix. With newer RealPlayers, RealPix is beginning to drop into the background in place of SMIL 2.0 capabilities. With RealText, however, this proprietary format will be useful for the near future.

Part III

Using SMIL: The Projects

15

SMIL in RealPlayer

If you had to pick a favorite player or browser for most SMIL authors, the most likely candidate would be RealPlayer by RealNetworks. As the first major player to support SMIL, RealPlayer has grown in capability with each passing release. It has kept up with the SMIL language and has a huge installed user base across multiple platforms. The latest release, RealONE, provides a full range of SMIL 2.0 support.

SMIL Through the RealPlayers

The first RealPlayer to support SMIL was called RealPlayer G2. As shown in Figure 15.1, appearance offered no doubt that G2 had its heart in being a stand-alone player. By this point in the development of RealPlayer, the plucky little streaming-media player already supported streaming audio, video, and Flash animation. What G2 offered was a coordinated assault on the problem of Web-based multimedia. Most streaming players could support one format at a time, but with addition of SMIL support in RealPlayer G2, now a way existed to offer the viewer multiple media types at the same time.

Figure 15.1   *G2 looks and feels like a media player.*

SMIL 1.0 support in RealPlayer G2, like the language itself, was extremely simple. By mastering the concepts of <seq> and <par> markup elements, most RealPlayer G2 authors were well on their way to offering basic but compelling Web multimedia presentations. Throw a little <layout> in, and Web multimedia authors could put the multimedia anywhere they wanted on the screen.

One of the most interesting aspects of RealPlayer G2 was its support of two proprietary SMIL-based authoring languages called RealPix and RealText. RealPix supported and organized streaming images. It created a number of basic but powerful effects within the RealPlayer itself. The immediate advantage is that these effects were enacted on the media client side, which meant that bandwidth-heavy encoding of visual transitions did not have to be included in the stream. Even in dial-up modem use, RealPix could be used to create a relatively sophisticated visual presentation.

RealPlayer G2 also offered RealText. Few things are lower in bandwidth require-ments than text. Being able to format and display text without having to burn it into a heavy image file gave RealPlayer G2 an even greater advantage in a low bandwidth world. This streaming hypertext also opened the door to a future RealPlayer that would be a full Web browser.

That is exactly the gradual transition that happened. Later versions of RealPlayer gained a URL line, a Search button, and the capability to have multiple player windows open at the same time. About the only thing keeping RealPlayer from working like a Web browser was a lack of support of HTML. The ninth version of RealPlayer is called the RealONE Player. As shown in Figure 15.2, RealONE Player supports all the features of a Web browser and then some.

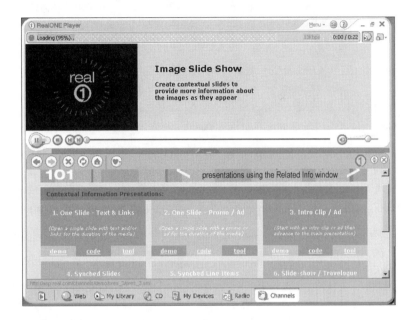

Figure 15.2   *RealONE is an integrated Web multimedia browser and entertainment package.*

Piggybacking off the capabilities of Internet Explorer in the Windows environment, RealONE Player is a full-featured Web presentation environment. What this means for the Web multimedia author is the capability to develop sophisticated and seamless Web-based presentations.

One final note: Both .smi and .smil are legal extensions for SMIL files, and both will be interpreted by the RealPlayers. However, Real has recently issued a recommendation that the extension .smil is used for SMIL presentations crafted for the RealPlayers. We have used .smi in this tutorial, but in the future, it may be wise to follow Real's recommendation and use the .smil extension.

The Catch

If a catch exists to authoring SMIL in RealONE Player, it is that the player is a major revision in the RealPlayer software. That is what you would expect from a player that has gained a whole new set of SMIL 2.0 features.

As a designer or developer of Web multimedia content, this means that the new player will be a little experimental for a while. Features will gradually settle in and the player will eventually do what you expect it to when giving it a SMIL 2.0 instruction. In the meantime, be prepared to be creative and flexible if you find that RealONE Player does not work exactly as expected.

Unlike its other major competitors, RealONE Player is a very mature SMIL 2.0 implementation. RealPlayer G2 was there first and RealNetworks has continually honed its capabilities. Web multimedia authors who want to focus on RealNetworks will find that they can easily choose how cutting edge they want to be in their streaming multimedia.

Tutorial Goals

The following tutorial is offered on our book Web site: `http://www.SMILBook.com`. You should play the tutorial, titled `main.smi`, and familiarize yourself with its source code before continuing on in this chapter. It is designed to play in the RealNetworks RealONE Player or later. Some portions of the markup, particularly the RealPix and RealText files, will play in RealPlayer G2 or later.

Because of the depth of capabilities in RealPlayer, providing an all-encompassing tutorial is a bit of a challenge. To highlight both older and newer approaches to delivering content for RealPlayer, this tutorial will demonstrate a project that is a bit contrived in its mix between older established SMIL 1.0-based RealPlayer G2 support and newer SMIL 2.0 RealONE Player support. In some situations, you might find the G2 capabilities of RealPlayer easier to use and more reassuring. In some cases, you might want to push the edge a bit and try something new.

This tutorial creates a short interactive presentation for a fictional travel company. It opens with a short Flash animation, followed by the display of three clickable regions that lead to multimedia presentations. A RealPix path shows the more established capabilities of RealPlayer G2. A SMIL 2.0-based streaming-image path shows the same type of material as could be authored for RealONE Player.

A RealMedia video path is also offered. All make use of transitions. This interactivity is powered by the new SMIL 2.0 <excl> element, which allows only one child element to be played at a time and imposes no sequential order. Its only concern is that only one element plays at a time. If an element begins to play while another element is playing, the new element takes charge and the old element is paused or stopped. This makes creating our interactivity much easier.

Building the Plan

Before we begin, let's take a look at what it is that we are building and the purpose behind it. The presentation we are about to construct is designed to advertise a tour marketed by a fictional travel company we've called "Villa Travel." The multimedia aspect of this marketing effort is meant to ignite enough interest in viewers that they would choose to sign up for the tour. We want to use our images, video, and sound to immerse viewers in the type of environment they would experience on this tour, so we will attempt to craft it in this manner.

As a side note, after the support files for this tutorial were created, we discovered that a real-life Villa Travel exists. The materials included here are not related to this real-life agency and are not meant as either an endorsement or advertisement for that company. Let's get underway with our planning.

As a multimedia author, I classify myself as a tinkerer. I work at most presentations one step at a time. That way, if the presentation suddenly stops working, I have a pretty good idea what went wrong. It's also a good idea to make frequent and incremental saves of your SMIL files. That way, in a worst-case scenario, you can always go back to something that should work. Authoring SMIL by hand takes time. It's only made worse when a machine gets cranky and corrupts a file.

However, even though I like to tinker at my multimedia, I also know that I can save time by planning. For that, I usually use a digital imaging tool such as Adobe Photoshop. In Photoshop, as shown in Figure 15.3, I can practice the visual look and arrange the content on layers that will mimic my final SMIL presentation. I usually start with a screenshot of the player environment itself. On top of this background file, I pull source media and begin arranging. If I wanted to, Photoshop would enable me to precisely position each element in my presentation. But as I said earlier, I like to tinker. So with my visual plan printed out, it's dead reckoning for me.

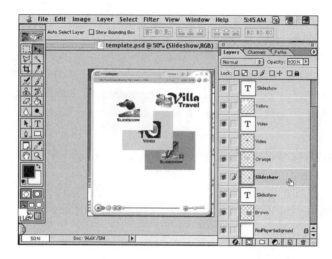

Figure 15.3 *Adobe Photoshop is perfect for designing the look and feel of the site before you even get to writing any SMIL.*

SMIL Namespace and Structure

My first step is to set up the overall structure of the SMIL presentation. Using a text editor, I rough in the structure in a text file called main.smi:

```
<smil xmlns="http://www.w3.org/2001/SMIL20/Language"
➥xmlns:rn="http://features.real.com/2001/SMIL20/Extensions">
    <head>
    </head>
    <body>
    </body>
</smil>
```

At this point, the document looks very much like an HTML file. Only the <smil> tags make it look different. What probably jumps out the most is the namespace declaration:

```
<smil xmlns="http://www.w3.org/2001/SMIL20/Language"
xmlns:rn="http://features.real.com/2001/SMIL20/Extensions">
```

The first namespace declaration lets the player know that this is a SMIL 2.0 document. The second namespace declaration enables support for special features that are specific to RealONE Player. Depending on what you make use of that is proprietary to a RealNetworks player, you may or may not need the second name-space reference. If the secondary namespace is not recognized by previous RealPlayers, it won't create any conflict; I put it in just to have it covered if it's needed.

Adding the Metainformation

Thankfully for me, metainformation support in RealONE Player is still pretty basic. My next code adds the metainformation between the two <head> tags:

```
. . .
<head>
    <meta name="title" content="Villa Travel Glass Blowing Trip" />
    <meta name="author" content="Tim Kennedy, Online Delivery" />
    <meta name="copyright" content="(c) Images and Video: Mary Slowinski,
➥ Music: Joodle Music/ASCAP" />
    <meta name="abstract" content="A multimedia look at Villa Travel's
➥ trip through glass blowing factories." />
    </head>
. . .
```

Here, the title, author, copyright, and abstract identifies the presentation to the outside world. In RealONE Player, some of this information will appear in the player title bar as the presentation plays. Where this info appears depends on the version of RealPlayer and the platform on which it is viewed.

Creating the Layout

One of the most critical sections in the <head> of a SMIL document belongs to <layout>. It is here that you tell the player exactly where you want your content to sit. It is here that my Photoshop plan for my presentation becomes extremely helpful. Using the plan as a guide, I drop the pixel measurements into the layout (lines 9–13). Notice that I add the layout information directly after the meta-information (line 8).

```
1: . . .
2: <head>
3:     <meta name="title" content="Villa Travel Glass Blowing Trip" />
4:     <meta name="author" content="Tim Kennedy, Online Delivery" />
5:     <meta name="copyright" content="(c) Images and Video: Mary Slowinski,
➥ Music: Joodle Music/ASCAP" />
6:     <meta name="abstract" content="A multimedia look at Villa Travel's
➥ trip through glass blowing factories." />
7:
```

```
 8:      <layout>
 9:           <root-layout width="500" height="400" backgroundColor=
➥"white" />
10:           <region id="flash" width="400" height="200" left="50"
➥top="100" backgroundColor="white" z-index="1" />
11:           <region id="rp" width="196" height="152" left="25" top="50"
➥z-index="2" />
12:           <region id="vid" width="196" height="152" left="150" top="125"
➥z-index="3" />
13:           <region id="img" width="196" height="152" left="275" top="200"
➥z-index="4" />
14:        <regPoint id="centered" regAlign="center" left="50%" top="50%" />
15:      </layout>
16: </head>
17: . . .
```

Most of the layout markup is almost the same in SMIL 1.0 and SMIL 2.0. The
<layout> tag pair wraps up our layout instructions within the <head>. Then comes
the <root-layout> in line 9:

```
<root-layout width="500" height="400" backgroundColor="white" />
```

The <root-layout> establishes the overall width and height of the RealPlayer
or RealONE Player window. Within this area, all visual content appears. In this
case, the playing space will be 500 pixels wide by 400 pixels tall. Because I plan to
lay out my work on a white field, backgroundColor="white" does just that for me.

Lines 10–14 are the individual named regions within the overall display area.
Let's look at line 11 as an example:

```
<region id="rp" width="196" height="152" left="25" top="50" z-index="2" />
```

A region can be as large as the <root-layout> or any size smaller. Each region is
given an id so that content can be placed in that region by name. The width and
height of the region is given in pixels. Because this region is smaller than the
<root-layout>, I also provide a starting point down from the top edge and over
from the left edge of the <root-layout>. Finally, it is possible for regions to
overlap. Because of this, SMIL supports a z-index. This is the vertical layering
of the document. Larger numbers "float" above smaller numbered layers in the
layout. Thus, in the following markup, my img region in line 13 sits above my
vid layer in line 12:

```
<region id="vid" width="196" height="152" left="150" top="125" z-index="3" />
<region id="img" width="196" height="152" left="275" top="200" z-index="4" />
```

A new `<layout>` element for SMIL 2.0 is `<regPoint>`. With `<regPoint>`, I can establish a point in any region to which I want to align content. In my example, I want to use smaller images and video than my individual regions. Within those regions, I want to center my content. So I declare a `<regPoint>` as follows:

```
<regPoint id="centered" regAlign="center" left="50%" top="50%" />
```

The `id` attribute names the `<regPoint>` so that I can call on it at will. My `regAlign` attribute tells the player that I want the object centered on the `<regPoint>`. Precisely placed, that means 50% down from the `top` and 50% over from the `left` edge of the region.

Adding the Flash Animation

Now that I have my `<layout>` built, it is time to figure out what content goes in that design. My first media object is an animation I have previously prepared in Macromedia Flash. The animation serves as an interesting "hook" for viewers and gets them interested in the tour immediately. I reference that clip with an `<animation>` element between the `<body>` tags:

```
. . .
<body>
    <par dur="indefinite">
        <animation src="animation/VillaFlash.swf" begin="00:00.0" region=
➥"flash" fill="remove" />
    </par>
</body>
. . .
```

The `src` attribute provides a path to where the file sits on the server. `begin="00:00.0"` starts the animation at the beginning of the presentation. `region="flash"` puts that animation in the previously established flash region in the `<head>` element. `fill="remove"` tells the player to remove the animation from the screen after it has completed it run. I use a `<par>` element to provide my first container for my animation because I know I will be adding more content shortly. Because I am building a menu that will play indefinitely, I set the duration for that value.

Painting the Screen with `<brush>`

My layout design calls for a splash of color here and there. I could go at this in several ways, including dropping the color into the `<region>` elements themselves.

But this is a great chance to try out the new `<brush>` element offered by SMIL 2.0. Directly after the `<animation>` element in the `<par>` element established earlier, I add several lines of code:

```
. . .
<par dur="indefinite">
    <animation src="animation/VillaFlash.swf" begin="00:00.0"
➡ region="flash" fill="remove" />
    <brush id="rp1" color="#FFFFCC" begin="00:05.5"
➡ region="rp" fill="hold" />
    <brush id="vid1" color="#FFCC66" begin="00:06.5"
➡ region="vid" fill="hold" />
    <brush id="img1" color="#CC9966" begin="00:07.5"
➡ region="img" fill="hold" />
. . .
```

These three `<brush>` elements paint three colored squares onscreen that fill the dimensions of the regions they are attached to. Web-safe colors, based on the Villa Travel company logo, are represented in standard Web hexadecimal. All three of these `<brush>` elements run in parallel with the Flash animation added earlier. However, with slightly different `begin` times, the three colored blocks will drop onscreen in a staggered fashion. Because I need these colored elements to stay onscreen for the rest of the presentation, I use a `fill="hold"` to hold them onscreen until the container ends. Because `<par dur="indefinite">`, the time container will never end and the colored blocks will stay onscreen indefinitely.

Adding `<transition>`

Dropping my colored `<brush>` blocks on the screen without any kind of transition gets boring in a hurry. I have already gone to the trouble to stagger their timing. Now I want to emphasize that with `<transition>`. My first step is to determine what `<transition>` type I want to use. You might want to consult Chapter 9, "From This to That: The Transition Effects Module," for a range of available transition effects. You can also consult the RealNetworks online documentation at the corporate Web site (`http://www.realnetworks.com/resources/`). I am in the mood for a slide wipe, so my first step is to enable and label the wipe `<transition>` in the `<head>` of the document:

```
. . .
<transition id="leftSlide" type="slideWipe" subtype="fromLeft" />
</head>
. . .
```

The id attribute labels the wipe so that I can call it from within any media element
I want. type and subtype identify the precise type of transition wipe I am using.
In this case, I am calling a digital slide wipe that will move in from the left side
of the region the media content sits in. Note that the attributes can be listed in
any order that is convenient for you as the author; playback is not affected by the
order of the attributes.

With the wipe identified, calling it is easy in SMIL. I use transIn to make that
wipe transition into the content. The code for the incoming transitions on my
<brush> elements looks like the following:

```
. . .
<par dur="indefinite">
    <animation src="animation/VillaFlash.swf" begin="00:00.0"
➡ region="flash" fill="remove" />
    <brush id="rp1" color="#FFFFCC" transIn="leftSlide" begin="00:05.5"
➡ region="rp" fill="hold" />
    <brush id="vid1" color="#FFCC66" transIn="leftSlide" begin="00:06.5"
➡ region="vid" fill="hold" />
    <brush id="img1" color="#CC9966" transIn="leftSlide" begin="00:07.5"
➡ region="img" fill="hold" />
. . .
```

Now the colored blocks wipe onto the screen. You can see the visual result in
Figure 15.4.

I want to make use of several transition types during my presentation. Personally,
I wouldn't use too many. But because this is a tutorial and a demonstration, I go
back and enable several additional variations for future use. You will find our old
friend leftSlide hanging out in the middle:

```
. . .
    <transition id="upSlide" type="slideWipe" subtype="fromBottom" />
    <transition id="ellipse" type="ellipseWipe" subtype="horizontal" />
    <transition id="leftSlide" type="slideWipe" subtype="fromLeft" />
    <transition id="fadeBrown" type="fade"
➡subtype="fadeToColor" fadeColor="#CC9966"/>
    <transition id="fadeOrange" type="fade"
➡subtype="fadeToColor" fadeColor="#FFCC66"/>
</head>
. . .
```

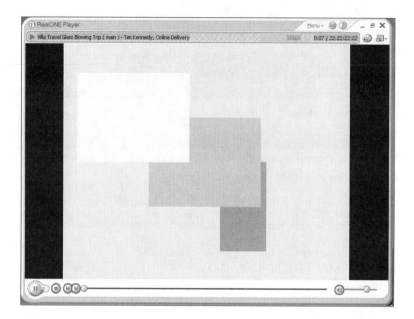

Figure 15.4 *Using <brush> and <transition>, I can wipe the colored squares into their planned background location.*

You can choose from a wide variety of transitions with SMIL 2.0 (see Chapter 9 for more information). The transitions also have been given subtypes to identify the exact effect that is desired. Here I have a mixture of wipes and fades. In slideWipe transitions, the destination media moves but the background does not; the effect is that the destination media is "sliding" across the background media. In this case, the subtype attribute determines that the slide will occur from the bottom of the region upward or from the left edge of the region, respectively. ellipseWipe transitions reveal the incoming media from the center out; subtype=horizontal indicates that the egg-shaped center will be elongated horizontally. fadeToColor will blend my graphics into the color declared here; I've matched the selected colors to those established by the <brush> elements. The effect will be that the graphics will fade into the same colors originally established in the regions using the <brush> element.

I now have the entire beginning of the SMIL document almost done. Before we move on, let's take a brief glimpse at the growing markup. The <head> section (line 2) contains the metainformation about the presentation (lines 3–6) and the graphical layout for the screen display (lines 8–15). The <head> section continues with the named transitions (lines 17–21), which will be called by their id attributes later in the document. The <body> section, which we have just begun to construct, so far directs the presentation to begin with the Flash animation (line 27) playing in parallel with the three regions filled with color using the <brush> element (lines 28–30). So far, so good.

```
 1: <smil xmlns="http://www.w3.org/2001/SMIL20/Language"
➥ xmlns:rn="http://features.real.com/2001/SMIL20/Extensions">
 2:     <head>
 3:         <meta name="title" content="Villa Travel Glass Blowing Trip" />
 4:         <meta name="author" content="Tim Kennedy, Online Delivery" />
 5:         <meta name="copyright" content="(c) Images and Video: Mary
➥ Slowinski, Music: Joodle Music/ASCAP" />
 6:         <meta name="abstract" content="A multimedia look at Villa Travel's
➥ trip through glass blowing factories." />
 7:
 8:         <layout>
 9:             <root-layout width="500" height="400"
➥ backgroundColor="white" />
10:             <region id="flash" width="400" height="200" left="50"
➥ top="100" backgroundColor="white" z-index="1" />
11:             <region id="rp" width="196" height="152" left="25" top="50"
➥ z-index="2" />
12:             <region id="vid" width="196" height="152" left="150" top="125"
➥ z-index="3" />
13:             <region id="img" width="196" height="152" left="275"
top="200"
➥ z-index="4" />
14:         <regPoint id="centered" regAlign="center" left="50%" top="50%" />
15:         </layout>
16:
17:     <transition id="upSlide" type="slideWipe" subtype="fromBottom" />
18:     <transition id="ellipse" type="ellipseWipe" subtype="horizontal" />
19:       <transition id="leftSlide" type="slideWipe" subtype="fromLeft" />
20:     <transition id="fadeBrown" type="fade" subtype="fadeToColor"
➥ fadeColor="#CC9966"/>
21:     <transition id="fadeOrange" type="fade" subtype="fadeToColor"
➥ fadeColor="#FFCC66"/>
22:     </head>
23:
24:
25:     <body>
26:         <par dur="indefinite">
27:             <animation src="animation/VillaFlash.swf" begin="00:00.0"
➥ region="flash" fill="remove" />
28:                 <brush id="rp1" color="#FFFFCC" transIn="leftSlide"
➥ begin="00:05.5" region="rp" fill="hold" />
29:                 <brush id="vid1" color="#FFCC66" transIn="leftSlide"
➥ begin="00:06.5" region="vid" fill="hold" />
```

```
30:                    <brush id="img1" color="#CC9966" transIn="leftSlide"
➥begin="00:07.5" region="img" fill="hold" />
31: . . .
```

Building the RealPix File

The beginning of my `main.smi` SMIL document is built. I need to put it aside and look into other issues. First, I need to take a moment and build a G2-capable RealPix file.

RealPix is written into its own text file the same as SMIL is. The difference is the elements and attributes used. But as a SMIL-based language, RealPix will feel reasonably comfortable by now. If not, take a closer look at Chapter 14, "SMIL That Isn't SMIL: RealNetworks's RealPix and RealText," which covers various RealPix elements and attributes.

I have six images that I am going to display in 30 seconds. To keep the markup easier to understand, I'm not going to get terribly fancy in my timing. The six images are titled blow.jpg, casting.jpg, glasscast.jpg, glasshead.jpg, glasspour.jpg and gloryhole.jpg; they can be found in the images directory alongside the `main.smi` document.

I start with a new text file that I name `blowpix.rp`. The first markup takes the following form:

```
<imfl>
<head timeformat="dd:hh:mm:ss.xyz" duration="30" width="176" height="132"
➥background-color="#FFFFCC" bitrate="23000" title="Glass blowing" author=
➥"Tim Kennedy" copyright="(c) Images by Mary Slowinski, Music by Joodle
➥Music" />
</imfl>
```

All RealPix sits between a pair of <imfl> tags, the same as all SMIL sits between <smil> tags. The <head> element sets up all the traditional information about the presentation, including title and copyright. But when used with a SMIL presentation, this information is not necessarily seen by viewers unless they go hunting for it.

`timeformat="dd:hh:mm:ss.xyz"` sets the time format for the remaining time references in the RealPix file. Because a seconds format is easier to understand than the default milliseconds, it is a good idea to set it in the <head>. Most of the other attributes follow the same SMIL conventions we have previously discussed, with the exception of bitrate. With most streaming-media formats, the bitrate for the data stream is encoded with the file. Streaming images are different. The author establishes the bitrate for streaming RealPix. So a little math is in order.

My streaming music, which will soon be added into the code of the main.smi document, was encoded at 11Kbps. I'm going to run that at the same time as my streaming images. Let's assume that I am preparing a RealPix presentation for a 56Kbps modem. RealNetworks suggests using 34Kbps as a bitrate mark to shoot for. This assumes that not all modems hit 56Kbps (they don't) and that some administrative overhead is required by the modem to function. 34Kbps is a pretty safe number for a 56Kbps stream. Therefore, if my music is using 11Kbps, that leaves 23Kbps left for the RealPix (34–11=23). bitrate="23000" is the bits per second equivalent for 23Kbps.

Loading the Images into RealPix

With the <head> of the RealPix document taken care of, I now load and identify my images to the RealPix document:

```
<imfl>
    <head timeformat="dd:hh:mm:ss.xyz" duration="30" width="176" height="132"
➥background-color="#FFFFCC" bitrate="23000" title="Glass blowing" author=
➥"Tim Kennedy" copyright="(c) Images by Mary Slowinski, Music by Joodle
➥Music" />
    <image handle="1" name="images/blow.jpg" />
    <image handle="2" name="images/casting.jpg" />
    <image handle="3" name="images/glasscast.jpg" />
    <image handle="4" name="images/glasshead.jpg" />
    <image handle="5" name="images/glasspour.jpg" />
    <image handle="6" name="images/gloryhole.jpg" />
. . .
```

Each <image> element has a handle and a name, as shown next:

```
<image handle="1" name="images/blow.jpg" />
```

handle is the unique sequential numeric identifier for an image. It is the RealPix equivalent of an id in SMIL. name is the path to the image on the server. It is the RealPix equivalent of a src attribute in SMIL. Now, I've got six images ready to go.

Fades and Crossfades in RealPix

Like SMIL transitions, RealPix supports a variety of fade and wipe effects. We see these in action in the last half of the RealPix file, which picks up right where we left off:

```
. . .
<fill start="0" color="#FFFFCC" />
<fadein start="1" duration="2" target="1" />
<crossfade start="5" duration="2" target="2" />
<crossfade start="10" duration="2" target="3" />
<crossfade start="15" duration="2" target="4" />
<crossfade start="20" duration="2" target="5" />
<crossfade start="25" duration="2" target="6" />
<fadeout start="28" duration="2" color="#FFFFCC" />
</imfl>
```

The first effect is the `fill` that starts the screen with a colored rectangle that will match one of the colored `<brush>` rectangles I set up in the SMIL document. `start="0"` tells the player to start with the colored rectangle at the beginning of the presentation. The `fill` is followed by a `fadein`, which begins one second after the presentation is begun:

```
<fadein start="1" duration="2" target="1" />
```

This `fadein` fades the first graphic in (`target="1"` corresponds to the graphic labeled `handle="1"`). The attribute `duration="2"` instructs the player to take two seconds to complete the transition. This graphic will then remain onscreen until the start time indicated by the following `crossfade`:

```
<fadein start="1" duration="2" target="1" />
<crossfade start="5" duration="2" target="2" />
```

Five seconds into the presentation, the image with `handle="1"` will dissolve or crossfade into the image with `handle="2"` and take two seconds to do so. In this manner, the `start` time of each subsequent effect determines how long the previous image is displayed onscreen. The end of the presentation comes with a `fadeout`:

```
<crossfade start="25" duration="2" target="6" />
<fadeout start="28" duration="2" color="#FFFFCC" />
```

The last image, known as `handle="6"` in the earlier RealPix markup, will fade out to the same color that we faded in from.

The Final RealPix

The final RealPix will play in RealPlayer or RealONE Player as a standalone document or as part of a larger SMIL presentation. The entire contents of `blowpix.rp` are as follows:

```
<imfl>
<head timeformat="dd:hh:mm:ss.xyz" duration="30" width="176" height="132"
➥background-color="#FFFFCC" bitrate="23000" title="Glass blowing" author=
➥"Tim Kennedy" copyright="(c) Images by Mary Slowinski, Music by Joodle
➥Music" />
<image handle="1" name="images/blow.jpg" />
<image handle="2" name="images/casting.jpg" />
<image handle="3" name="images/glasscast.jpg" />
<image handle="4" name="images/glasshead.jpg" />
<image handle="5" name="images/glasspour.jpg" />
<image handle="6" name="images/gloryhole.jpg" />
<fill start="0" color="#FFFFCC" />
<fadein start="1" duration="2" target="1" />
<crossfade start="5" duration="2" target="2" />
<crossfade start="10" duration="2" target="3" />
<crossfade start="15" duration="2" target="4" />
<crossfade start="20" duration="2" target="5" />
<crossfade start="25" duration="2" target="6" />
<fadeout start="28" duration="2" color="#FFFFCC" />
</imfl>
```

With the RealPix text file saved to the same directory as my main.smi SMIL file,
I'm ready to get back to business with the SMIL.

Referencing the RealPix in the SMIL

Now that I have my RealPix created, I can reference it in my SMIL, as shown in
the markup that follows:

```
<body>
    <par dur="indefinite">
        <animation src="animation/VillaFlash.swf" begin="00:00.0"
➥ region="flash" fill="remove" />
        <brush id="rp1" color="#FFFFCC" transIn="leftSlide"
➥ begin="00:05.5" region="rp" fill="hold" />

        <brush id="vid1" color="#FFCC66" transIn="leftSlide"
➥ begin="00:06.5" region="vid" fill="hold" />
        <brush id="img1" color="#CC9966" transIn="leftSlide"
➥ begin="00:07.5" region="img" fill="hold" />
        <par>
            <img src="blowpix.rp" region="rp" regPoint="centered" />
            <audio src="audio/piano.rm" />
        </par>
. . .
```

I plan to use my RealPix with a RealMedia streaming-audio file that adds some background music to the presentation. Because these two pieces need to run parallel with each other, I wrap them in a pair of <par> tags, as shown in the closer look at the markup that follows:

```
<par>
    <img src="blowpix.rp" region="rp" regPoint="centered" />
    <audio src="audio/piano.rm" />
</par>
```

Because the RealPix file is saved to the same directory as the SMIL file itself, I simply name the blowpix.rp file in the src attribute. region="rp" will put that in the region labeled rp. regPoint="centered" will put that RealPix aligned with the centered regPoint I set up earlier in the <layout>. Notice that this set of <par> tags is nested within the <par> tags we established earlier. The nesting of <par> and <seq> tags can be done as much as is necessary to create the presentation sequence desired.

Adding the Video

With the RealPix firmly planted in the first region, it is time to put the RealMedia video file into the second region called vid. Like our other media, the video contains footage of scenes the customer would experience on this tour and is intended to further entice the viewer into purchasing the tour package. Let's look at the code for this:

```
. . .
<par>
    <img src="blowpix.rp" region="rp" regPoint="centered" />
    <audio src="audio/piano.rm" />
</par>

<par>
    <video src="video/glassblow.rm" region="vid"
➡ transIn="ellipse" transOut="fadeOrange" regPoint="centered"
➡ fill="remove" />
</par>
```

Like the earlier RealPix file, I use the regPoint="centered" to center the video within the larger region colored by <brush>. Unlike the RealPix, which has its own internal fadeout, my video needs some transitions added to it. I use one of the transitions already coded into the <head> section—an ellipse transIn—to transition the video into the presentation, and another—one of the fade-out to color transitions—to transOut from the video at the end. fill="remove" removes the video from the region after the transition is over. This keeps it from flashing back up on the screen after the fade-out.

RealPix Without RealPix

Eventually, SMIL will replace RealPix for most RealONE Player authors. This was not possible with SMIL 1.0, but is achievable with SMIL 2.0 because of the additional modules that allow for transitions and timing. My third region uses this new SMIL 2.0 syntax and is filled with images and background music using the following parallel container:

```
. . .
<par>
    <audio src="audio/guitar.rm" />
    <seq>
        <img src="images/overhead.jpg" transIn="upSlide" dur="5"
➥ region="img" regPoint="centered" fill="transition">
            <param name="bitrate" value="2300"/>
        </img>
        <img src="images/paw.jpg" transIn="upSlide" dur="5" region="img"
➥ regPoint="centered" fill="transition">
            <param name="bitrate" value="23000"/>
        </img>
        <img src="images/smoke.jpg" transIn="upSlide" dur="5" region="img"
➥ regPoint="centered" fill="transition">
            <param name="bitrate" value="23000"/>
        </img>
        <img src="images/studio.jpg" transIn="upSlide" dur="5"
➥ region="img" regPoint="centered" fill="transition">
            <param name="bitrate" value="23000"/>
        </img>
        <img src="images/torch.jpg" transIn="upSlide" dur="5"
➥ region="img" regPoint="centered" fill="transition">
            <param name="bitrate" value="23000"/>
        </img>
        <img src="images/wheel.jpg" transIn="upSlide" transOut=
➥ "fadeBrown" dur="5" region="img" regPoint="centered" fill="transition"  >
            <param name="bitrate" value="23000"/>
        </img>
    </seq>
</par>
. . .
```

At first glance, this code appears to be a lot busier than it actually is. Early on, the <audio> and src establish the link to yet another music file. Being in a parallel block, this music file is set to run in parallel with the nested <seq> container. Each item within the <seq> container will play, as you should expect, in sequence. Therefore, the images sequentially play while the music plays in parallel with all of them.

A closer look at an <img> element in the preceding sample shows a few other tricks:

```
. . .
<img src="images/smoke.jpg" transIn="upSlide" dur="5" region="img"
↪regPoint="centered" fill="transition">
    <param name="bitrate" value="23000"/>
</img>
. . .
```

In this sample, we have the transition effects discussed earlier. The effects of all the transitions rival RealPix. But RealPix also establishes bitrate. Notice that the <img> tag does not end with a trailing forward slash (/). Instead, it breaks out to a tag pair to wrap a <param> element, which will establish a bitrate. Like the RealPix, the value is put at 23Kbps (or 23000 bps). Also notice yet another use of fill. fill="transition" holds the current image onscreen until the transition to the next content item is complete.

Interactivity with <excl>

The <excl> (exclusive) is a powerful new addition to SMIL 2.0 that makes building interactivity much easier than with SMIL 1.0. I now have three <par> time containers that each put content in their respective regions. But I want only one region to play at a time, and I want to be able to choose those regions by clicking them. First, I need to wrap all three <par> time containers with one set of <excl> tags, as shown next:

```
<excl dur="indefinite">
    <par id="yellow">
        <img src="blowpix.rp" region="rp" regPoint="centered" />
        <audio src="audio/piano.rm" />
    </par>

    <par id="orange">
        <video src="video/glassblow.rm" region="vid" transIn="ellipse"
↪transOut="fadeOrange" regPoint="centered" fill="remove" />
    </par>
```

```
    <par id="brown">
        <audio src="audio/guitar.rm" />
        <seq>
            <img src="images/overhead.jpg" transIn="upSlide" dur="5"
➥ region="img" regPoint="centered" fill="transition">
                <param name="bitrate" value="2300"/>
            </img>
            <img src="images/paw.jpg" transIn="upSlide" dur="5"
➥ region="img" regPoint="centered" fill="transition">
                <param name="bitrate" value="23000"/>
            </img>
            <img src="images/smoke.jpg" transIn="upSlide" dur="5"
➥ region="img" regPoint="centered" fill="transition">
                <param name="bitrate" value="23000"/>
            </img>
            <img src="images/studio.jpg" transIn="upSlide" dur="5"
➥ region="img" regPoint="centered" fill="transition">
                <param name="bitrate" value="23000"/>
            </img>
            <img src="images/torch.jpg" transIn="upSlide" dur="5"
➥ region="img" regPoint="centered" fill="transition">
                <param name="bitrate" value="23000"/>
            </img>
            <img src="images/wheel.jpg" transIn="upSlide" transOut=
➥ "fadeBrown" dur="5" region="img" regPoint="centered" fill="transition"  >
                <param name="bitrate" value="23000"/>
            </img>
        </seq>
        </par>
</excl>
```

A couple of things should be noted about <excl>. The time containers within the <excl> will play only one at a time. And because there is no established parallel or sequential time line to an <excl> container, there is no inherent duration to the container. By setting the duration as indefinite, I make sure the <excl> stays functioning (and waiting for user input) indefinitely.

Now I just need the <excl> interactive. I use a click action tied to the original <brush> elements I painted on the screen earlier. The <brush> element with an id of vid1 looks like this:

```
. . .
<brush id="vid1" color="#FFCC66" transIn="leftSlide" begin="00:06.5"
➥region="vid" fill="hold" />
. . .
```

If I want to make this area clickable, I simply reference the `id` in the element I want to play when clicked:

```
. . .
<par id="orange" begin="vid1.activateEvent">

    <video src="video/glassblow.rm" region="vid" transIn="ellipse"
➥ transOut="fadeOrange" regPoint="centered" fill="remove" />
</par>
. . .
```

With RealONE Player, `begin="vid1.activateEvent"` means that the connected parallel container will begin to play when the object labeled `id="vid1"` sends an `activateEvent` message, which is really just a mouse click. This is the familiar dot syntax approach that is detailed in Chapter 7, "Grouping Your Content: The SMIL Timing and Synchronization Module."

When one container within an `<excl>` starts playing, all the peer containers at the same level stop playing by default. Unfortunately, I have to force some child elements to also behave. In the third `<par>` group inside our `<excl>` element, I add some attributes as follows:

```
. . .
<par id="brown" begin="img1.activateEvent">
    <audio src="audio/guitar.rm" />
    <seq end="vid1.activateEvent; rp1.activateEvent">
        <img src="images/overhead.jpg" transIn="upSlide" dur="5"
➥ region="img" regPoint="centered" fill="transition">
            <param name="bitrate" value="2300"/>
        </img>
. . .
```

Notice the `<seq>` element. It carefully uses a set of `end` values to force the sequence to end when other elements are clicked:

```
<seq end="vid1.activateEvent; rp1.activateEvent">
```

This makes sure that only one container object at a time will be playing onscreen.

Keep in mind that the RealONE player is essentially still in its infancy. This presentation plays without problems in the player I am using to author; however, you may see some inconsistencies in playback depending on the version of the RealONE player you are using. Be sure to check your presentation on as many versions of the player that you can get your hands on, and try it on multiple platforms if possible. In any case, expect to tinker with the code as the RealONE player matures.

Bringing Regions to the Top

After an object in the stack plays, it would be nice to put it front and center. But if we look at our layers, we very quickly see that some layers are behind others.

Using <set>, I can animate a region to a new z-index. This will make the playing layer stand out in front. I've added the following code to the second <par> element inside our <excl> element to achieve this:

```
. . .
<par id="orange" begin="vid1.activateEvent">
    <set targetElement="vid" attributeName="z-index" to="4"/>
    <set targetElement="rp" attributeName="z-index" to="2"/>
    <set targetElement="img" attributeName="z-index" to="3"/>
    <video src="video/glassblow.rm" region="vid" transIn="ellipse"
➥transOut="fadeOrange" regPoint="centered" fill="remove" />
</par>
. . .
```

It is a little touch, but it does enhance the user experience.

Labeling the "Buttons"

Each display region doubles as a button or link to the multimedia presentations. But how does the audience know what they will get if they choose an area? To solve this problem, I slide an additional <par> block between the set of preexisting <excl> tags, which in turn will slide some transparent GIF graphics over the established color blocks:

```
. . .
<excl dur="indefinite">
    <par begin="00:09.0" >
        <img src="images/pour.gif" transIn="rightSlide" region="rp"
➥ regPoint="centered" fill="hold" >
            <param name="bitrate" value="23000"/>
        </img>
        <img src="images/heating.gif" transIn="rightSlide" region="vid"
➥ regPoint="centered" fill="hold" >
            <param name="bitrate" value="23000"/>
        </img>
        <img src="images/bigguy.gif" transIn="rightSlide" region="img"
```

```
➥regPoint="centered" fill="hold"  >
            <param name="bitrate" value="23000" />
        </img>
    </par>
. . .
```

This batch of images, which slide in after the Flash animation at 9 seconds, puts a label on each of the three regions. As with other media elements, I've added `id` attributes and declared the region in which they should be displayed. Each image will slide in from the right edge of the region and use the `regPoint` attribute to align in the center of the region. The `fill` attribute declares that the images should stay in place, and the `<param>` element dictates how much of the available bandwidth should be allocated to the load of the images. Because these are transparent GIF images, the background color of the region will show through.

Adding the Logo

Another nice (and important) touch is to add the company logo. I simply insert another `<img>` reference directly after the original `<brush>` statements:

```
. . .
<brush id="rp1" color="#FFFFCC" transIn="leftSlide" begin="00:05.5"
➥ region="rp" fill="hold" />
<brush id="vid1" color="#FFCC66" transIn="leftSlide" begin="00:06.5"
➥ region="vid" fill="hold" />
<brush id="img1" color="#CC9966" transIn="leftSlide" begin="00:07.5"
➥ region="img" fill="hold" />
<img src="images/smVillalogo.gif" transIn="leftSlide" begin="00:08.0"
➥ region="logo" fill="hold" />
. . .
```

Like the `<brush>` elements, the logo will slide onscreen and `hold` indefinitely.

Creating the RealText

The presentation is almost complete. I save my `main.smi` file and go off for one more short diversion. I have all my pictures in place, but I need to add descriptive text to the presentation. Like RealPix, RealText is a standalone text file that can either play separately or as part of a larger SMIL presentation. Next, I open a text editor and create a new text file named `text.rt`. The contents hold the following HTML-like markup:

```
<window>
<font face="Arial" size="5"><b>All About</b></font><br>
<font face="Impact" size="6">Glass!</font><br>
<font face="Arial" size="3"><b>Feel the heat on your face<br>
and don't forget your gloves.<br>
We tour the best glass studios<br>
in all of North America.</b><br></font><br>
<font face="Impact" size="5">$1999/person - (555) 555-1234</font>
</window>
```

This is about as simple as RealText gets. I simply put HTML-like markup between two <window> tags. RealText is capable of more, as shown in Chapter 14. I can time text or make it appear in different visual styles, like tickertape. But this text will be sufficient for this demonstration.

Dropping in the RealText

With the RealText completed, I need to reference it in the presentation. I drop the reference in right after <brush> and the company logo by using a <textstream/> element:

```
. . .
<brush id="rp1" color="#FFFFCC" transIn="leftSlide" begin="00:05.5"
➥ region="rp" fill="hold" />
<brush id="vid1" color="#FFCC66" transIn="leftSlide" begin="00:06.5"
➥ region="vid" fill="hold" />
<brush id="img1" color="#CC9966" transIn="leftSlide" begin="00:07.5"
➥ region="img" fill="hold" />
<img src="images/smVillalogo.gif" transIn="leftSlide" begin="00:08.0"
➥ region="logo" fill="hold" />
<textstream src="text.rt" begin="00:08.0" region="text" fill="hold" />
. . .
```

After I test the presentation on several machines (and if possible, on whatever versions of the RealPlayer I can find), I am ready to put my files on a server. Before we do that, let's take a moment to view what we've accomplished so far. You can sample the presentation from the Web site at http://www.SMILBook.com/. By now, the rather complex SMIL 2.0 document shown in Listing 15.1 should seem pretty comfortable.

Listing 15.1

```
 1: <smil xmlns="http://www.w3.org/2001/SMIL20/Language"
➥ xmlns:rn="http://features.real.com/2001/SMIL20/Extensions">
 2:     <head>
 3:         <meta name="title" content="Villa Travel Glass Blowing Trip" />
 4:         <meta name="author" content="Tim Kennedy, Online Delivery" />
 5:         <meta name="copyright" content="(c) Images and Video: Mary
➥ Slowinski, Music: Joodle Music/ASCAP" />
 6:         <meta name="abstract" content="A multimedia look at Villa
➥ Travel's trip through glass blowing factories." />
 7:
 8:         <layout>
 9:             <root-layout width="500" height="400"
➥ backgroundColor="white" />
10:             <region id="flash" width="400" height="200" left="50"
➥ top="100" z-index="1" />
11:             <region id="rp" width="196" height="152" left="25" top="50"
➥ z-index="4" />
12:             <region id="vid" width="196" height="152" left="150"
➥ top="125" z-index="3" />
13:             <region id="img" width="196" height="152" left="275"
➥ top="200" z-index="2" />
14:         <region id="logo" width="170" height="81" left="300" top="40"
➥ z-index="5" />
15:         <region id="text" width="300" height="175" left="25" top="225"
➥ z-index="1" />
16:         <regPoint id="centered" regAlign="center" left="50%" top="50%" />
17:         </layout>
18:
19:   <transition id="upSlide" type="slideWipe" subtype="fromBottom" />
20:   <transition id="ellipse" type="ellipseWipe" subtype="horizontal" />
21:   <transition id="rightSlide" type="slideWipe" subtype="fromRight" />
22:       <transition id="leftSlide" type="slideWipe" subtype="from
➥ Left" />
23:   <transition id="fadeBrown" type="fade" subtype="fadeToColor"
➥ fadeColor="#CC9966"/>
24:   <transition id="fadeOrange" type="fade" subtype="fadeToColor"
➥ fadeColor="#FFCC66"/>
25:     </head>
26:
27:
28:     <body>
29:         <par dur="indefinite">
30:             <animation src="animation/VillaFlash.swf" begin="00:00.0"
➥ region="flash" fill="remove" />
31:                 <brush id="rp1" color="#FFFFCC" transIn="leftSlide"
➥ begin="00:05.5" region="rp" fill="hold" />
32:                 <brush id="vid1" color="#FFCC66" transIn="leftSlide"
➥ begin="00:06.5" region="vid" fill="hold" />
33:                 <brush id="img1" color="#CC9966" transIn="leftSlide"
➥ begin="00:07.5" region="img" fill="hold" />
```

Listing 15.1   Continued

```
34:            <img src="images/smVillalogo.gif" transIn="leftSlide" begin=
➥ "00:08.0" region="logo" fill="hold" />
35:               <textstream src="text.rt" begin="00:08.0" region="text"
➥ fill="hold" />
36:
37:            <excl dur="indefinite">
38:
39:          <par begin="00:09.0" >
40:              <img src="images/pour.gif" transIn="rightSlide"
➥ region="rp" regPoint="centered" fill="hold" >
41:                  <param name="bitrate" value="23000"/>
42:              </img>
43:              <img src="images/heating.gif" transIn="rightSlide"
➥ region="vid" regPoint="centered" fill="hold" >
44:                  <param name="bitrate" value="23000"/>
45:               </img>
46:                 <img src="images/bigguy.gif" transIn="rightSlide"
➥ region="img" regPoint="centered" fill="hold"  >
47:                  <param name="bitrate" value="23000" />
48:               </img>
49:          </par>
50:
51:
52:          <par id="yellow" begin="rp1.activateEvent">
53:             <set targetElement="rp" attributeName="z-index" to="4"/>
54:             <set targetElement="vid" attributeName="z-index" to="3"/>
55:             <set targetElement="img" attributeName="z-index" to="2"/>
56:             <img src="blowpix.rp" region="rp" regPoint="centered" />
57:             <audio src="audio/piano.rm" />
58:          </par>
59:
60:          <par id="orange" begin="vid1.activateEvent">
61:             <set targetElement="vid" attributeName="z-index" to="4"/>
62:             <set targetElement="rp" attributeName="z-index" to="2"/>
63:             <set targetElement="img" attributeName="z-index" to="3"/>
64:             <video src="video/glassblow.rm" region="vid"
➥ transIn="ellipse" transOut="fadeOrange" regPoint="centered"
➥ fill="remove" />
65:          </par>
66:
67:
68:          <par id="brown" begin="img1.activateEvent">
69:             <set targetElement="rp" attributeName="z-index" to="2"/>
70:             <set targetElement="vid" attributeName="z-index" to="3"/>
71:             <set targetElement="img" attributeName="z-index" to="4"/>
72:             <audio src="audio/guitar.rm" />
73:             <seq end="vid1.activateEvent; rp1.activateEvent">
74:                 <img src="images/overhead.jpg" transIn="upSlide"
```

Listing 15.1   Continued

```
↪dur="5"
↪ region="img" regPoint="centered" fill="transition">
 75:                        <param name="bitrate" value="23000"/>
 76:                   </img>
 77:                   <img src="images/paw.jpg" transIn="upSlide" dur="5"
↪region="img" regPoint="centered" fill="transition">
 78:                        <param name="bitrate" value="23000"/>
 79:                   </img>
 80:                   <img src="images/smoke.jpg" transIn="upSlide" dur="5"
↪region="img" regPoint="centered" fill="transition">
 81:                        <param name="bitrate" value="23000"/>
 82:                   </img>
 83:                   <img src="images/studio.jpg" transIn="upSlide" dur="5"
↪region="img" regPoint="centered" fill="transition">
 84:                        <param name="bitrate" value="23000"/>
 85:                   </img>
 86:                   <img src="images/torch.jpg" transIn="upSlide" dur="5"
↪region="img" regPoint="centered" fill="transition">
 87:                        <param name="bitrate" value="23000"/>
 88:                   </img>
 89:                   <img src="images/wheel.jpg" transIn="upSlide"
↪transOut="fadeBrown" dur="5" region="img" regPoint="centered"
↪fill="transition"  >
 90:                     <param name="bitrate" value="23000"/>
 91:                   </img>
 92:                   <brush color="#CC9966" region="img" fill="hold"/>
 93:                   <img src="images/bigguy.gif" region="img"
↪regPoint="centered" fill="hold"  >
 94:                     <param name="bitrate" value="23000" />
 95:                   </img>
 96:                 </seq>
 97:              </par>
 98:         </excl>
 99:
100:          </par>
101:
102:      </body>
103:
104: </smil>
```

Putting It on a Web Server

The most accessible place for most people to put their RealPlayer and RealONE
Player SMIL files is on a traditional Web server. This can be a little tricky at first.
But it is easier than it first appears.

Like most streaming multimedia formats, RealMedia is more of an Internet technology than a Web technology. Because of this, a traditional Web browser needs to be told how to handle all these strange files that come its way, which is done with a RAM file.

The RAM file works as a stand-in and contains little more than the real URL to the first RealMedia file. When you write a link on a Web page, you write it to the RAM file. When the RAM file loads, it creates a handoff between the Web browser and the RealONE player. The RealONE player loads the RAM file, discovers the true location of your first RealMedia file (which is our SMIL file) and proceeds normally from there.

To create a RAM file, you need to create a file with a text editor. It is often helpful to name this file the same base name as your SMIL file; the difference is in the file extension. Instead of .smi or .smil, you use .ram. So if I am creating a RAM file for my main.smi SMIL file, I use main.ram for my RAM file.

There isn't a lot in the RAM file. No HTML. No SMIL. Just the absolute URL of where my SMIL file sits on the Web server. Thus, because it is the only text in my RAM file, I might type:

```
http://www.SMILBook.com/tutorials/main.smi
```

I then close that file and put it on the Web server along with my SMIL files. In a Web page, I write a link to the RAM file, as in the following:

```
<a href="http://www.SMILBook.com/tutorials/main.ram">A link</a>
```

That's all there is to it. After the SMIL file loads into RealONE Player, it takes over from there and loads the other supporting files as needed.

Serving your RealMedia content from a Web server is convenient, but it is typically not as efficient at delivering content as a true RealServer. Thankfully, the task on a RealServer is much easier.

Putting It on a RealServer

RealNetworks's RealServers come with a built-in RAM file generator called RAMGEN. This completely eliminates the need to link to a RAM file. To use RAMGEN, you pass the RealServer port number and RAMGEN command right in your link.

The URL for the file will now begin with "rtsp" instead of "http" to reflect the type of protocol used by Real (more information on streaming protocols is included in Chapter 2, "SMIL Authoring." Suppose you have a file that sits at the following URL:

```
rtsp://www.SMILBook.com/tutorials/main.smi
```

Next, after checking with the server system administrator, I would add the RealServer port number. Often this port will be something like 7070, which is the port we will use for our example. However, if you are loading your presentation onto a RealServer, be sure to check with the system administrator to determine the correct port number. Last, I add the RAMGEN command to that URL:

```
rtsp://www.SMILBook.com:7070/RAMGEN/tutorials/main.smi
```

Put into a Web page, the link looks like this:

```
<a href="rtsp://www.SMILBook.com:7070/RAMGEN/tutorials/main.smi">A
➥ link</a>
```

That is all there is to it. The RealServer receives the Web-based link and the RAMGEN command. It dynamically generates a RAM file for the location listed. Assuming that you have given it the right URL, your SMIL file loads up and begins to play.

{Note}

One important note is necessary on this tutorial. Not all versions of RealServer automatically support Flash. That is usually a value-added feature. You should talk with the server administrator and find out what is allowed by your version of RealServer.

The Final Presentation

With the last features installed and the files posted on the server, the final SMIL 2.0 markup for the RealNetworks RealONE Player is complete and the presentation is as shown in Figure 15.5.

Even with the rapid growth of Microsoft Internet Explorer as a SMIL browser, the RealNetworks RealONE Player is still the champion SMIL browser. With solid SMIL 1.0 support built in and SMIL 2.0 support rapidly developing, RealONE Player is ready for almost anything SMIL has to offer.

Figure 15.5   *The completed SMIL 2.0 presentation in the RealNetworks RealONE Player.*

16

SMIL in Internet Explorer

Working with SMIL in Microsoft Internet Explorer is addictive. Even when you consider the limitations inherent to the environment, this SMIL implementation is fun to work with and exciting to see.

Microsoft was originally a part of the effort that created SMIL 1.0. However, Microsoft's philosophy toward SMIL is different from most other implementations. Microsoft was not looking for implementation of SMIL within its Web multimedia player. Microsoft's goal was to incorporate SMIL within the Web browser itself.

Within months of the release of the SMIL 1.0 Recommendation, Microsoft and other industry partners offered a new proposal to the SMIL effort. Called Timed Interactive Multimedia Extensions for HTML (HTML+TIME for short), the new approach put a SMIL-like language in with the HTML. The HTML+TIME approach was initially offered in the Windows version of Internet Explorer 5.

Microsoft rejoined the SMIL effort as the 2.0 version of the language was drafted. At this point, HTML+TIME became XHTML+TIME, HTML+SMIL, or XHTML+SMIL, depending on which party you might be talking to. XHTML+SMIL, reflecting the XML changes in HTML and the official adoption of the approach into SMIL, is probably the most politically correct and generic name for the approach. But no matter what name you use, the end goal was the same: adding SMIL to the Web browser environment. For the sake of simplicity, I'll continue to use Microsoft's original name of HTML+TIME.

Internet Explorer 5.5 was one of the very first implementations of what was then the SMIL Boston draft. It offered behaviors in the Web browser that Microsoft referred to as *time2*. Internet Explorer offered additional support for such critical features as transitions.

The Catch

This growth in features from one browser to the next creates a bit of a catch for the author who wants to implement SMIL in Internet Explorer. The changes in the HTML+TIME implementation from 5.0 to 5.5 and 6.0 are significant enough to make any Web multimedia author nervous. As a Web multimedia author, you are taking big chances if you expect your audience to have the latest Web multimedia player. If they don't, you are taking big chances if you believe they will think that your content is important enough to download the latest player.

Now take a step back and assume we are not talking a small Web multimedia player but instead an entire browser. Although Web authors and developers change browsers constantly, the average public does not. To many, the Web browser is still this mystical thing that their ISP once gave them, and they are sticking to it.

Now take a step back further. Microsoft supports only HTML+TIME in its Windows versions of its browser. This is not a small market by any means. But in a competitive Web market, turning away business because the user does not have the "right" browser is stupid arrogance and commercial suicide.

So where can you use HTML+TIME? Obviously, you can detect the Web browser and feed a page designed for Internet Explorer. The more you can automate this approach, the more practical this solution is. If you have a closed intranet where all the machines accessing the content meet a standard right down to the version of the browser, you could roll out HTML+TIME content across an entire corporation. In such a closed environment with established learning labs where employees go for regular training, HTML+TIME becomes a very powerful solution.

The Beauty

Despite all the limitations, there is a beauty to SMIL in Internet Explorer that is hard to ignore. As Web multimedia players make the transition to Web multimedia browsers, Internet Explorer is already ahead of the game with an established browser that supports a variety of technologies. SMIL in Internet Explorer some-times feels more graceful than solving those same multimedia problems with other technologies. Although I firmly believe in cross-platform Web sites, I still feel drawn in by the capabilities that Internet Explorer offers.

About This Tutorial

The following tutorial is offered on our book Web site: `http://www.SMILBook.com`. You should play the tutorial and familiarize yourself with its source code before continuing on this chapter. It is designed to play in the Windows version of Microsoft Internet Explorer 6 and later.

No single tutorial can address every capability of HTML+TIME in Internet Explorer. Likewise, any language typically offers multiple approaches that can be used to address the same multimedia problem. This tutorial emphasizes the transition and animation functions of Internet Explorer. Occasionally, I use different approaches to redundant problems so that you can see some of the variations allowed. Finally, the form of the markup leaves something to be desired. The focus here is markup oversimplification and clarity. Many additional standard Web page elements, such as image sizing, for example, are intentionally omitted.

With that in mind, this tutorial (as shown in Figure 16.1) creates a very short Web advertisement for a European trip package, the Art and Architecture Tour, offered by a fictional travel company called Villa Travel. The presentation features transitions between still images and text and adds in some background music. After completing the work on the support files for the tutorial section of this book, we discovered that a real-world Villa Travel actually exists. Our sample presentation is not meant as an endorsement or advertisement for this company; instead, it is intended only as an example of SMIL and its capabilities.

It uses a number of images and one audio track. It focuses on the transitions and timing of the elements on the screen. As with any HTML+TIME presentation, it could be embellished with additional HTML, images, media, JavaScript, and links to outside resources.

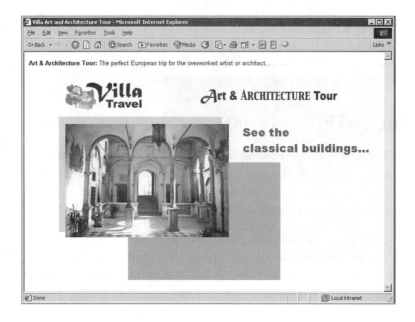

Figure 16.1 *You can create a short and compelling SMIL presentation easily with HTML+TIME in Internet Explorer.*

My approach to this tutorial will be a bit gradual. It is possible to figure out all your pieces in advance and slap the bulk of the page together in one shot. But I write markup like most people put up a Christmas tree. First I stand the tree up and make sure it will not fall over. Then I put up one ornament at time and make sure it works in its location. I build a presentation the same way. I establish the structure and then put each element into the presentation one piece at a time. I make gradual and sequentially named saves of the document I am authoring. When working with SMIL and HTML+TIME in particular, it is quite easy to make an authoring mistake or discover an undocumented "feature." Working in steps will make it easier to backtrack and fix the problem.

Planning the Presentation

Before I begin to write any code, I need to first consider the desired end result of my efforts and then craft the presentation accordingly. As mentioned previously, we are creating a short Web advertisement for a European Art and Architecture

Tour offered by our fictitious travel agency Villa Travel. Because the main goal of the presentation is to attract clients, I'll first choose some engaging images that represent the highlights of such a tour. Because of the short duration of the presentation, I choose four images that represent the art, architecture, and beauty of Europe and place the images in a loose sequence. Then, putting on my copywriter's cap, I craft a few phrases to add continuity to the presentation and provide information about Villa Travel and how to contact them. Knowing that they will be needed, I also grab an image of Villa Travel's logo and create a title graphic containing the name of the tour; both of these can be resized if necessary. Finally, I choose some background music.

Visually, this rough draft appears as follows: The presentation begins with the logo of Villa Travel. The word "presents" is then displayed, followed by the image that contains the title of the tour. When the word "presents" is first displayed onscreen, the background music begins. Several other images follow, and then a succession of text blocks and images begins. Each text block or phrase is preceded by an image that illustrates the following text. The text blocks state "See the classical buildings…/…the sculpture…/…the cathedrals…/…the beauty./See the best art and architecture Europe has to offer./$3599 per person 555-555-1234."

Now that I have a rough idea of what I want to put into the presentation, I have to determine how I want to place it on the screen.

Roughing Out the Page

As shown in Figure 16.2, I usually start by roughing out the presentation page in an image editing program such as Adobe Photoshop. This enables me to get a rough feel for the overall look of the page and specifically where the elements will sit. It also enables me to think through the various layers that will appear in the presentation. Even if you don't start with an electronic layout, a quick sketch on a piece of paper will still put you ahead of the game as you create your presentation. If you go this route, you may later decide to turn to an imaging software program to determine exact pixel measurements for your layout, if you are so inclined. I myself prefer to tinker.

At this stage, I also determine that I will need a large logo and a small one, as well as a small tour title graphic and a large one. I go ahead and create this now.

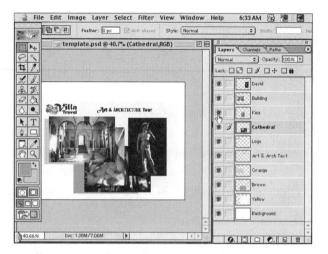

Figure 16.2 *Planning your work in a layered graphics tool such as Photoshop can save considerable time in authoring.*

Getting Started with a Template

All HTML+TIME documents start with a template of basic markup needed to bring SMIL to your Web pages. It takes the following form:

```
<html xmlns:t="urn:schemas-microsoft-com:time">
<head>
    <style>
        .time {behavior: url(#default#time2);}
    </style>
    <?import namespace=t urn=":schemas-microsoft-com:time" implementation="
➥#default#time2">
</head>
<body>

</body>
</html>
```

The first reference of `xmlns:t="urn:schemas-microsoft-com:time"` declares the XML namespace. Between the `<style>` tags, the Cascading Style Sheet (CSS) class attribute of `.time` allows us to associate selected elements with the `time2` behavior. The line that begins `<?import` imports the `time2` behavior into that namespace. `time2`, having replaced `time`, is currently the most up-to-date behavior set. It is this behavior set that will bring SMIL to the Web browser.

With all the technical pieces in place that tell the browser which namespace to use, and that bring in the class and behavior set used to bring in SMIL, it is time to put together a basic presentation. The trunk of our tree, to reference my earlier analogy, is now complete.

Putting Up the Structure

With the template in place, my next step is to rough out the structure of the presentation. This enables me to ensure that all the components are included. Referring again to my Christmas tree analogy, this is where I add the branches. Here we will bring in the images and text that make up the bare bones of our presentation, without any adornments. Therefore, my first markup would look like Listing 16.1.

Listing 16.1

```
1: <html xmlns:t ="urn:schemas-microsoft-com:time">
2: <?import namespace="t" implementation="#default#time2">
3: <head>
4:      <title>Villa Art and Architecture Tour</title>
5:      <style>
6:          .time {behavior: url(#default#time2);}
7:      </style>
8: </head>
9: <body>
10:
11:      <t:img class="time" src="images/Villalogo.gif" id="logo"
  ➥width="346" height="126" />
12:
13:      <div class="time" id="presents">
14:          presents
15:      </div>
16:
17:      <t:img class="time" src="images/anatour.gif" id="artarch"
  ➥width="525" height="125" />
18:
19:      <t:audio class="time" ID="audio" src="audio/bach.asf" />
20:
21:      <t:img class="time" src="images/smVillalogo.gif" id="smlogo"
  ➥width="170" height="81" />
22:
23:      <t:img class="time" src="images/smanatour.gif" id="smartarch"
  ➥width="300" height="34" />
24:
```

Listing 16.1   Continued

```
25:      <t:img class="time" src="images/santam.jpg" id="building"
 ➥width="350" height="236" />
26:
27:      <div class="time" id="classical">
28:          See the classical buildings...
29:      </div>
30:
31:      <t:img class="time" src="images/david.jpg" id="david" width="200"
 ➥height="298"/>
32:
33:      <div class="time" id="sculpture">
34:          ...the sculpture...
35:      </div>
36:
37:      <t:img class="time" src="images/cathedr.jpg" id="cathedral" width=
 ➥"350" height="236" />
38:
39:      <div class="time" id="cathedrals" >
40:          ...the cathedrals...
41:      </div>
42:
43:      <t:img class="time" src="images/kiss.jpg" id="kiss" width="200"
 ➥height="298" />
44:
45:      <div class="time" id="beauty">
46:          ...the beauty.
47:      </div>
48:
49:      <div class="time" id="best" >
50:          See the best art and architecture Europe has to offer.
51:      </div>
52:
53:      <div class="time" id="price">
54:          $3599/person   555-555-1234
55:      </div>
56:
57: </body>
58: </html>
```

Initially, the code might look pretty busy. But all that it is doing is loading eight images, seven text blocks, and one audio file. Let's take a look at a sample of each.

Lines 11, 17, 21, 23, 25, 31, 37, and 43 all add images. A typical image markup looks like this (taken from line 11 in Listing 16.1):

```
<t:img class="time" src="images/Villalogo.gif" id="logo" width="346"
 ➥height="126" />
```

This is really not that different from a typical SMIL image tag. The main difference is that you must add `t:`, which references the namespace and extensions established in lines 1 and 2 in Listing 16.1. You must also use the `class` attribute to call in the behavior set declared earlier in line 6. Also, note the use of the `id` to name this element. That way, I will have a reference I can hook to for SMIL interactivity and timing.

Now let's look at lines 13–15. Because I know that I will want to control the timing of the text blocks, I'll enclose them within `<div>` `</div>` tags. This will allow me to attach time behavior to text blocks by adding the `class` attribute to the `<div>` tag. Here is the code for the text "presents," which appears in line 13 of Listing 16.1 and uses the following technique:

```
<div class="time" id="presents">
    presents
</div>
```

Finally, nothing fancy exists with the one audio file that we add in line 19. This particular file will play locally and it is small enough to download quickly online. Following, we see the reference to an audio time behavior of `t:audio`:

```
<t:audio class="time" ID="audio" src="audio/bach.asf" />
```

Currently, Internet Explorer is not terribly picky about the use of various media designations in the HTML+TIME time containers. In the preceding example, I could just as easily refer to the audio file with `t:media`. Because Microsoft may make a difference in its implementation of HTML+TIME later, I would encourage you to do it right from the beginning.

With the structure of the page established, it is time to start decorating.

Adding Timing

Now that I have the images, text, and sound in place, my next step is to establish the timing for the display of these elements. Adding timing is simply a matter of building in `begin`, `end`, and/or `dur` (for duration). First, glance at our growing markup sample in Listing 16.2:

Listing 16.2

```
1: <html xmlns:t ="urn:schemas-microsoft-com:time">
2: <?import namespace="t" implementation="#default#time2">
3: <head>
4:     <title>Villa Art and Architecture Tour</title>
```

Listing 16.2   Continued

```
 5:      <style>
 6:           .time {behavior: url(#default#time2);}
 7:      </style>
 8: </head>
 9: <body>
10:
11:      <t:img class="time" begin="0" dur="5" src="images/Villalogo.gif"
➥id="logo" width="346" height="126" />
12:
13:      <div class="time" begin="logo.end" dur="2" id="presents">
14:           presents
15:      </div>
16:
17:      <t:img class="time" src="images/anatour.gif" id="artarch"  begin=
➥"presents.end" dur="5" width="525" height="125" />
18:
19:      <t:audio class="time" ID="audio" src="audio/bach.asf" begin=
➥"presents.begin" />
20:
21:      <t:img class="time" begin="artarch.end+1" dur="indefinite" src=
➥"images/smVillalogo.gif" id="smlogo" width="170" height="81" />
22:
23:      <t:img class="time" begin="artarch.end+1" dur="indefinite" src=
➥"images/smanatour.gif" id="smartarch" width="300" height="34" />
24:
25:      <t:img class="time" begin="smartarch.begin+2" dur="5" src=
➥"images/santam.jpg" id="building" width="350" height="236" />
26:
27:      <div class="time" begin="smartarch.begin+3" dur="3" id=
➥"classical">
28:           See the classical buildings...
29:      </div>
30:
31:      <t:img class="time" begin="smartarch.begin+7" dur="5" src=
➥"images/david.jpg" id="david" width="200" height="298" />
32:
33:      <div class="time" begin="smartarch.begin+8" dur="3" id=
➥"sculpture">
34:           ...the sculpture...
35:      </div>
36:
37:      <t:img class="time" begin="smartarch.begin+12" dur="5" src=
➥"images/cathedr.jpg" id="cathedral" width="350" height="236" />
38:
39:      <div class="time" begin="smartarch.begin+13" dur="3" id=
➥"cathedrals">
40:           ...the cathedrals...
41:      </div>
42:
43:      <t:img class="time" begin="smartarch.begin+17" dur="indefinite" src=
➥"images/kiss.jpg" id="kiss" width="200" height="298" />
```

Listing 16.2   Continued

```
44:
45:     <div class="time" begin="smartarch.begin+18" dur="3" id="beauty">
46:         ...the beauty.
47:     </div>
48:
49:     <div class="time" begin="smartarch.begin+21" dur="indefinite" id=
➥"best">
50:         See the best art and architecture Europe has to offer.
51:     </div>
52:
53:     <div class="time" begin="smartarch.begin+22" dur="indefinite" id=
➥"price">
54:         $3599/person  555-555-1234
55:     </div>
56:
57: </body>
58: </html>
```

Again, as you grow accustomed to the markup, you will see that it is really not
that complex. I know that my audio file lasts approximately 30 seconds, so I have
timed out my materials within that limit. Take a look at line 11 again for a basic
timing example:

```
<t:img class="time" begin="0" dur="5" src="images/Villalogo.gif" id="logo"
➥width="346" height="126" />
```

All I have added to my previous example of this markup is `begin="0"` and
`dur="5"`. Simply enough, my first graphic will load with the Web page at 0 seconds
and display for 5 seconds. The text that follows the graphic in lines 13–15 is a
little more interesting. Its timing uses the following form:

```
<div class="time" begin="logo.end" dur="2" id="presents">
    presents
</div>
```

Here, I have taken advantage of the `id` attached to the first image.
`begin="logo.end"` means that this text will begin when the item with `id="logo"`
ends. This is the "dot syntax" we've grown accustomed to in Chapter 7, "Grouping
Your Content: The SMIL Timing and Synchronization Module" and in Chapter
15, "SMIL in RealPlayer." In the same manner, I can designate the beginning of
an element to coincide with the beginning of another element, as I did in line 19,
with the audio:

```
<t:audio class="time" ID="audio" src="audio/bach.asf" begin=
➥"presents.begin" />
```

`begin="presents.begin"` means that this audio file will begin promptly when the text labeled with `id="presents"` starts. Of course, the audio file in this example will have to load before it can play, but I'll address that later in this tutorial.

I can also add and subtract time from the reference of when another element begins or ends, as shown next, taken from lines 23–25 in the preceding code listing:

```
<t:img class="time" begin="artarch.end+1" dur="indefinite" src=
➥"images/smanatour.gif" id="smartarch" width="300" height="34" />
```

```
<t:img class="time" begin="smartarch.begin+2" dur="5"
➥src="images/santam.jpg" id="building" width="350" height="236" />
```

In this sample, the first graphic, which is the small version of our tour title image, will begin 1 second after the graphic labeled with `id="artarch"` ends. The second graphic, which is the image that precedes the text block "See the classical buildings…," will load 2 seconds after the first graphic (`id="smartarch"`) begins. Using this approach, I can sequentially load the following element in reference to the preceding one. Why would I want to do this? Authoring in this approach can be easier than giving absolute times. If you end up inserting another element, the entire presentation timing will ripple to match the changes.

One other issue to note in the preceding markup sample is the use of the `dur="indefinite"` attribute in the first line. Although most of my graphics will come and go onscreen, several will stay for the duration of the presentation. In this case, a graphic of the tour title will sit on the screen from when it appears until the Web page is closed or reloaded. Because this timing is `indefinite`, I cannot load the second graphic in relation to when the title ends. I cannot time off of an `end` that will never come. That is why my second graphic loads in relation to `smartarch.begin+2`.

Time to Add Time Containers

My structure is built and my timing is added. My layout is built. Now it is time to add time containers that, in SMIL, include the `<par>`, `<seq>`, and `<excl>` elements. Through the use of time containers, and in particular the `<par>` (parallel) element, I can group my content to load and display as sets. This allows me to ensure that the media elements and text are grouped together logically and that Internet Explorer will accept the transitions I'll add in the next step. First, look at our growing Web page, shown in Listing 16.3:

Listing 16.3

```
1: <html xmlns:t ="urn:schemas-microsoft-com:time">
2: <?import namespace="t" implementation="#default#time2">
3: <head>
4:     <title>Villa Art and Architecture Tour</title>
5:     <style>
6:         .time {behavior: url(#default#time2);}
7:     </style>
8: </head>
9: <body>
10:
11:     <t:img class="time" begin="0" dur="5" src="images/Villalogo.gif"
➥id="logo" width="346" height="126" />
12:
13:     <div class="time" begin="logo.end" dur="2" id="presents">
14:         presents
15:     </div>
16:
17:     <t:par>
18:         <t:img class="time" src="images/anatour.gif" id="artarch"
➥begin="presents.end" dur="5" width="525" height="125" />
19:     </t:par>
20:
21:     <t:audio class="time" ID="audio" src="audio/bach.asf" begin=
➥"presents.begin" />
22:
23:     <t:par>
24:         <t:img class="time" begin="artarch.end+1" dur="indefinite"
➥src="images/smVillalogo.gif" id="smlogo" width="170" height="81" />
25
26:         <t:img class="time" begin="artarch.end+1" dur="indefinite" src=
➥"images/smanatour.gif" id="smartarch" width="300" height="34" />
27:
28:     </t:par>
29:
30:     <t:par>
31:         <t:img class="time" begin="smartarch.begin+2" dur="5" src=
➥"images/santam.jpg" id="building" width="350" height="236" />
32:         <div class="time" begin="smartarch.begin+3" dur="3" id=
➥"classical">
33:             See the<br>classical buildings...
34:         </div>
35:     </t:par>
36:
37:     <t:par>
38:         <t:img class="time" begin="smartarch.begin+7" dur="5" src=
➥"images/david.jpg" id="david" width="200" height="298" />
39:         <div class="time" begin="smartarch.begin+8" dur="3" id=
➥"sculpture">
40:             ...the sculpture...
```

Listing 16.3   Continued

```
41:            </div>
42:        </t:par>
43:
44:        <t:par>
45:            <t:img class="time" begin="smartarch.begin+12" dur="5" src=
➥"images/cathedr.jpg" id="cathedral" width="350" height="236" />
46:            <div class="time" begin="smartarch.begin+13" dur="3" id=
➥"cathedrals">
47:                ...the cathedrals...
48:            </div>
49:        </t:par>
50:
51:        <t:par>
52:            <t:img class="time" begin="smartarch.begin+17" dur=
➥"indefinite" src="images/kiss.jpg" id="kiss" />
53:            <div class="time" begin="smartarch.begin+18" dur="3"
➥id="beauty">
54:                ...the beauty.
55:            </div>
56:        </t:par>
57:
58:        <t:par>
59:            <div class="time" begin="smartarch.begin+21" dur="indefinite"
➥id="best">
60:                See the best art and architecture Europe has to offer.
61:            </div>
62:            <div class="time" begin="smartarch.begin+22" dur="indefinite"
➥id="price">
63:                $3599/person   555-555-1234
64:            </div>
65:        </t:par>
66:
67: </body>
68: </html>
```

The <par> elements I've added in lines 17, 23, 30, 37, 44, 51, and 58 in Listing 16.3 (and their corresponding closing <par> tags) look remarkably like any other SMIL <par> tags. The only difference here is the addition of the t: just inside the tag; this references, once again, the namespace and the extensions we declared in lines 1 and 2.

Decorating with Transitions

Now it's time to decorate the presentation with transitions. To start off, I'll add some fades that will fade the images and text on and off the screen, and I'll add timing to these transitions. I'll also add some proprietary transitions specific to HTML+TIME. At this point, the markup will begin to look very complex, as you can see in Listing 16.4. But do not fear, you will find that it gets comfortable soon enough:

Listing 16.4

```
 1: <html xmlns:t ="urn:schemas-microsoft-com:time">
 2: <?import namespace="t" implementation="#default#time2">
 3: <head>
 4:     <title>Villa Art and Architecture Tour</title>
 5:     <style>
 6:         .time {behavior: url(#default#time2);}
 7:     </style>
 8: </head>
 9: <body>
10:
11:     <t:img class="time" begin="0" dur="5" src="images/Villalogo.gif"
➥id="logo" width="346" height="126" />
12:         <t:transitionFilter targetElement="logo" type="fade" begin=
➥"logo.end-2" dur="2" mode="out" from="0.0" to="1.0" calcmode="linear" />
13:     </t:img>
14:
15:     <div class="time" begin="logo.end" dur="2" ID="presents">
16:         <t:transitionFilter targetElement="presents"
➥begin="presents.begin" dur="1" mode="in" type="fade"/>
17:         <t:transitionFilter targetElement="presents"
➥begin="presents.end-1" dur="1" mode="out" type="fade"/>
18:         presents
19:     </div>
20:
21:     <t:par>
22:         <t:img class="time" src="images/anatour.gif" id="artarch"
➥begin="presents.end" dur="5" width="525" height="125" />
23:             <t:transitionFilter targetElement="artarch" type="fade"
➥begin="artarch.begin" dur="2" mode="in" from="0.0" to="1.0"
➥calcmode="linear" />
24:             <t:transitionFilter targetElement="artarch" type="fade"
➥begin="artarch.end-2" dur="2" mode="out" from="0.0" to="1.0"
➥calcmode="linear" />
25:     </t:par>
26:
27:     <t:audio class="time" id="audio" src="audio/bach.asf" begin=
➥"presents.begin" />
28:
29:     <t:par>
30:         <t:img class="time" begin="artarch.end+1" dur="indefinite"
➥src="images/smVillalogo.gif" id="smlogo" />
```

Listing 16.4   Continued

```
31:          <t:img class="time" begin="artarch.end+1" id="smartarch"
➡dur="indefinite" src="images/smanatour.gif" width="300" height="34" />
32:             <t:transitionFilter targetElement="smartarch" type=
➡"progid:DXImageTransform.Microsoft.Pixelate()" begin="smartarch.begin"
➡dur="2" mode="in" from="0.0" to="1.0" calcmode="linear" />
33:          </t:par>
34:
35:       <t:par>
36:          <t:img class="time" begin="smartarch.begin+2" dur="5" src=
➡"images/santam.jpg" id="building" width="350" height="236" />
37:             <t:transitionFilter targetElement="building" type=
➡"progid:DXImageTransform.Microsoft.RandomDissolve()" begin="
➡building.begin" dur="1" mode="in" from="0.0" to="1.0" calcmode="linear" />
38:             <t:transitionFilter targetElement="building" type=
➡"progid:DXImageTransform.Microsoft.RandomDissolve()" begin=
➡"building.end-1" dur="1" mode="out" from="0.0" to="1.0" calcmode=
➡"linear" />
39:          </t:img>
40:          <div class="time" begin="smartarch.begin+3" dur="3"
➡id="classical">
41:             <t:transitionFilter begin="classical.begin" dur="1"
➡mode="in" type="fade"/>
42:             <t:transitionFilter begin="classical.end-1" dur="1"
➡mode="out" type="fade"/>
43:             See the classical buildings...
44:          </div>
45:       </t:par>
46:
47:       <t:par>
48:          <t:img class="time" begin="smartarch.begin+7" dur="5" src=
➡"images/david.jpg" id="david" width="200" height="298" />
49:             <t:transitionFilter targetElement="david" type=
➡"progid:DXImageTransform.Microsoft.RandomDissolve()" begin="david.begin"
➡dur="1" mode="in" from="0.0" to="1.0" calcmode="linear"   />
50:             <t:transitionFilter targetElement="david" type=
➡"progid:DXImageTransform.Microsoft.RandomDissolve()" begin="david.end-1"
➡dur="1" mode="out" from="0.0" to="1.0" calcmode="linear" />
51:          </t:img>
52:          <div class="time" begin="smartarch.begin+8" dur="3" id=
➡"sculpture">
53:             <t:transitionFilter begin="sculpture.begin" dur="1"
➡mode="in" type="fade"/>
54:             <t:transitionFilter begin="sculpture.end-1" dur="1"
➡mode="out" type="fade"/>
55:          ...the sculpture...
56:          </div>
57:       </t:par>
58:
59:       <t:par>
```

Listing 16.4   Continued

```
60:            <t:img class="time" begin="smartarch.begin+12" dur="5" src=
➥"images/cathedr.jpg" id="cathedral" width="350" height="236" />
61:              <t:transitionFilter targetElement="cathedral" type=
➥"progid:DXImageTransform.Microsoft.RandomDissolve()"
➥begin="cathedral.begin" dur="1" mode="in" from="0.0" to="1.0"
➥calcmode="linear" />
62:              <t:transitionFilter targetElement="cathedral" type=
➥"progid:DXImageTransform.Microsoft.RandomDissolve()"
➥begin="cathedral.end-1" dur="1" mode="out" from="0.0" to="1.0"
➥calcmode="linear" />
63:            </t:img>
64:            <div class="time" begin="smartarch.begin+13" dur="3" id=
➥"cathedrals">
65:              <t:transitionFilter begin="cathedrals.begin" dur="1"
➥mode="in" type="fade"/>
66:              <t:transitionFilter begin="cathedrals.end-1" dur="1"
➥mode="out" type="fade"/>
67:                ...the cathedrals...
68:            </div>
69:        </t:par>
70:
71:        <t:par>
72:          <t:img class="time" begin="smartarch.begin+17" dur="indefinite"
➥src="images/kiss.jpg" id="kiss" width="200" height="298" />
73:              <t:transitionFilter targetElement="kiss" type=
➥"progid:DXImageTransform.Microsoft.RandomDissolve()" begin="kiss.begin"
➥dur="1" mode="in" from="0.0" to="1.0" calcmode="linear" />
74:            </t:img>
75:            <div class="time" begin="smartarch.begin+18" dur="3"
➥id="beauty">
76:              <t:transitionFilter begin="beauty.begin" dur="1" mode="in"
➥type="fade"/>
77:              <t:transitionFilter begin="beauty.end-1" dur="1"
➥mode="out" type="fade"/>
78:                ...the beauty.
79:            </div>
80:        </t:par>
81:
82:        <t:par>
83:          <div class="time" begin="smartarch.begin+21" dur="indefinite"
➥id="best">
84:              <t:transitionFilter begin="best.begin" dur="1" mode="in"
➥type="fade"/>
85:              See the best art and architecture Europe has to offer.
86:            </div>
```

Listing 16.4   Continued

```
87:          <div class="time" begin="smartarch.begin+22" dur="indefinite"
➥id="price" >
88:              <t:transitionFilter begin="price.begin" dur="1" mode="in"
➥type="fade"/>
89:              $3599/person   555-555-1234
90:          </div>
91:      </t:par>
92:
93: </body>
94: </html>
```

Before you get lost in the mind-numbing nature of the growing markup, let's
highlight a couple of critical sections of transitions. The opening graphic, with
the attribute id="logo" (line 11 in Listing 16.4), appears immediately, but then
transitions out with a slow fade:

```
<t:img class="time" begin="0" dur="5" src="images/Villalogo.gif" id="logo"
➥width="346" height="126" />
    <t:transitionFilter targetElement="logo" type="fade" begin="logo.end-2"
➥dur="2" mode="out" from="0.0" to="1.0" calcmode="linear" />
```

The magic of this transition is created with the addition of a <transitionFilter>
element. Because my graphic is named with id="logo", I can apply that transition
to that graphic by using the targetElement="logo" attribute and value. The
type of transition I am declaring is fade. Graphics can either fade in or out, so
mode="out" declares this to be a fade-out. My begin and end times use the familiar
format, but you will notice the use of subtracting from the end value to control
when the fade-out starts. My from values declare that it will be a complete fade
from zero to full fade-out. Finally, the calcmode of linear means that the
fade-out will be a smooth and even transition.

Now that you understand a basic fade, let's look at the same approach attached to
fade-in and fade-out the text block "presents," which appears on lines 15–19 in
Listing 16.4:

```
<div class="time" begin="logo.end" dur="2" ID="presents">
    <t:transitionFilter targetElement="presents" begin="presents.begin"
➥dur="1" mode="in" type="fade"/>
    <t:transitionFilter targetElement="presents" begin="presents.end-1"
➥dur="1" mode="out" type="fade"/>
        presents
</div>
```

In this example, I used the `<div>` element to wrap the `<transitionFilter>` elements in with the text. Because the elements are already wrapped in with the text, I did not need to use the `targetElement`. However, I typically use `targetElement` just to play it safe. This example also demonstrates both in and out modes of transition. I have also streamlined this example by omitting the `from` and `calcmode` values; leaving them out causes the browser to simply substitute the defaults for these attributes. The default values for these attributes are the same as the values we have been coding into our previous transitions; the default `from` value is 0.0 and the default value of `calcmode` is `linear`.

Now let's try something a little more ambitious. Internet Explorer supports the standard range of SMIL transitions. But it also offers a continually expanding proprietary set of transitions, as shown in these two excerpts that follow, taken from lines 31 and 32 and lines 72 and 73 in Listing 16.4:

```
<t:img class="time" begin="artarch.end+1" id="smartarch"
➥dur="indefinite" src="images/smanatour.gif" width="300" height="34" />

    <t:transitionFilter targetElement="smartarch" type=
➥"progid:DXImageTransform.Microsoft.Pixelate()" begin="smartarch.begin"
➥ dur="2" mode="in" from="0.0" to="1.0" calcmode="linear" />
. . .
<t:img class="time" begin="smartarch.begin+17" dur="indefinite" src=
➥"images/kiss.jpg" id="kiss" width="200" height="298" />
            <t:transitionFilter targetElement="kiss" type=
➥"progid:DXImageTransform.Microsoft.RandomDissolve()" begin="kiss.begin"
➥dur="1" mode="in" from="0.0" to="1.0" calcmode="linear" />
```

In the first example, the transition creates a blocky type of digital effect that focuses in to reveal the image of the small tour title graphic. The second example creates a digitally grainy fade to the image of the sculpture of Eros and Psyche kissing. For educational purposes, I have shown a couple of different effects in this tutorial. But be careful about overdoing it. Just because you can use an effect does not mean you should.

As shown in Figure 16.3, roaming through the HTML+TIME `transitionFilter` section of the Microsoft Developer Network Library (`http://msdn.microsoft.com/library/default.asp` under Web Development, Web Multimedia, HTML+TIME) will reveal what new tricks your target version of the browser offers.

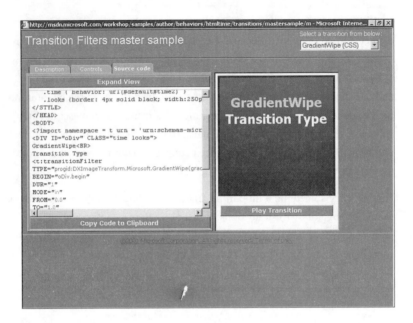

Figure 16.3   *The MSDN Library offers an interactive* `transitionFilter` *demonstrator.*

Matching the Planned Layout

My presentation is structured and timed. I have time containers that group elements together, and I have added the transitions. Now I can layout my pictures and text in their locations on the page. Using my Photoshop template as a guide, I can roughly position the elements with style sheets, as shown in Listing 16.5:

Listing 16.5

```
 1: <html xmlns:t ="urn:schemas-microsoft-com:time">
 2: <?import namespace="t" implementation="#default#time2">
 3: <head>
 4:     <title>Villa Art and Architecture Tour</title>
 5:     <style>
 6:         .time {behavior: url(#default#time2);}
 7:         p { font-family:arial; color:black; font-size:10pt }
 8:         div { font-family:arial black; font-size:18pt; color:black }
 9:     </style>
10: </head>
11: <body>
12:
13:     <t:img class="time" begin="0" dur="5" src="images/Villalogo.gif"
➡id="logo" style="position:absolute; top:150px; left:220px" width="346"
➡height="126" />
```

Listing 16.5   Continued

```
14:          <t:transitionFilter targetElement="logo" type="fade" begin=
➥"logo.end-2" dur="2" mode="out" from="0.0" to="1.0" calcmode="linear" />
15:
16:      <div class="time" begin="logo.end" dur="2" id="presents" style=
➥"position:absolute; top:200px; left:300px; font-size:28pt; color:gray">
17:          <t:transitionFilter begin="presents.begin" dur="1" mode="in"
➥type="fade"/>
18:          <t:transitionFilter begin="presents.end-1" dur="1" mode="out"
➥type="fade"/>
19:          presents
20:      </div>
21:
22:      <t:par>
23:          <t:img class="time" src="images/anatour.gif" id="artarch"
➥begin="presents.end" dur="5" style="position:absolute; top:150px;
➥left:130px; z-index:5" width="525" height="125" />
24:          <t:transitionFilter targetElement="artarch" type="fade"
➥begin="artarch.begin" dur="2" mode="in" from="0.0" to="1.0"
➥calcmode="linear" />
25:          <t:transitionFilter targetElement="artarch" type="fade"
➥begin="artarch.end-2" dur="2" mode="out" from="0.0" to="1.0"
➥calcmode="linear" />
26:      </t:par>
27:
28:      <t:audio class="time" id="audio" src="audio/bach.asf" begin=
➥"presents.begin" />
29:
30:      <t:par>
31:          <t:img class="time" begin="artarch.end+1" dur="indefinite"
➥src="images/smVillalogo.gif" id="smlogo" style="position:absolute;
➥top:52px; left:300px; z-index:1" width="170" height="81" />
32:          <t:animateMotion targetElement="smlogo" values="0,0; -210,0"
➥begin="artarch.end+1" dur="2" calcMode="spline" keyTimes="0;1"
➥keySplines="0 0 .35 1" fill="freeze" />
33:          <t:img class="time" begin="artarch.end+1" dur="indefinite"
➥src="images/smanatour.gif" id="smartarch" style="position:absolute;
➥top:75px; left:375px; z-index:3" width="300" height="34" />
34:          <t:transitionFilter targetElement="smartarch" type=
➥"progid:DXImageTransform.Microsoft.Pixelate()" begin="smartarch.begin"
➥dur="2" mode="in" from="0.0" to="1.0" calcmode="linear" />
35:      </t:par>
36:
37:      <t:par>
38:          <t:img class="time" begin="smartarch.begin+2" dur="5" src=
➥"images/santam.jpg" id="building" style="position:absolute; top:150px;
➥left:90px; z-index:5" width="350" height="236" />
39:          <t:transitionFilter targetElement="building" type=
```

Listing 16.5   Continued

```
➥"progid:DXImageTransform.Microsoft.RandomDissolve()"
➥begin="building.begin" dur="1" mode="in" from="0.0" to="1.0"
➥calcmode="linear" />
 40:            <t:transitionFilter targetElement="building" type=
➥"progid:DXImageTransform.Microsoft.RandomDissolve()"
➥begin="building.end-1" dur="1" mode="out" from="0.0" to="1.0"
➥calcmode="linear" />
 41:        </t:img>
 42:        <div class="time" begin="smartarch.begin+3" dur="3" id=
➥"classical" style="position:absolute; top:150px; left:470px; z-index:6">
 43:            <t:transitionFilter begin="classical.begin" dur="1"
➥mode="in" type="fade"/>
 44:            <t:transitionFilter begin="classical.end-1" dur="1"
➥mode="out" type="fade"/>
 45:        See the<br>classical buildings...
 46:        </div>
 47:    </t:par>
 48:
 49:    <t:par>
 50:        <t:img class="time" begin="smartarch.begin+7" dur="5" src=
➥"images/david.jpg" id="david" style="position:absolute; top:135px;
➥left:450px; z-index:5"  width="200" height="298" />
 51:            <t:transitionFilter targetElement="david" type=
➥"progid:DXImageTransform.Microsoft.RandomDissolve()" begin="david.begin"
➥dur="1" mode="in" from="0.0" to="1.0" calcmode="linear" />
 52:            <t:transitionFilter targetElement="david" type=
➥"progid:DXImageTransform.Microsoft.RandomDissolve()" begin="david.end-1"
➥dur="1" mode="out" from="0.0" to="1.0" calcmode="linear" />
 53:        </t:img>
 54:        <div class="time" begin="smartarch.begin+8" dur="3"
➥id="sculpture" style="position:absolute; top:250px; left:175px; z-index:6">
 55:            <t:transitionFilter begin="sculpture.begin" dur="1"
➥mode="in" type="fade"/>
 56:            <t:transitionFilter begin="sculpture.end-1" dur="1"
➥mode="out" type="fade"/>
 57:            ...the sculpture...
 58:        </div>
 59:    </t:par>
 60:
 61:
 62:    <t:par>
 63:        <t:img class="time" begin="smartarch.begin+12" dur="5" src=
➥"images/cathedr.jpg" id="cathedral" style="position:absolute; top:220px;
➥left:290px; z-index:5" width="350" height="236" />
 64:            <t:transitionFilter targetElement="cathedral" type=
➥"progid:DXImageTransform.Microsoft.RandomDissolve()" begin=
➥"cathedral.begin" dur="1" mode="in" from="0.0" to="1.0" calcmode=
➥"linear" />
```

Listing 16.5   Continued

```
65:              <t:transitionFilter targetElement="cathedral" type=
➥"progid:DXImageTransform.Microsoft.RandomDissolve()" begin=
➥"cathedral.end-1" dur="1" mode="out" from="0.0" to="1.0" calcmode=
➥"linear" />
66:          </t:img>
67:          <div class="time" begin="smartarch.begin+13" dur="3"
➥id="cathedrals" style="position:absolute; top:160px; left:450px;
➥z-index:6">
68:              <t:transitionFilter begin="cathedrals.begin" dur="1"
➥mode="in" type="fade"/>
69:              <t:transitionFilter begin="cathedrals.end-1" dur="1"
➥mode="out" type="fade"/>
70:              ...the cathedrals...
71:          </div>
72:      </t:par>
73:
74:
75:      <t:par>
76:          <t:img class="time" begin="smartarch.begin+17" dur="indefinite"
➥src="images/kiss.jpg" id="kiss" style="position:absolute; top:150px;
➥left:295px; z-index:5" width="200" height="298" />
77:              <t:transitionFilter targetElement="kiss" type=
➥"progid:DXImageTransform.Microsoft.RandomDissolve()" begin="kiss.begin"
➥dur="1" mode="in" from="0.0" to="1.0" calcmode="linear" />
78:          </t:img>
79:          <div class="time" begin="smartarch.begin+18" dur="3"
➥id="beauty" style="position:absolute; top:375px; left:565px; z-index:6">
80:              <t:transitionFilter begin="beauty.begin" dur="1"
➥mode="in" type="fade"/>
81:              <t:transitionFilter begin="beauty.end-1" dur="1"
➥mode="out" type="fade"/>
82:              ...the beauty.
83:          </div>
84:      </t:par>
85:
86:
87:      <t:par>
88:          <div class="time" begin="smartarch.begin+21" dur="indefinite"
➥id="best" style="position:absolute; top:220px; left:90px; font-size:12pt;
➥z-index:6">
89:              <t:transitionFilter begin="best.begin" dur="1" mode="in"
➥type="fade"/>
90:              See the best<br>art and architecture<br>Europe has to
➥offer.
91:          </div>
```

Listing 16.5 Continued

```
92:          <div class="time" begin="smartarch.begin+22" dur="indefinite"
➥id="price" style="position:absolute; top:320px; left:565px;
➥font-size:16pt; z-index:6">
93:              <t:transitionFilter begin="price.begin" dur="1" mode="in"
➥type="fade"/>
94:              $3599/person<br><br>555-555-1234
95:          </div>
96:      </t:par>
97:
98: </body>
99: </html>
```

Right up top in the <head> element, in lines 5–9, I address some basic text formatting needs of the layout using style sheets:

```
<style>
    .time {behavior: url(#default#time2);}
    p { font-family:arial; color:black; font-size:10pt }
    div { font-family:arial black; font-size:18pt; color:black }
</style>
```

From then on, whether I am using a <p> or <div>, some base text characteristics are covered. I will not go into style sheets in depth. But a quick look at a sample from lines 13–18 in Listing 16.5 shows style-sheet positioning in action for both an image and a text block:

```
<t:img class="time" begin="0" dur="5" src="images/Villalogo.gif" id="logo"
➥style="position:absolute; top:150px; left:220px" width="346"
➥height="126" />
. . .
<div class="time" begin="logo.end" dur="2" id="presents" style=
➥"position:absolute; top:200px; left:300px; font-size:28pt; color:gray">
</div>
```

In the first example, the top-left corner of the image will be positioned 150 pixels down and 220 pixels from the left edge of the display. In the second example, the text is placed down 200 pixels and over from the left 300 pixels. It is also sized up to 28 points and colored gray.

Some full disclosure is in order. I'm working from a finished tutorial. That is kind of like one of those cooking television shows in which the chef magically turns to the oven and pulls out a completed and beautiful culinary creation. Multimedia authoring is messy and I like to tinker. Typically, I continue to tweak my position values as I tweak my presentation. Sure, I could probably accurately measure things to the pixel in Photoshop. The artist in me personally prefers to dead reckon and see what I get. Use whichever world view you like.

Putting a Graphic in Motion

You might have noticed a new addition to our latest version of our growing presentation. In Listing 16.5, it appears in line 31 and 32. Let me highlight it for you:

```
<t:img class="time" begin="artarch.end+1" dur="indefinite" src=
"images/smVillalogo.gif" id="smlogo" style="position:absolute; top:52px;
left:300px; z-index:1" width="170" height="81" />
    <t:animateMotion targetElement="smlogo" values="0,0; -210,0" begin=
"artarch.end+1" dur="2" calcMode="spline" keyTimes="0;1" keySplines=
"0 0 .35 1" fill="freeze" />
```

Here, I have used an `<animateMotion>` element to dynamically change the position of the small logo. The previous `position` has already placed that logo down 52 pixels and over to the right 300 pixels. Now `<animateMotion>` causes that graphic to move from its current position to a new home 210 pixels to the left. It does that with the `values` attribute: `0,0` starts the graphic at its current location. `-210,0` gives the graphic a final resting place. It tells the graphic to stay at the same height (or *y* coordinate) but now subtract 210 pixels from the previous 300 pixel *x* coordinate. Now we have set up starting and ending places in which the `<animateMotion>` can occur.

You might have also noticed four other interesting attributes. `calcMode="spline"` tells the browser we are going to calculate the location between the first and starting position by means of spline animation. In other words, I'm going to do some easing on our graphic as it slides into its new location. `keyTimes="0;1"` tells the browser to calculate between the two extremes of the starting and ending point. My spline effect will go from the beginning of the animation to the end. `keySplines="0 0 .35 1"` sets the spline control points that control the animation. You will probably want to visit Chapter 10, "Bringing Graphics to Life: The

Animation Modules," for a full discussion on keySplines. My first pair of numbers tell the beginning of the animation to start at full speed. .35 1 tells the end of the animation to calculate a speed curve based off a control point plotted in a motion graph at .35,1. This is kind of abstract in numeric form. But if you look at a graph, as shown in Figure 16.4, you see the curve will chart a slowdown in speed (more time over less distance) toward the end of the curve in the upper-right corner of the graph.

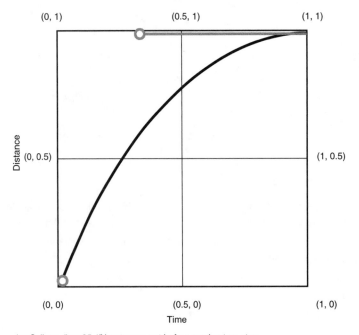

keySplines="o o.35 1" is an ease out before coming to a stop

Figure 16.4 *In this motion graph of the keySplines="0 0 .35 1" values, notice how distance covered slows in relation to time spent covering that distance.*

This spline animation will start out at full speed and slow into (or ease into) an eventual stop. A final attribute of fill="freeze" tells the graphic to stay put at its new place after the animation has concluded.

Building the Background

Our stage is now mostly set. All I need to finish up is to add an interesting backdrop for the presentation to be displayed against. This will keep the display space visually interesting to the viewer. Using Web-safe colors based on the logo, I create a series of colored boxes on the screen, which will be added to our document just after the audio element on line 28 in Listing 16.5:

```
. . .
<t:par dur="indefinite">
    <span id="orange" style="position:absolute;top:230px;
➥left:75px;height:0px; width:350px; background-color:#FFCC66; z-index:4">
        <t:animate targetElement="orange" attributeName="top" from="230"
➥to="135" begin="artarch.end-1" dur="2" fill="freeze" />
        <t:animate targetElement="orange" attributeName="height" from="0"
➥to="240" begin="artarch.end-1" dur="2" fill="freeze" />
    </span>
    <span id="brown" style="position:absolute;top:230px;left:225px;
➥height:0px; width:325px; background-color:#CC9966; z-index:3">
        <t:animate targetElement="brown" attributeName="height" from="0"
➥to="245" begin="artarch.end-1" dur="2" fill="freeze" />
    </span>
    <span id="yellow" style="position:absolute;top:230px;left:300px;
➥height:0px; width:450px; background-color:#FFFFCC; z-index:2">
        <t:animate targetElement="yellow" attributeName="top" from="230"
➥to="50" begin="artarch.end-1" dur="2" fill="freeze" />
        <t:animate targetElement="yellow" attributeName="height" from="0"
➥to="385" begin="artarch.end-1" dur="2" fill="freeze" />
    </span>
</t:par>
. . .
```

This code generates three boxes through style sheets. It appears just after our opening graphics. The other graphics and text float above these colored boxes in the Web browser. Because all these exist within <t:par> tags, they'll all be grouped together. To cut down on the clutter, let's focus on the code for just one:

```
<span id="orange" style="position:absolute;top:230px;left:75px;height:0px;
➥width:350px; background-color:#FFCC66; z-index:4">
```

There's nothing fancy here. Using top, left, height, and width values within a <span> (which does not have a t: before it because it is defining its style inline), I have defined a square and filled in its background color with the hexadecimal equivalent of orange(#FFCC66). The z-index value, which layers elements with higher values over those with lower values, floats those squares on a layer underneath the graphics (or other squares) in the layout. But take a closer look at the height. A height of 0 pixels? This is not a box, this is an invisible line. You see, I'm going to grow that line into my colorful background box. To do that, I need to move the top value up the screen and add to the height value:

```
. . .
<span id="orange" style="position:absolute;top:230px;left:75px;height:0px;
➥width:350px; background-color:#FFCC66; z-index:4">
    <t:animate targetElement="orange" attributeName="top" from="230"
➥to="135" begin="artarch.end-1" dur="2" fill="freeze" />
    <t:animate targetElement="orange" attributeName="height" from="0"
➥to="240" begin="artarch.end-1" dur="2" fill="freeze" />
</span>
. . .
```

That is exactly what I have done with the generic animate element. Using attributeName to tell the browser which attribute to change, I animate that numeric value from one value to another. For example, the starting height of the "orange" element is 0. In the second <animate> element, the attributeName tells us that the height of the targeted element (orange) should be altered from 0 to 240 pixels. It also declares that this should begin a second after the end of the element with an ID of "artarch"; it should occur over 2 seconds and freeze on the screen when it is completed. As shown in Figure 16.5, the resulting box literally grows on the screen over the specified 2-second duration. It replaces the fading title graphic floating on a layer above.

As with our earlier animated company logo, fill="freeze" sticks that box at its new setting permanently. A dur="indefinite" in the outer <t:par> time container tells all the boxes to stay onscreen until the Web page is closed or reloaded. I now have a stage in which to make my graphics and text appear.

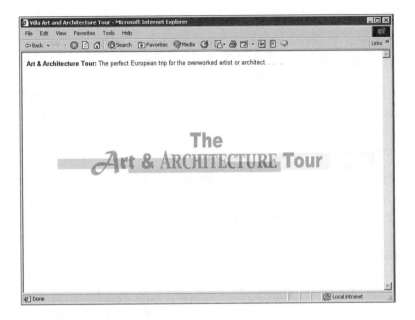

Figure 16.5 *As the title graphic fades out, the squares* animate *into full size on the layer beneath.*

Dealing with Bandwidth

At some point in any Web multimedia presentation, the issue of available bandwidth is going to rear its ugly head. In most Web multimedia players, dealing with bandwidth is an integral issue in developing content. You should continually keep an eye on how fast you can stream content within a given moment in time.

A Web browser approach to Web multimedia offers some advantages and disadvantages. In some ways, loading and caching content in memory is easier to understand than similar functions in a streaming multimedia player. In most cases, material loads as it is displayed and is stored in local memory until the user is done with the Web page. Usually, that means storing (or caching) the content in memory begins almost immediately as the page loads. But the timing in a SMIL document changes how the page is loaded and what appears on the page in relation to time. The catch is that, unlike a streaming multimedia player, preloading is not usually built in as part of that process.

With a streaming multimedia player, preloading content often happens before the material starts playing and as the presentation plays. That is a integral part to streaming multimedia over the Web. A Web browser is different. A Web browser is designed for connecting to the server, grabbing the content it needs, and displaying that content until the user changes the Web page. The page usually doesn't appear until all the content is loaded. Smooth preloading of visual material as the presentation unfolds is not a part of how a Web browser is designed to function.

Therefore, this presentation creates a bit of a dilemma in terms of bandwidth. The three major media elements in this presentation are text, audio, and images. Text is a low-bandwidth solution no matter how you use it. About the only issue involved in text display is how fast the computer can draw what you want on the screen. In the Villa Travel example, our audio is also fairly simple. If I was streaming the audio, it would play on your computer at a precise bandwidth. This tutorial file is designed for local playback off your hard drive and is compressed small enough to load before playing, in most circumstances, on a reasonably solid Web connection. Streaming the file from a streaming server would make that process even smoother. And in a worst-case scenario, the audio is not a critical component to the presentation. If it doesn't play, the text and visual information will still deliver the primary content.

It is the visual information that gets tricky. Unlike RealNetworks RealPlayer or RealONE player, I'm not streaming my images into Microsoft Internet Explorer. Therefore, they are not preloading into the player and loading the next image while the first is being displayed. If the HTML+TIME calls for an image and it is not there, the presentation grinds to a halt.

In all fairness, SMIL 2.0 does offer new features in controlling how a presentation plays if the media has not loaded. These features include the `syncBehavior`, `syncMaster`, and `syncTolerance` attributes of the Timing and Synchronization Module. As a very complete implementation of SMIL 2.0, Internet Explorer supports these features. In practice, I have found they currently work with mixed results. As the implementation matures, these areas will function with greater regularity in the browser. But even under the best circumstances, `syncBehavior`, `syncMaster`, and `syncTolerance` deal with missing material by shutting down the presentation in some way, which is not an ideal way to deal with media loading.

My presentation needs to preload the images. Web authors have used a number of tricks to preload images for future use by the Web browser. For example, I could use JavaScript to preload and cache all the required images as the page loads.

Another quick, easy, and bulletproof trick involves resizing the image to one pixel by one pixel. You then load the image at the top of the Web page and try not to make it too noticeable. When the image is called again by the browser to display it at its proper size, the image is already loaded in the cache. In our example, suppose I had the following timed display of the image planned:

```
. . .
<t:img class="time" begin="intro.click" dur="5" src="images/Villalogo.gif"
➥id="logo" style="position:absolute; top:150px; left:220px" width="346"
➥height="126" />
. . .
```

At the very beginning of the Web page, I could preload that image by using the following markup:

```
. . .
<img src="images/Villalogo.gif" width="1" height="1">
. . .
```

The user sees a small one-pixel by one-pixel dot at the top of the screen. Depending on the graphic and Web page background, it might not even be noticeable. When that graphic is called again by the presentation, it will already have been "displayed" on the page and it can call it from the Web browser cache for quick redisplay.

When in Doubt...Stall!

Preloading the images works great if the browser is given time to preload the images. But launching the presentation immediately is going to put me right back where I started: with images that still need to be loaded while the presentation plays. I have one other trick I can use to help buy time for the images to load. I stall.

In the early days of CD-ROM multimedia (or even its floppy disk-based predecessor), it took time to load content into the computer before it could be displayed onscreen. Therefore, multimedia authors got creative in how they stalled the viewer. Low memory title sequences and other distractions hid the fact that the content was frantically loading like mad behind the scenes. As CD-ROM drives and computers got faster, this approach faded. It began to reappear as Web multimedia came into existence. Again, multimedia authors needed to stall as content loaded frantically over the network.

One great way to stall is to give the user something short to read and a button to click. Most users will pause for a moment to get their bearings. In every second that they pause to figure out what to do next, you can be preloading material behind the scenes. What I need, then, is an interactive pause just before my presentation. I can do that by adding some simple code at the very beginning of my document:

```
<p>
    <b>Art & Architecture Tour:</b> The perfect European trip for the
➥overworked artist or architect.
    <div class="time" begin="0" end="intro.click">
        <button id="intro">Play Presentation</button>
    </div>
</p>
```

What is going on here? We have already seen that SMIL 2.0 supports timing off the begin and end events of playing objects. It also supports timing off mouse events such as a click. The form is the object id value followed by a dot and then click or onClick. In the preceding example, I have created a button in HTML and assigned the name intro to it. When the user clicks that button named intro, a mouse click event is noticed by the Web browser. In this case, the button will end on the mouse click because end="intro.click".

What is neat about this use of SMIL in HTML+TIME is that it opens a great deal of interactivity to the designer and developer that used to require more complex scripting with a language such as JavaScript. In Internet Explorer, almost anything that can be labeled with an id can be made clickable. I could even make the text itself clickable by modifying the paragraph tag with <p id="intro">. In practice, I have found click behavior to sometimes be a little quirky in early versions of HTML+TIME-capable versions of Internet Explorer. Again, as the browser continues to develop and mature, these issues will likely fade away quickly.

If I incorporated these image preloading and stalling tactics into the beginning of the document, it would look something like this:

```
. . .
<p>
    <b>Art & Architecture Tour:</b> The perfect European trip for the
➥overworked artist or architect.
    <img src="images/Villalogo.gif" width="1" height="1">
    <img src="images/anatour.gif" width="1" height="1">
    <img src="images/smVillalogo.gif" width="1" height="1">
    <img src="images/smanatour.gif" width="1" height="1">
    <img src="images/santam.jpg" width="1" height="1">
    <img src="images/david.jpg" width="1" height="1">
    <img src="images/cathedr.jpg" width="1" height="1">
    <img src="images/kiss.jpg" width="1" height="1">
    <div class="time" begin="0" end="intro.click">
```

```
        <button id="intro">Play Presentation</button>
    </div>
</p>

<t:img class="time" begin="intro.click" dur="5" src="images/Villalogo.gif"
➥id="logo" style="position:absolute; top:150px; left:220px" width="346"
➥height="126" />
. . .
```

As you can see in this sample, I have given the viewer text to read and I have begun loading images behind the scenes using the one pixel workaround discussed previously. After most of the images have started loading, the browser will begin rendering the Play button. When users gets their bearings and click that button, it will communicate a click event to the browser. The Play button will disappear (end="intro.click") and the first graphic in the timeline will appear with begin="intro.click". It's all downhill from here as the presentation begins to play.

Final Code and Final Thoughts

With the last features installed, the final HTML+TIME markup for Internet Explorer 6 is complete and the presentation is as shown in Figure 16.6.

Figure 16.6   *The completed HTML+TIME presentation in Internet Explorer 6.*

Now that we have finished the presentation, be sure to view it from the Web site at http://www.SMILBook.com/. Having worked through the examples, our completed markup in Listing 16.6, which is updated to include the style-sheet information for the <p> and <div> elements, the animated boxes, and the preloading/stalling tricks, should seem fairly understandable now:

Listing 16.6

```
 1: <html xmlns:t ="urn:schemas-microsoft-com:time">
 2: <?import namespace="t" implementation="#default#time2">
 3: <head>
 4:     <title>Villa Art and Architecture Tour</title>
 5:     <style>
 6:         .time {behavior: url(#default#time2);}
 7:         p { font-family:arial; color:black; font-size:10pt }
 8:         div { font-family:arial black; font-size:18pt; color:black }
 9:     </style>
10: </head>
11: <body>
12:
13:     <p>
14:         <b>Art & Architecture Tour:</b> The perfect European trip for
➥the overworked artist or architect.
15:         <img src="images/Villalogo.gif" width="1" height="1">
16:         <img src="images/anatour.gif" width="1" height="1">
17:         <img src="images/smVillalogo.gif" width="1" height="1">
18:         <img src="images/smanatour.gif" width="1" height="1">
19:         <img src="images/santam.jpg" width="1" height="1">
20:         <img src="images/david.jpg" width="1" height="1">
21:         <img src="images/cathedr.jpg" width="1" height="1">
22:         <img src="images/kiss.jpg" width="1" height="1">
23:         <div class="time" begin="0" end="intro.click">
24:             <button id="intro">Play Presentation</button>
25:         </div>
26:     </p>
27:
28:     <t:img class="time" begin="intro.click" dur="5" src=
➥"images/Villalogo.gif" id="logo" style="position:absolute; top:150px;
➥left:220px" width="346" height="126" />
29:         <t:transitionFilter targetElement="logo" type="fade" begin=
➥"logo.end-2" dur="2" mode="out" from="0.0" to="1.0" calcmode="linear" />
30:
31:     <div class="time" begin="logo.end" dur="2" id="presents" style=
➥"position:absolute; top:200px; left:300px; font-size:28pt; color:gray">
32:         <t:transitionFilter begin="presents.begin" dur="1" mode="in"
➥type="fade"/>
33:         <t:transitionFilter begin="presents.end-1" dur="1" mode="out"
➥type="fade"/>
34:         presents
35:     </div>
36:
```

Listing 16.6   Continued

```
37:     <t:par>
38:         <t:img class="time" src="images/anatour.gif" id="artarch"
➥begin="presents.end" dur="5" style="position:absolute; top:150px;
➥left:130px; z-index:5" width="525" height="125" />
39:             <t:transitionFilter targetElement="artarch" type="fade"
➥begin="artarch.begin" dur="2" mode="in" from="0.0" to="1.0" calcmode=
➥"linear" />
40:             <t:transitionFilter targetElement="artarch" type="fade"
➥begin="artarch.end-2" dur="2" mode="out" from="0.0" to="1.0"
➥calcmode="linear" />
41:     </t:par>
42:
43:     <t:audio class="time" id="audio" src="audio/bach.asf" begin=
➥"presents.begin" />
44:
45:     <t:par dur="indefinite">
46:         <span id="orange"
➥style="position:absolute;top:230px;left:75px;
➥height:0px;width:350px; background-color:#FFCC66; z-index:4">
47:             <t:animate targetElement="orange" attributeName="top"
➥from="230" to="135" begin="artarch.end-1" dur="2" fill="freeze" />
48:             <t:animate targetElement="orange" attributeName="height"
➥from="0" to="240" begin="artarch.end-1" dur="2" fill="freeze" />
49:         </span>
50:
51:         <span id="brown" style="position:absolute;top:230px;
➥left:225px; height:0px;width:325px; background-color:#CC9966; z-index:3">
52:             <t:animate targetElement="brown" attributeName="height"
➥from="0" to="245" begin="artarch.end-1" dur="2" fill="freeze" />
53:         </span>
54:
55:         <span id="yellow" style="position:absolute;top:230px;
➥left:300px; height:0px;width:450px; background-color:#FFFFCC; z-
➥index:2">
56:             <t:animate targetElement="yellow" attributeName="top"
➥from="230" to="50" begin="artarch.end-1" dur="2" fill="freeze" />
57:             <t:animate targetElement="yellow" attributeName="height"
➥from="0" to="385" begin="artarch.end-1" dur="2" fill="freeze" />
58:         </span>
59:     </t:par>
60:
61:     <t:par>
62:         <t:img class="time" begin="artarch.end+1" dur="indefinite" src=
➥"images/smVillalogo.gif" id="smlogo" style="position:absolute; top:52px;
➥left:300px; z-index:1" width="170" height="81" />
63:             <t:animateMotion targetElement="smlogo" values="0,0; -210,0"
➥begin="artarch.end+1" dur="2" calcMode="spline" keyTimes="0;1"
➥keySplines="0 0 .35 1" fill="freeze" />
64:         <t:img class="time" begin="artarch.end+1" dur="indefinite"
```

Listing 16.6   Continued

```
➥src="images/smanatour.gif" id="smartarch" style="position:absolute;
➥top:75px; left:375px; z-index:3" width="300" height="34" />
 65:           <t:transitionFilter targetElement="smartarch" type=
➥"progid:DXImageTransform.Microsoft.Pixelate()" begin="smartarch.begin"
➥dur="2" mode="in" from="0.0" to="1.0" calcmode="linear" />
 66:      </t:par>
 67:
 68:      <t:par>
 69:           <t:img class="time" begin="smartarch.begin+2" dur="5" src=
➥"images/santam.jpg" id="building" style="position:absolute; top:150px;
➥left:90px; z-index:5" width="350" height="236" />
 70:           <t:transitionFilter targetElement="building" type=
➥"progid:DXImageTransform.Microsoft.RandomDissolve()" begin=
➥"building.begin" dur="1" mode="in" from="0.0" to="1.0" calcmode="linear" />
 71:           <t:transitionFilter targetElement="building" type=
➥"progid:DXImageTransform.Microsoft.RandomDissolve()" begin=
➥"building.end-1" dur="1" mode="out" from="0.0" to="1.0" calcmode=
➥"linear" />
 72:           </t:img>
 73:           <div class="time" begin="smartarch.begin+3" dur="3" id=
➥ "classical" style="position:absolute; top:150px; left:470px; z-index:6">
 74:                <t:transitionFilter begin="classical.begin" dur="1"
➥mode="in" type="fade"/>
 75:                <t:transitionFilter begin="classical.end-1" dur="1"
➥mode="out" type="fade"/>
 76:           See the<br>classical buildings...
 77:           </div>
 78:      </t:par>
 79:
 80:      <t:par>
 81:           <t:img class="time" begin="smartarch.begin+7" dur="5" src=
➥"images/david.jpg" id="david" style="position:absolute; top:135px;
➥left:450px; z-index:5" width="200" height="298" />
 82:           <t:transitionFilter targetElement="david" type=
➥"progid:DXImageTransform.Microsoft.RandomDissolve()" begin="david.begin"
➥dur="1" mode="in" from="0.0" to="1.0" calcmode="linear" />
 83:           <t:transitionFilter targetElement="david" type=
➥"progid:DXImageTransform.Microsoft.RandomDissolve()" begin="david.end-1"
➥dur="1" mode="out" from="0.0" to="1.0" calcmode="linear" />
 84:           </t:img>
 85:           <div class="time" begin="smartarch.begin+8" dur="3"
➥id="sculpture" style="position:absolute; top:250px; left:175px;
➥z-index:6">
 86:                <t:transitionFilter begin="sculpture.begin" dur="1"
➥mode="in" type="fade"/>
 87:                <t:transitionFilter begin="sculpture.end-1" dur="1"
➥mode="out" type="fade"/>
 88:                ...the sculpture...
 89:           </div>
 90:      </t:par>
```

Listing 16.6   Continued

```
91:
92:     <t:par>
93:         <t:img class="time" begin="smartarch.begin+12" dur="5" src=
➥"images/cathedr.jpg" id="cathedral" style="position:absolute; top:220px;
➥left:290px; z-index:5" width="350" height="236" />
94:             <t:transitionFilter targetElement="cathedral" type=
➥"progid:DXImageTransform.Microsoft.RandomDissolve()" begin=
➥"cathedral.begin" dur="1" mode="in" from="0.0" to="1.0" calcmode=
➥"linear" />
95:             <t:transitionFilter targetElement="cathedral" type=
➥"progid:DXImageTransform.Microsoft.RandomDissolve()" begin=
➥"cathedral.end-1" dur="1" mode="out" from="0.0" to="1.0" calcmode=
➥"linear" />
96:         </t:img>
97:         <div class="time" begin="smartarch.begin+13" dur="3"
➥id="cathedrals" style="position:absolute; top:160px; left:450px;
➥z-index:6">
98:             <t:transitionFilter begin="cathedrals.begin" dur="1"
➥mode="in" type="fade"/>
99:             <t:transitionFilter begin="cathedrals.end-1" dur="1"
➥mode="out" type="fade"/>
100:            ...the cathedrals...
101:        </div>
102:     </t:par>
103:
104:     <t:par>
105:        <t:img class="time" begin="smartarch.begin+17" dur="indefinite"
➥src="images/kiss.jpg" id="kiss" style="position:absolute; top:150px;
➥left:295px; z-index:5" width="200" height="298" />
106:            <t:transitionFilter targetElement="kiss" type=
➥"progid:DXImageTransform.Microsoft.RandomDissolve()" begin="kiss.begin"
➥dur="1" mode="in" from="0.0" to="1.0" calcmode="linear" />
107:        </t:img>
108:        <div class="time" begin="smartarch.begin+18" dur="3"
➥id="beauty" style="position:absolute; top:375px; left:565px; z-index:6">
109:            <t:transitionFilter begin="beauty.begin" dur="1"
➥mode="in" type="fade"/>
110:            <t:transitionFilter begin="beauty.end-1" dur="1"
➥mode="out" type="fade"/>
111:            ...the beauty.
112:        </div>
113:     </t:par>
114:
115:     <t:par>
116:        <div class="time" begin="smartarch.begin+21" dur="indefinite"
➥id="best" style="position:absolute; top:220px; left:90px; font-family:
➥arial black; font-size:12pt; color:black; z-index:6" fill="freeze">
117:            <t:transitionFilter begin="best.begin" dur="1" mode="in"
➥type="fade"/>
118:            See the best<br>art and architecture<br>Europe has to
```

Listing 16.6   Continued

```
offer.
119:          </div>
120:            <div class="time" begin="smartarch.begin+22" dur="indefinite"
➥id="price" style="position:absolute; top:320px; left:565px; font-family:
➥arial black; font-size:16pt; color:black; z-index:6" fill="freeze">
121:               <t:transitionFilter begin="price.begin" dur="1" mode="in"
➥type="fade"/>
122:               $3599/person<br><br>555-555-1234
123:          </div>
124:        </t:par>
125:
126: </body>
127: </html>
```

Despite early limitations, HTML+TIME is worth a close look by any Web multimedia designer or developer. Compared to other interactive and programming
technologies, HTML+TIME in Internet Explorer is a simple and even fun language
in which to author. As other players, browsers, and computer platforms increasingly
borrow from Internet Explorer for Web-browsing capability, HTML+TIME may
mature into a common approach to creating SMIL.

Part IV

Appendices

Appendix A

SMIL 2.0 Modules, Elements, and Attributes

The following list is a chapter-by-chapter breakdown of the SMIL 2.0 modules, an alphabetical listing of their corresponding elements, and their associated attributes.

Structure Module (See Chapter 4)

Elements:

body	Contains content and pathways to content, as well as information related to the timing of the presentation.
head	Typically the home of such areas as layout and metainformation, this element contains information about the presentation that is not related to the timing or display of the media elements.
smil	The outer container element of a host-language conformant SMIL document.

Attributes:

class	Similar to id, class has the added flexibility of allowing the identifier to be used across several objects and elements.
id	Attaches a unique identifier to any element or object so that another element or object can reference the original element or object for another purpose (such as to enable animation, interactivity, and so on).

`xml:lang`	Specifies the language code that determines spoken or written language presented in the content.
`xmlns`	Declares the namespace of the SMIL document, often used to enable additional player-specific features.
`title`	Used to let the user know something about the object or element to which it is attached.

Metainformation Module (See Chapter 5)

Elements:

`meta`	Used to provide information about the content in the presentation.
`metadata`	A highly extensible approach to providing very detailed information about the content in the presentation.

Attributes:

`content`	Offers descriptive content that matches the type of metainformation identified with `name`.
`name`	Used with `content`, this attribute specifies the name for the type of metainformation supplied.

Layout Modules (See Chapter 6)

Elements:

`layout`	Used to create a graphical layout and control audio playback.
`region`	Designates space for media playback or layout.
`regPoint`	A registration point for arranging regions and media.
`root-layout`	Defines the overall screen dimensions for a presentation.
`topLayout`	The top-level layout when using multiple display windows or layouts.

Attributes:

`background-color`	Deprecated in favor of `backgroundColor`.
`backgroundColor`	Used to designate a background color for a presentation display area.
`bottom`	Used to declare the bottom edge or point of a display area.
`close`	Provides control for closing multiple display windows.
`fit`	Designates how media is handled when it does not fit into its assigned display area.
`height`	Used to declare the height of a display area.
`left`	Designates the left edge of a display area.

open	Provides control for opening multiple display windows.
regAlign	Used with media objects to precisely align the element with a registration point.
regPoint	Refers to previously defined regPoint by id value.
region	Refers to previously defined region by id value or regionName.
regionName	A unique identifier for a region.
right	Designates the right edge or point of a display area.
showBackground	Determines whether a background color will be visible.
soundLevel	Used to control the volume of audible media.
top	Designates the top edge or point of a display area.
type	Identifies the layout language to be used by the presentation.
width	Declares the width of a presentation space.
z-index	Used to identify the layer on which the display space or media object occurs.

Timing and Synchronization Module (See Chapter 7)

Elements:

excl	Declares an exclusive time container where one element or time container from a group of elements or time containers is played exclusively.
par	Declares a parallel time container where two or more elements or time containers can run at the same time.
seq	Declares a sequential time container where one element or time container follows another in sequence.
priorityClass	Used with an excl element to control the playback characteristics of other elements and time containers when an element or time container is chosen to play exclusively.

Attributes:

begin	Specifies the begin time or event for an element or time container.
dur	Specifies the duration time for an element or time container.
end	Specifies the end time or event for an element or time container.
endsync	Synchronizes the end of children in a <excl> or <par> group based on the behavior of one of the elements or objects in the group.
fill	Describes how an element or object looks on its end in a timeline.

fillDefault	Describes the default fill behavior for a block of elements.
higher	Used with <priorityClass> to describe the playback characteristics of parent elements or objects when another element or object is playing exclusively.
lower	Used with <priorityClass> to describe the playback characteristics of child elements or objects when another element or object is playing exclusively.
max	Defines the maximum active duration for an element.
min	Defines the minimum active duration for an element.
pauseDisplay	Used with <excl> and <priorityClass> to control the display of elements or object paused when an element or object is playing exclusively.
peers	Used with <priorityClass> to describe the playback characteristics of peers when another element or object is playing exclusively.
repeat	Allows an element to repeat for a specified whole number of times.
repeatCount	Allows an element to repeat for a specified whole or fractional number of times.
repeatDur	Declares that an element will continue to repeat until a specified duration ends.
restart	Controls the behavior of how an element can be restarted in a timeline.
restartDefault	Controls the default behavior of how a block of elements can be restarted in a timeline.
syncBehavior	Controls how elements and objects stay synchronized under varying network conditions.
syncBehaviorDefault	Declares a default for a block of elements that controls how elements and objects stay synchronized under varying network conditions.
syncMaster	Synchronizes the playback of all elements to one master element.
syncTolerance	Specifies how tightly or loosely elements and objects stay synchronized under varying network conditions.
syncToleranceDefault	Declares a default for a block of elements that specifies how tightly or loosely elements and objects stay synchronized under varying network conditions.
timeAction	Specifies the action that is taken on an element when it is in the timeline.
timeContainer	Allows timing and synchronization elements to be used in another XML-compliant language (such as XHTML).

Media Object Modules (See Chapter 8)

Elements:

animation	Used to call a media source file—usually animated vector graphics or other animated format—into a presentation.
audio	Used to call a media source file—usually with audio content—into a presentation.
brush	Allows a solid color to be used as a media object.
img	Used to call a media source file into a presentation, usually containing a still image.
param	Declares a runtime parameter for a media object. Often used to pass situation-specific adjustments to a media object.
ref	A generic catch-all element used to call a media source file into a presentation.
text	Used to call a media source file consisting of text or HTML into a presentation.
textstream	Used to call a media source file that contains moving text into a presentation.
video	Used to call a media source file—usually with video content—into a presentation.

Attributes:

abstract	A brief description of a media object that can be used when generating a table of contents.
alt	Specifies text to be displayed in place of a media object. Also used by assistive devices.
author	Identifies the author of the media object.
clip-begin	Deprecated in favor of clipBegin.
clipBegin	Specifies the start of playback offset from the start of the media object.
clip-end	Deprecated in favor of clipEnd.
clipEnd	Specifies the stop of playback offset from the start of the media object.
color	Defines the color that is painted when using the brush element.
copyright	Declares the copyright notice for the media object.
erase	Determines whether a media object will continue to display after it has reached the end of its duration.
longdesc	A URI link that leads to a long text description of the media object.
mediaRepeat	Used with media objects that loop either to support the looped behavior of the object or to override the looping behavior.

name	Names a runtime parameter declared by the <param> element.
readIndex	Dictates the order in which assistive devices will read aloud the alt, title, and longdesc values, if declared.
src	Provides the address used to locate and retrieve a media object.
sensitivity	Declares whether user actions are applied to the media object that is closest to the surface in a layered environment.
title	Provides a very brief description about the media object.
type	Identifies the MIME type of a media object and can be used to influence which helper application is used to play back a media file.
value	Used in conjunction with the name and valuetype attributes to define a runtime parameter for a media object.
valuetype	Defines the type of information being passed to a player using the param element along with the name and value attributes.

Transition Effects Module (See Chapter 9)

Elements:

transition	Used to define a transition class that is applied to media objects in the body of the presentation.
transitionFilter	Animates the progress of a transition and allows for full control over the timing of the progress of a transition.

Attributes:

begin	Specifies the begin time for a <transition> or <transitionFilter>. Defined fully in the Timing and Synchronization modules (Chapter 7).
borderColor	Specifies the content of a border generated along a wipe edge.
borderWidth	Specifies the width of a border generated along a wipe edge.
by	Specifies a relative offset value for the progress of a transitionFilter. Defined in the BasicAnimation module (Chapter 10).
calcMode	Declares the interpolation mode of the progress of the <transitionFilter>. Defined fully in the BasicAnimation module (Chapter 10).
direction	Specifies the direction that a transition will run.
dur	Declares the duration of a <transition> or <transitionFilter>.
end	Specifies the end time for a transition or <transitionFilter>. Defined in the Timing and Synchronization module (Chapter 7).
endProgress	Declares the amount of progression through a <transition> at which to end execution.

fadeColor	Specifies the start or end color when using the type attribute value of "fade" with a subtype value of "fadeToColor" or "fadeFromColor".
from	Declares the amount of progression through a `<transitionFilter>` at which to begin execution.
href	Indicates the target element to which a `<transitionFilter>` is applied using a URI.
horzRepeat	Declares how many times to perform the given transition along a horizontal axis.
mode	Indicates whether the parent element will transition in or out.
repeatCount	Allows an element to repeat for a specified whole or fractional number of times. Fully defined in the Timing and Synchronization module (Chapter 7).
repeatDur	Declares that an element will continue to repeat until a specified duration ends. Fully defined in the Timing and Synchronization module (Chapter 7).
startProgress	Declares the amount of progression through a `<transition>` at which to begin execution.
subtype	Defines the subtype of a transition, determined by the type attribute of the transition in question.
targetElement	Specifies the element to which a `<transitionFilter>` is applied using the identifier (or id attribute value) of the element.
to	Specifies the amount of progression through a `<transitionFilter>` at which to end execution.
transIn	Indicates that a transition should begin at the beginning of the media object to which it is attached.
transOut	Indicates that a transition should end at the end of the media object to which it is attached, or at the end of its fill state.
type	Declares the type or family of a transition. Required.
values	A semicolon-separated list of one or more values specifying the progress of the `<transitionFilter>`.
vertRepeat	Defines how many times to perform a given transition along a vertical axis.

Animation Modules (See Chapter 10)

Elements:

animate	A generic animation element that starts an animated effect.
animateColor	Used to animate the color change of an element.
animateMotion	Used to animate the motion of an element.
set	Changes an attribute to a set value for a limited period of time.

Attributes:

accumulate	Controls whether the animation is cumulative.
actuate	Used with the href attribute; follows the link to the target element automatically.
additive	Controls whether the animation is additive.
attributeName	Specifies the name of the target attribute.
attributeType	Specifies the type of the named attribute.
by	Specifies the relative offset value of the animation.
calcMode	Determines the interpolation approach for the animation.
from	Declares a starting point for an animation.
href	Declares the target element to be animated by using an XLink locator.
keySplines	Defines control points that describe the speed (easing) of a spline animation.
keyTimes	Controls the pacing of a spline animation.
origin	Used by <animateMotion> to declare the origin of motion for the animation.
path	Uses coordinate values to describe the curve used by spline animation in <animateMotion>.
show	Used with the href attribute; specifies that the link does not include additional content.
targetElement	Used to specify which element the animation effect is being targeted to.
to	Declares the ending value for the animation.
type	Used with the href attribute; declares the type of XLink used.
values	Used to provide values needed by a supporting element or attribute.

Linking Modules (See Chapter 11)

Elements:

a	Allows for a hyperlink to be associated with a media object that has a visual display.
anchor	Deprecated in favor of the area element.
area	Used to define a portion of a media object's visual display area as a hyperlink.

Attributes:

accesskey	Defines a keyboard key that can be used to activate a hyperlink.
actuate	Declares whether user action is necessary for a hyperlink to be activated.
alt	Provides alternative text to be displayed along with a hyperlink or in place of it. Also used by assistive devices for the visually impaired.
coords	Used to identify a set of spatial coordinates that define a clickable space on the display area of a media object.
destinationLevel	Sets the audio level of a resource when a link is followed.
destinationPlaystate	Determines whether a resource begins playing when a link is followed.
external	Identifies whether the destination resource should be opened using the current application or an external one.
fragment	Allows for a SMIL presentation to overlay and/or override links in embedded media.
href	Identifies the URI of a destination resource in a hyperlink.
nohref	Specifies that a space declared using the area element does not have a URI associated with it.
shape	Designates the clickable shape of an area on the display surface of a media object.
show	Controls how the source presentation display responds when a hyperlink is followed.
sourceLevel	Sets the audio level of the presentation that contains a hyperlink when the link is followed.
sourcePlaystate	Determines the temporal behavior of the source presentation when a hyperlink is followed.
tabindex	Allows for the manual assignment of a tab order for links within a presentation should they be navigated by keyboard.
target	Identifies the display environment into which a destination resource should be opened.

Content Control Modules (See Chapter 12)

Elements:

customAttributes	Allows for the definition of one or more author-defined custom test attributes.
customTest	Defines specific custom test attributes.

prefetch   Allows for media files to be retrieved, or preloaded, prior to
                  being called up by the presentation.

switch   Used to enclose a set of presentation alternatives from which
                  one can be chosen for implementation, based on the evalua-
                  tion of its accompanying test attributes.

Attributes:

bandwidth   Defines how much bandwidth should be used to
                                   prefetch files.

customTest   Used to call a custom test attribute by its identifier.

defaultState   Determines the initial state for a named custom test
                                   variable.

mediaSize   Declares how much of a file to prefetch based on the
                                   size of the file.

mediaTime   Declares how much of a file to prefetch based on the
                                   duration of the file.

override   Used to determine whether a user has the capability
                                   to override the initial state of a custom test variable.

skip-content   Determines whether the content of an element is
                                   skipped or evaluated.

system-overdub-or-caption   Deprecated in favor of systemOverdubOrSubtitle
                                   and systemCaptions.

systemAudioDesc   A test attribute used to determine whether closed
                                   audio descriptions should be rendered.

systemBitrate   A test attribute used to deliver presentations that
                                   match the user's bandwidth capabilities.

systemCPU   A test attribute that can assist with specifying the
                                   CPU on which the SMIL player is operating.

systemCaptions   A test attribute that allows for the display of text
                                   equivalent to the audio portion of a presentation.

systemComponent   A test attribute that provides a URI that is used to
                                   identify a component of the playback system.

systemLanguage   A test attribute that can be used to match the presen-
                                   tation's language to that of the viewer.

systemOperatingSystem   A test attribute that can assist with specifying the
                                   operating system of a viewer.

systemOverdubOrSubtitle   A test attribute that determines whether a viewer
                                   prefers overdubbing or captioning, when available.

systemRequired   A test attribute used to provide an extension mecha-
                                   nism for new elements or attributes.

systemScreenDepth	A test attribute that can be used to specify the depth of the screen color palette required for display.
SystemScreenSize	A test attribute that can be used to specify the screen size necessary for the given element to be displayed.
uid	Identifies a URI identifier for a given custom test that is to be used persistently.

Time Manipulations Module (See Chapter 13)

Attributes:

accelerate	Accelerates the timeline of a media object or time container from stopped to full speed.
autoReverse	Reverses the playback of a timeline of a media object or time container when its end is reached.
decelerate	Decelerates the timeline of a media object or time container from full speed to stopped.
speed	Slows down or speeds up the timeline of a media object or time container.

Appendix B

Online Resources

The Definitive Authority: The World Wide Web Consortium (W3C) SMIL Pages

http://www.w3.org/AudioVideo/

Maintained by the standards body for the Web and the authors of SMIL, this site is the official resource for SMIL 1.0 and 2.0. It includes links to the specification documentation for both versions, as well as the history of SMIL and other useful resources.

Companion Site for This Book

Technology moves forward quickly. As we write this book, the SMIL community is constantly gaining new browsers, players, tools, and authoring techniques. But at some point with each chapter, we have to close the file and send what we have to the publisher. SMILBook is our way of keeping you up to date on the world of SMIL.

SMILBook

http://www.smilbook.com/

Check here to keep posted on the changes and developments that occurred after this book was published.

Downloadable Media Players

Media players are necessary for the playback of SMIL presentations and their associated media files. The players that support playback of SMIL presentations are available using the following URLs.

Supported platforms: Mac and Win-98/Me/NT4/2000

RealPlayer 8.0

http://www.real.com/

This version of RealPlayer supports playback of SMIL 1.0 presentations, as does the earlier G2 version. The next generation of this player, called RealONE, was released as a preview in late September of 2001. When the final version of RealONE is released, it will be available at this same location.

QuickTime 5.0

http://www.apple.com/quicktime/download/

Apple's QuickTime player can be used to playback SMIL 1.0 presentations. The next version of this player, due out in early winter of 2002, is expected to support SMIL 2.0.

Internet Explorer 6

http://www.microsoft.com/windows/ie/default.htm

Microsoft's browser is able to play back SMIL 2.0 presentations that are authored using its HTML+TIME language profile.

GRiNS-SMIL 2 Player (Oratrix)

http://www2.oratrix.nl/Products/G2P?zone=G2P

Oratrix was one of the first companies to create a player to support SMIL 2.0 files. Available as a free download for both Macintosh and Windows platforms, the GRiNS player is part of a commercial venture by Oratrix that includes a SMIL authoring tool.

SOJA Cherbourg 2

http://www.helio.org/products/smil/

A Java-based SMIL player available for download.

Authoring Tools

Although SMIL presentations can be hand-coded, software is available that allows for a more intuitive approach to authoring followed an automated output of code. The URLs that follow provide information on most of the tools now available.

RealSlideShow

`http://www.realnetworks.com/products/slideshow/index.html`

This tool provides an intuitive interface for creating RealPlayer-based image presentations timed to music.

Fluition

`http://www.confluenttechnologies.com/`

This tool uses an object-oriented approach to authoring. To take full advantage of this software, some SMIL authoring knowledge is helpful.

GRiNS

`http://www2.oratrix.nl/`

GRiNS is designed with the multimedia artist in mind and is part of the Oratrix SMIL package.

HomeSite (Allaire)

`http://www.allaire.com/products/homesite/index.cfm`

Long respected as an HTML authoring tool, HomeSite can also output SMIL files.

SMIL 2.0 Authoring Resources

This section provides links to articles, tutorials, and other resources for creating SMIL 2.0 presentations.

JustSMIL (Streaming Media World)

`http://smw.internet.com/smil/smilhome.html`

One of the early comprehensive online resources for all things SMIL. One of the authors of this book, coincidentally, is the founder of the JustSMIL site.

HTML+Time 2.0

```
http://msdn.microsoft.com/library/default.asp?url=/workshop/
author/behaviors/time.asp
```

A primer on how to use Microsoft's updated HTML+Time for SMIL presentations in Internet Explorer 5.0 and later.

RealSystem Production Guide: Assembling a Presentation with SMIL 2.0

```
http://service.real.com/help/library/guides/production8/realpgd.htm
```

The URL listed is a link to the RealSystem Production Guide currently in use. When the new generation of RealPlayer that supports SMIL 2.0 is announced (October 2001), this link should provide access to the updated Production Guide.

The CWI SMIL Page

```
http://www.cwi.nl/~media/SMIL/
```

Based in the Netherlands, CWI (Centrum voor Wiskunde en Informatica) is the National Research Institute for Mathematics and Computer Science. They offer workshops around the world on implementing SMIL.

Universal SMIL

```
http://www.empirenet.com/~joseram/universal/universal.html
```

Media formats and content that is playable on all players. A convenient chart.

Webopedia

```
http://webopedia.internet.com/TERM/S/SMIL.html
```

Contains a brief definition of SMIL and some links.

Web Review Looks at the Future of SMIL

```
http://www.webreview.com/1999/10_08/designers/10_08_99_1.shtml
```

An article describing the differences and new features of SMIL 2.0.

SMIL 2.0: Codeless Animation in HTML

```
http://hotwired.lycos.com/webmonkey/01/24/index3a.html
```

An article by Rodney Reid for Webmonkey on the use of SMIL 2.0 for animation.

SMIL 1.0 Resources

This section provides links to articles, tutorials, and other resources for creating SMIL 1.0 presentations.

JustSMIL (Streaming Media World)

http://smw.internet.com/smil/smilhome.html

As listed previously, a comprehensive online resource for all things SMIL, including many articles and tutorials on SMIL 1.0.

A Primer on SMIL

http://www.webtechniques.com/archives/1998/09/bouthillier/

Larry Bouthillier, in an article for Web Techniques, provides the background of SMIL's introduction as a W3C standard.

SMIL: Multimedia Markup

http://hotwired.lycos.com/webmonkey/98/23/index1a.html?tw=authoring

Another introductory article to the use of SMIL 1.0 for creating multimedia presentations. This article was written by Shvatz for Webmonkey.

An Overview of Using SMIL 1.0

http://hotwired.lycos.com/webmonkey/00/41/index4a.html?tw=authoring

Steve McCannell, in an article for Webmonkey, gives an overview of SMIL 1.0.

RealSystem Production Guide: Assembling a Presentation with SMIL 1.0

http://service.real.com/help/library/guides/production8/realpgd.htm

Areas of interest in the Production Guide include Chapter 6: "Assembling a Presentation with SMIL 1.0," Chapter 7: "Extending SMIL," Appendix D: "SMIL Quick Reference," and Appendix E: "SMIL Language Codes."

Apple QuickTime's SMIL 1.0 Pages

http://www.apple.com/quicktime/authoring/qtsmil.html

http://www.apple.com/quicktime/authoring/qtsmil2.html

A little bit of info on how to make use of QuickTime's SMIL extensions.

RealNetwork's SMIL 1.0 Tutorial

`http://www.realnetworks.com/devzone/tutorials/authoring/smil/index.html`

A concise, step-by-step introduction to using SMIL 1.0.

RealNetworks SMIL 1.0 Evaluator

`http://www.realnetworks.com/devzone/howto/`
`↪contentcreation/smilevaluator/index.html`

Try this validator to check for common SMIL 1.0 coding errors.

WebReview SMIL 1.0 Articles

`http://www.webreview.com/2000/05_05/designers/05_05_00_1.shtml`

Follow the links on the bottom of this article to access several additional WebReview articles on SMIL.

Some Additional SMIL 1.0 Online Tutorials

`http://www.webreview.com/1999/03_12/designers/03_12_99_1.shtml`

`http://www.helio.org/products/smil/tutorial/index.html`

`http://www.empirenet.com/%7Ejoseram/index.html`

Three additional basic introductions to SMIL 1.0.

GLOSSARY

A

active duration   The length of time during which the *element* plays normally. If no repeating behavior is specified and an end is not specified, the active duration is the same as the *simple duration*, or the natural duration of the element. If the element is set to play repeatedly, the active duration is defined by how many times the simple duration is repeated.

active time   Time measured in relation to the *element*'s *active duration*. Active time is measured from the beginning of the element.

architecture   See *closed architecture*, *open architecture*, and *streaming media architecture*.

attributes   Code contained within an *element*. In the example `<region id="main">`, id is an *attribute* of the *element* `region`. Attributes are generally used to extend or refine an element's function and to provide information about the data, in contrast to being data itself. See also *element*, *value*.

authoring tool   A program or application that helps create a hypertext, graphical, or multimedia presentation. Usually provides a graphical interface that allows the user to drag and drop media objects onto a layout and/or into a timeline. The tool then automatically creates the underlying code and/or scripting to implement the user's decisions.

average data rate   Represents the average amount of data per time unit that a presentation outputs. Calculated by dividing a presentation's combined file size by its duration.

B

bandwidth   The amount of data that can pass through a network connection in a given time period. Usually measured in *kilobits* per second (*Kbps*) and primarily dependent on the hardware, software, and connection rate of a client machine.

bit   The smallest unit of data measurement. Assigned a binary value of 1 or 0. Eight bits are in a *byte*.

bit rate   A measurement of bandwidth and also the rate at which a presentation is streamed. Usually expressed as *kilobits* per second (*Kbps*). See also *constant bit rate* and *variable bit rate*.

buffering   Receiving and storing data before it is played back. Initial buffering of a presentation is called *preroll*, during which files are accessed by the *client* machine. Extensive buffering during a presentation can stall playback entirely.

byte   A common data measurement. One byte consists of eight bits.

C

cascading style sheets (CSS)   Adds formatting information to *HTML* and *XML* in layers, where each layer overrules the previous one.

child element   An element *nested* within another one, with the outer element referred to as the *parent element*.

client   An application that receives data from a *server*. For instance, a *RealPlayer* receives data from a RealServer, the same as a Web browser receives data from a Web server.

clip   A media file within a presentation. Many clips have internal timelines.

clock-value   The numeric means of representing time. *Full*, *partial*, or *time-count* clock-values are permitted in SMIL coding.

closed architecture   A proprietary system owned by a manufacturer. Usually only products and devices from the manufacturer will function in a closed system. *HTML+Time* is an example of a closed architecture that functions only in the Internet Explorer browser on Windows machines. See also *open architecture*.

codec   A compression/decompression software component that translates data between its uncompressed and compressed forms. Reduces the *bandwidth* required by a streaming clip.

constant bit rate (CBR)   A method of encoding audio and video files so that the *bit rate* of the file remains the same throughout the entire file. See also *bit rate* and *variable bit rate (VBR)*.

continuous media   Media that is naturally time-based and generally supports intrinsic timing and duration (although the duration might be indefinite). These media are sometimes described as "time-based" or "played" media. This includes most audio, video, and time-based animations. See also *discrete media*.

CSS   See *cascading style sheets*.

D

data rate   The number of *byte*s per second used to represent a media object. Usually measured in *kilobytes* per second (*KBps*) or megabytes per second (MBps).

definite time   Time resolved to a finite, non-indefinite value. See also *desired time*, *effective time*, *explicit time*, and *implicit time*.

discrete media   Media that does not have intrinsic timing or intrinsic duration. This includes images, text, and some vector media. See also *continuous media*.

duration   See *active duration* and *simple duration*.

E

effective time   Time that is actually observed at document playback. It reflects both the constraints of the timing model as well as real-world issues, such as media delivery. See also *desired time*, *explicit time*, and *implicit time*.

element   The most basic unit of code, which acts as a container for data presentation and modification. In the example `<region id="main">`, `<region>` is the element. See also *attribute* and *value*.

encoding   Usually found in a *streaming media architecture*, the encoding process translates data into a compressed form that is understood by the architecture's *player* or *plug-in*.

explicit time   A time that has been specified by the author, using the SMIL syntax. See also *implicit time*.

eXtensible Markup Language   See *XML*.

F

full clock-value   A means to represent a moment in time measured in hours, minutes, and seconds. For example, 01:15:25.12 would be interpreted as 1 hour, 15 minutes, 25 seconds and 12 milliseconds. See also *partial clock-value* and *timecount value*.

H

helper application   A program or file that adds functionality to another program. Often browsers use these applications to play back multimedia. Also called a *plug-in*.

host-language conformant profile   A SMIL 2.0 *language profile* that incorporates a Structure module, which in turn contains the <smil> element. *Profiles* further enhance the potential for smooth playback of multimedia presentations across *players* and browsers. The main host-language conformant profiles are the *SMIL 2.0 Language Profile* and the *SMIL 2.0 Basic Language Profile*. See also *integration-set conformant profile*.

HTML (Hypertext Markup Language)   An authoring language used to define the structure and layout of a Web document.

HTML+Time (HTML+Timed Interactive Multimedia Extensions)   A proposal put forth to the *W3C* by Microsoft at the time *SMIL* 1.0 was adopted that extends *HTML* and enables timing and interactivity without using scripting languages. Supported only by the Internet Explorer browser on Windows machines. In SMIL 2.0, this approach can be found in the *XHTML+SMIL 2.0 Language Profile*.

HTTP (Hypertext Transfer Protocol)   The underlying protocol used by the World Wide Web. Can be used for *streaming* media. See also *TCP*.

Hypertext Markup Language   See *HTML*.

I

implicit time   Time that is defined intrinsically by the element media (for example, based on the length of a movie) or by the time model semantics (such as duration of a par time container). See also *explicit time.*

integration-set conformant profile   A SMIL 2.0 *language profile* that does not include the root <smil> element, but instead incorporates the SMIL code into an HTML document that is displayed as a Web page. *HTML+Time* is an example of this type of language profile. See also *host-conformant language profile.*

intrinsic duration   The natural duration of a media file when it follows its timeline from start to finish.

K

Kbps   *Kilobits* per second. A common measurement of *bandwidth.*

KBps   *Kilobytes* per second, also referred to as "Kps." A common measurement of a file's *data rate.*

kilobit (Kb)   1024 bits.

kilobyte (KB)   A common data measurement equal to 1024 bytes.

L

language profile   Also called *profiles*, these standards combine modules and present established characteristics for playing back multimedia. The intent behind profiles is an effort to enhance the potential for smooth playback of multimedia presentations across *players* and browsers. Currently, two types of language profiles make use of SMIL 2.0: *host-language conformant profile* and *integration-set conformant profile.*

layout   The graphical or visual structure of a document or presentation.

M

media objects   The files that make up a multimedia presentation, including audio, video, still image, animation, HTML pages, and/or text files. Called through the use of text-only coding, the links to these objects make up a significant portion of a *SMIL* presentation. See also *Web objects.*

media time   Time measured in relation to the object's *duration*. Media time is measured from the beginning of the media, as modified by any `clipBegin` or `clipEnd` attributes.

meta-information   *Meta* is a common prefix that means "about." Therefore, meta-information is information about the data being presented and commonly includes information about the author, copyright, keywords, and other indexing and presentation data. In *SMIL* 2.0, the Metainformation module provides the arena for exchanging this information.

MIME types   MIME is an acronym for multipurpose Internet mail extensions, which is a specification for formatting non-ASCII messages so that they can be sent over the Internet. Web browsers support various MIME types, which identify the file type for graphics, audio, and video files, among others.

N

nested   Embedding one object within another object of the same type. This structure often occurs in programming and code writing when an *element* is nested within another element. See also *child element* and *parent element*.

non-temporal   Not related to time or attached to a timeline.

O

open architecture   A system with publicly published specifications and standards. Allows the system to connect easily with other devices, programs, and systems that also conform to the published standards. *SMIL* and *HTML* are both examples of open architecture systems. See also *closed architecture*.

P

packets   A unit of data sent over the Internet using *HTTP* and *TCP* protocols. Files and documents are broken into packets by *TCP*, which then reassembles the data at the *client* end. If any data is damaged or missing, the packets are re-sent.

parent element   When elements are *nested*, the parent element is the outer element. *Child element*s are then *nested* within the parent element.

partial clock-value   A means to represent a moment in time in which unused time components are hidden. For example, begin="00:30.25" will cause the element to start playing at 30.25 seconds. See also *full clock-value* and *timecount value*.

player   The *client* application that plays back multimedia that has been encoded for use by the player. See also *streaming media architecture*.

plug-in   A program or file that adds functionality to another program. Often browsers use these applications to play back multimedia. Also called *helper applications*.

preroll   The initial *buffering* of a presentation during which files are accessed by the *client* machine.

profiles   New in SMIL 2.0, profiles combine modules and present established characteristics for playing back multimedia. The intent behind profiles is an effort to enhance the potential for smooth playback of multimedia presentations across players and browsers. See also *language profile*.

progressive download   A file that is transmitted from a standard *HTTP*/Web server using *TCP*/IP and is downloaded to the *client* machine. Playback begins when enough data has been received for the entire file to play back without interruption. Often mistaken for streaming. Also called "pseudo-streaming."

pseudo streaming   See *progressive download*.

Q

QuickTime   Developed by Apple Computers, QuickTime is an architecture for the creation and delivery of multimedia. The QuickTime architecture provides a popular *player* and *plug-in*, as well as *server* software and an *encoding* device. The QuickTime player also has the capacity to play back many well-known file formats that are not specifically QuickTime files. A robust and well-distributed system for Web multimedia, QuickTime currently supports SMIL 1.0 playback. The next version of the player is expected to support SMIL 2.0. See also *streaming architecture*.

R

RealMedia   A blanket term used to refer to the various "Real" data types that can be streamed using a *RealPlayer*. File types referred to as RealMedia include RealAudio and RealVideo (.rm), RealFlash, *RealPix (.rp)*, and *RealText (.rt)*.

RealPix (.rp)   A file type that uses a proprietary markup language to stream still images along with special effects, such as zooms and fades. Requires a *RealPlayer* for viewing.

RealPlayer   The player for *RealMedia* files. Supports *SMIL* 1.0 playback and will support SMIL 2.0 with the release of the RealONE version of the player.

RealSlideshow   A RealNetworks tool that uses SMIL 1.0 to create streaming slideshows. See also *streaming architecture*.

RealSystem   An *architecture* for the delivery of multimedia developed by RealNetworks, which includes *RealPlayer* (*player* and *plug-in*), RealServer (*server* software), and RealProducer (*encoding* device).

RealText (.rt)   A file type that uses a proprietary markup language to present streaming text. Requires a *RealPlayer* for viewing. See also *streaming architecture*.

real-time   Delivery that occurs simultaneously with an event or playback of a file.

region   In *SMIL* coding, an area designated for playback of media elements.

RTP (Real-Time Protocol)   The Internet standard protocol for the transport of *real-time* data. None of the commercial *streaming* products currently use RTP, but the protocol is expected to be adopted by streaming vendors over time. See also *RTSP*, *TCP*, and *UDP*.

RTSP (Real-Time Streaming Protocol)   An open, standards-based control protocol developed by RealNetworks and Netscape. RTSP works with established protocols such as *UDP* and *TCP* to stream multimedia to *RTP*-based client players, including RealPlayer. See also *TCP*.

S

Scalable Vector Graphics (SVG)   An *XML*-based standard language for vector graphics recommended by the *W3C*.

server   A computer that other computers connect to for the purpose of retrieving information. The machines that are connecting to the server are called *client* machines.

simple duration   The _duration_ defined by the basic `begin` and `dur` markup. It does not include any of the effects of playing repeatedly or of `fill`. If the _explicit time_s are not specified, the simple duration is defined as the element's implicit duration. See also _active duration_.

simple time   Time measured in relation to the element's _simple duration_. Simple time is measured as an offset from the beginning of a particular instance of the _simple duration_.

SMIL (Synchronized Multimedia Integration Language)   A simple but powerful _XML_-compliant markup language that coordinates how and when multimedia files play back on _client_ machines. Created using a _text editor_ or any other software that saves output as plain text with line breaks.

SMIL 2.0 Basic Language Profile   A stripped-down version of the _SMIL 2.0 Language Profile_, intended for use with personal digital devices, mobile phones, and entertainment devices. This language profile is also a _host-conformant language profile_ currently making use of the SMIL 2.0 modules.

SMIL 2.0 Language Profile   The main _host-conformant language profile_ currently making use of the SMIL 2.0 modules. Incorporates a Structure module and the use of the `<smil>` element.

SMIL Boston   The name given to the working draft of _SMIL_ 2.0.

specification (W3C)   A publicly available recommendation made by the _World Wide Web Consortium_ that describes the building blocks of the Web. See also _W3C_.

spline   A smooth curve that passes through two or more points.

streaming   A technique for transferring data as a steady and continuous stream that allows data to be viewed before the entire file is transmitted. Also used to refer to transferring data in _real-time_.

streaming media architecture   A system for delivering multimedia over the Web. Usually an architecture includes server software, an _encoding_ device, and a _player_ or _helper application_. _QuickTime_, _RealNetworks_, and _Windows Media_ are all streaming media architectures. See also _streaming_.

syntax   The spelling and grammar of a programming language.

T

TCP (Transmission Control Protocol)   A protocol used by *HTTP* to ensure reliable document transfer. Before sending, TCP breaks the data into *packets*, which are then reassembled at the *client* end. If any data is missing or damaged, the entire document is re-sent. See also *RTSP* and *UDP*.

temporal   Having to do with time and timelines.

text editor   An application that enables writing and saving plain text files with line breaks. Used to create *HTML* and *SMIL* documents "by hand." Notepad (Windows) and SimpleText (Macintosh) are examples of text editors.

timecount value   A means to represent a moment in time in which time divisions are abbreviated. Using timecount values, the moment in time of 1 hour, 30 minutes, and 15 seconds becomes "1h30m15s." See also *full clock-value* and *partial clock-value*.

true streaming   See *streaming*.

U

UDP (User Datagram Protocol)   A protocol for the delivery of media over the Web, and the alternative to *TCP*. UDP forsakes TCP's error correction and allows data dropout to maintain real-time delivery of a presentation. The best choice for live broadcasts because all viewers get the same information simultaneously. A downside of UDP is that the transmissions are often blocked by network firewalls.

URI (Uniform Resource Identifier)   The generic term for an absolute or relative address of a resource. When the address given is absolute, as in `http://www.example.com`, the first part of the address indicates what protocol to use, and the second part specifies the IP address or the domain name where the resource is located. When the address is relative, as in `page.html`, the address indicates the path to the resource relative to the document in which it appears. A URL is one kind of URI.

V

value   In coding, the data assigned to an *attribute* within an *element*. In the example `<region id="main">`, the element is `<region>`, id is the attribute, and main is the value. Values should always be enclosed in quotation marks.

variable bit rate (VBR)   A method of *encoding* that changes the bit rate over the course of the file. This allows the encoder to allocate more bits to areas that are harder to encode and fewer bits to areas that are easier, which creates higher-quality compressed files. See also *bit rate* and *constant bit rate (CBR)*.

W

W3C (World Wide Web Consortium)   A group of researchers and industry representatives who develop *specifications*, guidelines, software, and tools that are universally adaptable for the Web. One particular task of the W3C is to produce *specifications*, or recommendations, that describe building blocks for the Web. The *SMIL* specifications are examples of these recommendations that are public and available to all.

Web objects   The online files used in a multimedia presentation, including Web sites and links to audio, video, still image, animation, and/or text files on the Web. Called into action through the use of text-only coding, the links to these objects make up a significant portion of a *SMIL* presentation. See also *media objects*.

Windows Media Player   Formerly called NetShow. An architecture for the delivery of multimedia using the Internet Explorer browser. Still in development for use on the Macintosh OS. See also *streaming architecture*.

X

XHTML+SMIL 2.0 Language Profile   A *language profile* that is *integration-set conformant* rather than *host-language conformant* and makes use of the *SMIL* 2.0 modules. This profile does not include the root `<smil>` element; instead, it incorporates the SMIL code into the Web page along with *HTML*.

XML (eXtensible Markup Language)   Separates content from formatting. Allows for the creation of customized element sets to provide functionality not available with *HTML*. XML is a language for defining languages. *SMIL* is an XML-compliant markup language.

Index